MY
LOVELY
ENEMY

MY
LOVELY
ENEMY

A NOVEL BY

Rudy Wiebe

McClelland and Stewart

The Canadian Publishers
McClelland and Stewart Limited
25 Hollinger Road
Toronto
M4B 3G2

Canadian Cataloguing in Publication Data
    Wiebe, Rudy, 1934 –
        My lovely enemy
    ISBN 0-7710-8989-9
    I. Title.
    PS8545.I415M9   C813′.54   C83-094114-2
    PR9199.3.W54M9

The content and characters in this book are fiction. Any resemblance to actual persons or happenings is coincidental.

Excerpts from "On Hearing a Name Long Unspoken" in *Flowers for Hitler*, by Leonard Cohen and "I Cry Love" in *I've Tasted My Blood* by Milton Acorn are reproduced by permission of McClelland and Stewart Limited.

Excerpts from "Billboards" and "White Dwarfs" in *There's A Trick with a Knife I'm Learning to Do*, published by McClelland and Stewart Limited is reproduced by permission of the author.

Excerpt from "The Snow Girl's Ballad" in *Collected Poems: The Two Seasons*, by Dorothy Livesay is reproduced by permission of McGraw-Hill Ryerson Ltd.

Every reasonable attempt has been made to attribute copyright material used in this publication. Information regarding inadvertent errors or omissions of copyright information would be welcomed by the publisher, and efforts will be made to correct same in future editions.

Printed and bound in Canada by
T. H. Best Printing Company Limited

To the memory of
my mother and my father

Blessed are the dead who die
in the faith of Christ

Books by Rudy Wiebe

FICTION:

My Lovely Enemy (1983)
The Angel of the Tar Sands (1982)
The Mad Trapper (1980)
Alberta / A Celebration (1979, with
 Harry Savage and Tom Radford)
The Scorched-Wood People (1977)
Where is the Voice Coming From? (1974)
The Temptations of Big Bear (1973)
The Blue Mountains of China (1970)
First and Vital Candle (1966)
Peace Shall Destroy Many (1962)

ESSAYS:

A Voice in the Land (1981, edited by W.J. Keith)

EDITED:

More Stories from Western Canada
 (1980, with Aritha van Herk)
Getting Here (1977)
Double Vision (1976)
Stories from Pacific and Arctic Canada
 (1974, with Andreas Schroeder)
Stories from Western Canada (1972)
The Story-Makers (1970)

DRAMA:

Far as the Eye Can See (1977, with
 Theatre Passe Muraille)

Old folk say that when a person sleeps
the soul is turned upside down so that it hangs
head downwards, only clinging to the body
by its big toe. That is why
we also believe that death and sleep
are sisters.
> —quoted by Knut Rasmussen,
> *The Intellectual Culture of the Iglulik Eskimo*

The day will come when, having mastered the ether,
the winds, the tides and gravity, we will harness
the energies of love for God. And then,
for the second time in the history
of the world, we will discover
fire.
> —Teilhard de Chardin,
> *The Evolution of Chastity*

MAY

ONE

There can be nothing on earth as peaceful and rewarding as working with the dead. I know, for I once was a public school teacher, for nine years and had worked my way up – the Teachers' Association considered it up – to vice-principal of a twenty-room junior high before ulcers got to me and I had to either quit or bleed to death. So I slid sideways into business, a multinational corporation so enormous only seven or eight countries in the world have a larger annual budget. I had always enjoyed the cold precision of mathematics, the absolute impersonal logic of it that makes conscience, may the maker of all be thanked, unnecessary: who ever heard of scarring the psyche of a computer, or disciplining it either? No patrolling the halls at coffee break with pen and detention list in hand (the black strap only a sacred memory), no parents adamant that the hefty dossier of their sweet little Johnny's annotated nastiness actually disguised the litmus paper soul of a *wunderkind*. A computer's only purpose is that it keeps spinning in or out data twenty-four hours a day every day of the year, its only possible problem that this process foul up, somehow. When that happens it must be corrected instantaneously, give or take fifteen seconds, but better yet yesterday, which was when you would have fixed it if only your logic had been clear enough to anticipate the breakdown. As it should have been. At least that is the way IBS looked at it; you simply kept working until it was fixed, and one morning when I got home again at 3:30 and was setting the alarm for 7:15 – since I'd been at work

1

twenty hours straight I thought I might steal an extra half-hour's sleep that morning – Liv opened one sleep-bleary eye at me dropping my shorts – I wear nothing in bed – and murmured,

"Why don't you just sleep at IBS?"

At 3:30 a.m. her voice is marvelously deep and I'm high, high, every cell in my body spinning like computer reels gone ingloriously berserk.

"I don't own any pyjamas. I'd terrorize the caretakers like this."

I slid under the cool covers, reaching, the skin inside her curled thigh as familiar and warm as the bottoms of her breasts.

"I'd be happy to have you without half your stomach," she said into my passing ear. "It'd be better than never having you at all."

That's why I'm now in the Micro-materials Reading Room in the basement of Cameron Library at the University of Alberta. A psychologist friend told me years ago that any man aging in the seventies who hasn't changed his career at least twice will either have a heart attack, an ulcer operation, be catatonic or dead by the time he is sixty-five. That was immensely reassuring to me. From the window of my office at the university I look across the North Saskatchewan River and see the Lear jet scoot up from behind downtown Edmonton and scatter to the power places of the world, but I'm behind that desk only in the mornings. Afternoons and occasionally evenings and Saturdays and holidays I'm in this quiet micro-material darkness snooping around through the past; if I keep on doing this long enough I'll become the world expert (or as Liv has it "ex-spurt" – a has-been under discernible pressure) on nineteenth-century western Canadian Indian and fur trade history. A reassuring mouthful too.

To be an historian is to be a time-traveller and a voyeur; I like that. Accumulating, sorting, matching and cross-referencing such data, and clues and hints of data as your diligent, imaginative research can uncover, you watch people as intensely as the records and your trained ingenuity permit; they cannot object. Indeed, they can't be disturbed in any way or have any idea this is happening because of course you didn't exist when they were alive. You can read every scrap of their most intimate correspondence; they're exposed to you, alone, in serene unconsciousness, actually the record of their factuality (that is, all the things they have physically done) is already complete; they will never "do" anything again and so the data of their life is now completed, ended and available for study. Obviously, this stands in total contrast to the way in which life happens before our eyes all the time, where we can't really understand who is doing what, or why because the "doing" humans are still alive and so always becoming something—or perhaps un-becoming. A living stream never at rest and forever moving into an unknown land. We have memory of course, and expectation—what more can we have with the present the slit it is between past and future, the point where we may *do*, but mostly remember and anticipate, fearfully hope? Philosophers sometimes speak of us as living in a wider 'fictive' or 'specious' present in which we continually try to remember past facts so that we can create a sound present understanding of character and world in the light of an expected future, but we still have only our one, particular, point of view and we are inevitably subject to the 'anthropocentric illusion,' we ourselves are tangled in these memories and expectations, we always are. Life our one long journey to our long home. People have to live it, and are often happy to do so without thought. On the other hand, by the very nature of my discipline as an historian I stand outside whatever I am observing; in my research the people and events have happened a century ago so there is no way I personally can be involved in the facts I am trying to uncover. There is no rush whatever for me to find anything: I can spend years gathering what data I can from as many diverse sources as I have time to unearth; my knowledge will be limited only by my own industry and by the records that remain extant. I can, actually, look upon the completed facts of nineteenth-century western Canada very much as we must imagine God himself looks upon them: knowing (within the uncertainty of human limits and the mutability of its records) all.

"You of course still believe in God," my psychologist friend said to me at the party on Saturday. Her name is, inappropriately, Joy.

"Still," I agreed. "Don't you say that to me every year about this time?"

"We shouldn't meet so often," she said, her classically white, lengthened face set in what must by now be her confirmed existentialist irony. In fact, when I think of a "modern" face the image of Joy's rises before me immediately, though she is exactly as old as I. In the past few years it seems essential to her that everyone she meets, even people who have known her since grade two, must understand very clearly once again that she believes in nothing. Such persistence always makes me intemperate in the opposite direction. Especially at parties.

"I keep hoping," Joy would not let it go, "that history might help you. Schools are zoos and computers of course can't teach anyone anything except the technology of spinning things, but history ... one would hope," she paused, her wine glass held so thoughtfully high. If she could have grown a beard her chin would have been greatly enhanced. "If you really are rooting about in past civilizations, surely..." she shrugged. It was all so self-evident that I'd be damned if I didn't evade it.

"History," I was full of wise saws and modern instances, "can tell us of no people that did not believe in God."

"A god," she amended instantly, "or several dozen. Not even that gives you pause?"

"No," not when she asked the question, "I will brook no paws."

Her brother Harold, a first-year member of the history department, pushed by with a very tall glass of something alcoholic ostentatiously at his teeth; eight years younger. He was beneath my notice my few years in small-town Vulcan but I knew even then he was a voyeuristic brat. Maybe that's why he's technically a better historian than I – he started so early. But technically only, not in the sweet heart's core, oh no, sing them over again to me, wonderful words –

"Hey, listen to me," Joy did not hesitate to jostle. I had

4

known her too long to be rude and leave; she would simply pursue. "You believe in a god as people always have, to quote you, a god to whom you pray about future events in hope that he'll manipulate them in some way and benefit you – your god can change the future?"

"If he pleases, of course, well?"

When I was a businessman we had met just as often, which is annually at Albert and Ardyth's spring party, and she had never bothered to snipe at what she supposed I believed, but now – perhaps my present label sets her off: I am a 'professor,' to 'profess' is very different than to 'business,' ah, to leave a name at which the world grows pale.

"Well, if your god has the power to change the future, at your request, then surely at your request he can also change the past."

"Of course," I said, much too quickly.

"But that," Joy had at me squarely with her main thrust, "that is patently ridiculous and if you're an historian you know it."

"What do you mean, *if* I'm an historian?"

"Well, you are, so you know it's ridiculous. You dig around in the past as if – you know you do – as if it had already all happened, whatever you find is absolutely unchangeable. Could you," she was very nearly laughing now: only a defeated opponent could make her name come true, "the most famous event in your area, could you pray that Louis Riel should not be hanged, today, right now in 1980? And your god would answer your prayer – suddenly Riel would *not* have been hanged?"

But she did not quite laugh; her eyes below her plucked brows suddenly gained a clear grey wideness; almost like distant longing. Perhaps I just wanted to see that, groping frantically as I was to distract her historical absurdity; I tried peevishness.

"Oh it's always that praying Riel, don't you know of anyone else in the nineteenth century, always —"

"What does it matter who?"

"Try Darcy McGee, George A. Custer, anyone."

"I don't know McGee [I nearly roared!] and Custer was

5

involved with Indians, I wouldn't want to make it too complicated for your Christian god."

"So considerate!"

"Well? He's not hanged?" Her philosophic bloodhounds undetracted.

"You choose Riel, I suppose, because his death is a very commonly known [she did not notice my McGee jab] 'hard historic fact,' as it were?"

She hesitated; I might out-expert her. "He was hanged in 1885, wasn't he?"

"I said *is*, not *was*, it is right now a hard historic fact, you'd say?"

"Yes, okay, yes, *is*."

"In other words, the actual action of the hanging is completed, now. Riel is not being hanged now, in Regina or anywhere else."

"Yes of course. So?"

I wasn't sure of 'so' myself, but I had to keep throwing out the, in this case, rotten fish of Professor Becker's argument since at the moment my flailing mind striated by wine could seem to hook into nothing else.

"You're talking," I continued, "not about changing the actual historical event but about changing the record of that event [I was contradicting my own operational theory and attempted practice, but she could not know that], which is a very different thing. Because historians always deal exclusively with the records, not with the events themselves which happen only once and are, by the very nature of human life, unrepeatable. History after all is not physics. The historian must reach conclusions using all the miscellaneous and often chance records of all sorts of people who observed with untrained eyes something which certainly wasn't as controlled as even the sloppiest laboratory experiment, and their observations can never be tested for accuracy by any repetition. Therefore," Joy was trying to interrupt but I was in lecture now, I would (could?) brook no pause, "therefore each historian inevitably makes a personal selection of the facts he chooses to consider, *so* — you see, I got to your so — so what if

6

an historian came along today who had some reason to doubt the mass of records about Riel's hanging? Elementary, my dear Doctor Lemming. He might believe, as some Metis do to this day, that Riel was not hanged but was actually rescued by Dumont and his riders from Montana, that the police and the government, to avoid humiliation and to give Macdonald his political coup in the East (which was why Riel was hanged anyway), he might believe the authorities just did an incredible cover-up, maybe even hanged someone else so they'd have a body to bury. Ergo, all the extant written records were systematically falsified and then our oddball historian would find one ancient Metis who told him just before she died that she had seen Riel walking on a street in St. Vital with his grandchildren in 1906. Eh, what about that?"

"Why would Riel go along with —"

"They bought him off, silly, the haves have always unendingly destroyed the have nots!"

Joy now had me by the shoulders; both hands. "What has that got to do with my question?"

"Listen my friend," I was groping in the salty muck at the bottom of the barrel, "the simple statement, 'In November 1885 Louis Riel was hanged in the Northwest Territories' is historically not so simple. Quite a number of people were hanged then, do you know how many?"

"No, but—do you?"

"Yes," I said. "I do. Every one. Are their hangings historical facts also? If so, why should God change Riel's hangings and not—just to stick with hangings associated with the so-called Rebellion—not Wandering Spirit's hanging, or Iron Body's or Round the Sky's or Miserable Man's? Your one little generalization about one past event is made up of millions of individual facts and if we had a William Faulkner—God spare us!—to write the stories of all those hangings we'd see pretty quick how infinitely complex any little human —"

"James! Stop it!"

Where was Liv? Didn't she have eyes? I suddenly realized that Albert and Ardyth always gave stupid parties; there was never a single idiot standing about, listening, who would

7

help me destroy this conversation with one good joke.

"Could your god," Joy said steadily, "now change the fact that Riel was hanged in 1885, *now?*"

"Well," I said heavily; we were back to the main event. "Why would you expect ... God to be ... randomly capricious...."

"Why not?"

"There's no reason ... for reason, it just happens to be the way he's set up the universe. It's not chaos, stars spin in a certain order, you walk off the High Level Bridge and you fall two hundred feet to —"

"You can't step off," her forehead was almost touching mine, "while praying for levitation?"

"O you can, of course. Pray, of course."

"But don't expect much!"

"Well...."

She had left me nothing but my appeal to order, and now that stood tottering. We were both seven when we first met and her grey-eyed, sometimes immovable seriousness pinned me immediately; I remember once after a May rain I ate an earthworm for her because she wanted a description – not the taste itself, only a description – of how it tasted. I almost swallowed it too, and certainly got enough to be able to describe the taste forever. Green and variously squitchy.

"And your poor friend Louis R certainly was and certainly will remain hanged." She sounded almost sad; I remembered again with a bitterness only years can engrain how gently she held my head as I got rid of the worm and my somewhat earlier lunch. So I suppose a mind frantically searching, clutching for anything can be considered in a state of prayer, at least when one-upmanship fades before a possible glimmer of understanding. I sometimes believe in that, too.

"I've never prayed to change the past," I said, and realized what I was saying, "not the research past ... personal is different ..." between heads and shoulders I saw a girl with long hair so dark it appeared black, so long it seemed momentarily she was wearing nothing else. "To tell the truth, I've never even thought of doing that."

"Out of the mouths of babes," Joy said, "and atheists." So

confirmed in her blithe irony that it made me suddenly desperate O dear God to force one tiny sliver of faith between her perfect ironical teeth.

"But ... if I did, pray that," I had no guide to wherever I might be going. Albert with drinks moved by and across the room the girl was turning an incredible face towards me so that I had to quickly close my eyes, concentrate, follow words blind one after the other as they made the path I was walking, "but if I could and ... God answered that prayer, then ... Riel would ... never actually have been hanged, at all."

Joy stared at me, her eyes slightly glazed.

"That's it." I said. "Of course, because the hanging would have had to *not take place in 1885*! Of course!" I was amazed once I dared admit it, almost staggered, "All records actually could have all been falsified and every historian now would only find evidence that he had been hanged, but the fact is that he would have had to be *not hanged then*! And he would not have been, then!"

"No, no!" Joy's hand clamped onto my sleeve, "I mean suddenly, *now*. So we all know God can do it, now!"

"No! Don't you see, Joy, you're thinking as if God were living in time sequence with us but of course he doesn't, he's by necessary definition *not* human, time is nothing to him."

"You're just weaseling out of it, you're —"

"No, listen, for God you have to set it up differently. 1980 and 1885 are as it were the same instant to him and he would know in 1885 that I in 1980 would make this prayer, 'O Lord have mercy, don't let them hang Riel,' and he would answer my prayer, he would move those thousands, then, in 1885, to not hang him. And all the millions now dead who have always believed him hanged—they had to believe it because they were told that, none of them actually saw him dangling or even handled the original sworn death witness statements as I have, and I've never had reason to doubt their veracity—all those people have thought wrongly for generations that he was hanged."

"For your prayer to be answered, would you have to know he was never hanged?"

The black-haired girl spoke beside me, though not looking

at me. Her dress was gold and cotton lamé to the floor; her face purest porcelain, and her voice.

"Wha ... no, no, I guess not, what would it matter? Maybe they did fake all the records, I mean everybody knows the sheriff refused to officiate at the hanging, he sent his deputy, and the body was shipped in an unmarked boxcar to St. Boniface, there were a million chances to ... actually it's more than possible he never was hanged and there's so much talk now about pardoning him in the House of Commons, you'll see, one of these days they'll 'discover' some secret memos, some —"

"Jakie," Joy murmured, almost plaintively. "Jakie?"

"Joy," I said. Sadness turned me round to her like a wave, my schoolboy name caught in the memory of her particular voice, her eyes glancing up in momentarily indefensible discouragement. "Joy." I would never have dared think it, out of myself, and I felt suddenly very warm toward her, almost happy. All Vulcan past was not only bleak, my very childhood ... but the black-haired girl was gone.

I stared an empty circle around the crowded room; where she had first turned toward me there was only a blank window with the strewn lights of Edmonton far below. And her voice, it seemed perhaps ... perhaps still speaking softly, somewhere.

"God..." I hesitated; but the word itself was an anchor. "God has done ... what he does, whatever the records say after."

"And he can change ... past facts?" Joy stared at me.

"God's 'consciousness' has no sequence. All is now."

But when your head nods in the cone of a microfilm reader on Tuesday afternoon, such a thought is barely short of professional blasphemy. Especially when you continue to hear a voice singing as it seems, softly somewhere: "History is a needle/for putting men asleep/anointed with the poison/of all they want to keep."

SASKATCHEWAN HERALD, Battleford, N.W.T. (Canada), Monday, August 25, 1878. / TELEGRAPHIC NEWS will be found on the fourth page. / ON THE WING-J.D. Doherty and Joseph McIntyre, who have been in Battleford for some time with a photographic gallery, folded their tents one day last week and moved off for Carleton, Prince Albert, and all points East.

Here are the facts: every single letter of each word with every punctuation mark and space of that newspaper was set individually by the hands of P.G. Laurie, Editor and Proprietor. Facts one hundred and two years old. Who would pray to change them? It is possible someone has. Would it be easier if I could see the pictures Messrs. Doherty and McIntyre showed to those lonely settlers and startled, gaping Indians inside their square tents on the Battle River flats? Perhaps they also had brought a camera, had themselves taken pictures. Of Mr. Laurie breaking up a form of type so he could set the next font of heavy cast letters he had hauled by oxcart from Winnipeg, barely enough to print a single page – but what difference could a picture make? The grouped letters I see shift before my eyes as I slowly turn the handle of the microfilm reader are nothing more than slightly transparent shadows of his original ink, not actually the imprint of the letters themselves, leave alone the letters, leave alone the hand of the wordmaker; leave by far alone his personal reflective consciousness which dared to begin the *Saskatchewan Herald* when there were perhaps two hundred English speakers scattered about the unsettled bush and no more than fifty of them could read.

A kind of prayer-manoeuvred *1984*, dear god on the trail that was Battleford's only street.

The air conditioning whirs relentlessly, and burps somewhere deep in its bowels. Except for one other reader pyramid of light, the Reading Room is indeterminate grey, I am within ashes. I look at my hand, at my other hand: known flesh, patterns of skin creases, hair, nail shapes. When I draw my hands out of the light that lays the demarcated shadows of P.G. Laurie's words over them, when I hold them against the ashen depthlessness of the room, I can still see them – there, the thumbs touch – but I may be looking through them. They now appear to be without substance or dimension, transparent, if I dared turn them on edge they might not even make a line. We the living in our endlessly moving slit

11

of present are variable and complex and transparent beyond comprehension, and if one dare not trust the dead, then who....

"Professor Dyck?"

At certain moments your name spoken is more than a touch because it enters you more deeply. The question of one's formal name – I hear my own every day in any tone, anger or neutrality or respect or fawning, that – I have held certain positions which elicit such responses – a face materializes out of greyness, long hair and narrow Egyptian nose and wide black eyes. That tawny imperial skin. I can only stare; she is at my shoulder.

"You are ... Dr. James Dyck ... History."

The hair and lamé girl from the party ... woman, definitely woman.

"Yes."

"Oh." She has known it but is nevertheless mildly surprised. We seem to be tangled in each other's eyes; I cannot blink and neither does she. She is tilting closer, she has nothing further to ask me, I cannot tell whether her mouth is opening to say anything because I am being moved into the sheer blackness of her eyes – 'I swear she casts a shadow white as stone' – my voice saying something:

"... just looking, at my hands...."

and there they are on either side of her face, I notice that peripherally and I can feel her long hair on the backs of my hands though I cannot see it against the dark room, it parts soft as air under my fingers and the warmths of our faces are coming together, mine moving up the hard beam of her look and her face blurs out of focus as I feel her lips breathe her breath, there. Somewhere something is pounding, rapidly, rapidly.

Skin between black eyebrows at the bridge of a nose; an ear exposed through a fall of hair in the angled glare from my micro reader. I reach and switch off the light, my glasses are smeared anyway.

"Thank you," she says slowly. For the light I think; her face moves a little and I feel her sit on my knee, legs bent be-

12

tween mine. She is wearing worn jeans. "There is no one else here."

"You taste ... sweet ..." I can only be obvious. But the dark gives a presence no light can create and I have to mumble, already instinctively secretive. "The archivist Eddie Dalrymple likes to bring me things ... things he thinks I want."

"I know," she says away from me and I know that momentarily she is facing where she will see the grey oblong of the door if it opened, down the phalanx of unlit readers. "Do you ... want them?"

"What?"

"The things, he brings?"

"I have, once or twice. You were at Albert and Ardyth's party."

"The view was fine, from the window."

"But the party pretty awful."

Our cheeks are touching, our mouths beside each other's ears; someone should be sitting at the next reader so he would never know we are saying anything. We aren't saying anything. Our mouths may be moving to keep our hands motionless.

"You looked so sad and troubled," she murmurs, "Joy Lemming talking to you."

"An old friend. She's troubled me since we were seven."

"I have old friends like that too."

"'For man is born for trouble as the sparks fly upwards.'"

"I don't believe everything in Job is a necessity," past my ear.

It is like stepping through a mirror and feeling someone you have never seen but realize you have known forever, not a doppelgänger—she is shaped nothing like me!—but a sudden knowing that is edged with ... possible ... I could move my hands anywhere on her full body and she could move hers over mine yet at the moment I do not want that nor does she. We motionlessly place some words in this air-rushing darkness, we will never again feel so innocent inside an accepting innocence we did not know we had and which we are already committed to leave without question because this certain se-

13

crecy envelops us also, it is my heart nudging the soft side of her breast, it is a texture of cheek and shallow quick breathing and my left hand lying on her thigh, closed so that her warmth comes against the backs of my fingers, the inside tip of my thumb. Certainly tenderness, possibly terror.

"She ... she was baiting me with God, and you asked me such a good question and I looked for you, in every room, but...."

"You were letting go, a little."

"I don't drink much."

"That's not what I mean."

"I wanted to talk to you, to ask you ... something."

She is silent, against me so close that very soon I will see her frightening thoughts behind my eyelids. And her next words do startle me, more than her materialization at my shoulder.

"You're still too careful. Whole lands, peoples, may exist and we don't know it. Borges wrote a story about how an entire planet was eventually discovered through the conjunction of a mirror and a defective, out-of-date version of the *Encyclopaedia Britannica.*"

"What?"

"A whole planet, unknown till then. Borges, the Argentinian writer, I think in his story the discovery of the planet Tlön begins when he accidentally reads the encyclopaedia in a mirror."

"Backwards?"

"I suppose so," she says against my ear as if she were whispering a secret neither of us could audibly voice. "And then he discovers a whole encyclopaedia has been written about Tlön that describes everything, its languages and the different Tlön peoples, their history, all the fauna and flora and climate—forty-eight volumes, twice as big as the *Britannica.*"

"All the possible human and natural history of a planet that never existed?"

"Yes ... but how can you be sure it didn't? He finds only one volume, the other forty-seven have disappeared because only one copy of each was ever printed and then —"

"Only *one* copy, how ...?"

I cannot even formulate a question; her voice singing in my ear like trees.

"It's about a planet," she explains with tender patience, "invented in the nineteenth century by an enormous number of brilliant men hired to do that on the whim of a tycoon, and when they've done it he has another whim and destroys it. The encyclopaedia. So Borges says in his story."

"But the catch is, the tycoon missed one volume and so the planet became known?"

"The one volume was found again," she whispers in my ear, "only after Tlön was separately discovered in a mirror."

Accidentally facing an opened, defective *Encyclopaedia Britannica*. I know, yes; whatever place those brilliant men thought they were inventing actually already existed. In mirrors. The use of a mirror is not to be painted upon. Surface is not all, nor ashes.

There is not light enough in the Micro-materials Room to see any mirror, but if we have not stepped through it we must be still inside. Since she appeared I am simply in now, including her round weight on my leg, her breast against my chest. But there is the world I have lived until this ineffable revelation, just over the brow of the hill as it seems of my present sensations and it will materialize before me at some moment, I know that too; how inappropriately.

"We are God's inventions," she says. "He could wave his... hand, rod, whatever, over these microfilms and worlds would vanish, whole races replete with history appear and who could know the difference? For us they would always have been, or never."

"God can be no capricious tycoon."

"Thank God," she says.

And rises just as I am aware my leg is numb. I stand with her: I seem to be sighting down the faint, white part of her hair towards the grey door as if she were some new, terrifying weapon.

"I wanted to ask you, at the party did you sing, somewhere, 'History is a needle ...'?"

"Leonard Cohen."

"Your voice has been talking to me, round and round."

"Are you like that too?"

"A pack rat, the strangest things I've read or heard, clusters of words."

"Catalogues and want ads too?"

"Well, my subconscious has some discernment."

Her breath tugs in small laughter. "You were so busy lecturing each other, I stood there and told you that very quietly, but you didn't notice."

"You were there for a while, beside me?"

"Yes. I'm Gillian Overton, Joy's my sister-in-law."

"You're ... Harold's...."

"Yes, his wife."

A needle of my Vulcan past slides deep into me: Harold. Harold Lemming came to teach in our department last summer, I was the junior member on his hiring committee and did not mention I had ever known him. Graduate of Queen's and Toronto and Oxford; absolutely brilliant. There was "Married" on the c.v. yes, but like this, and ten years younger? At least, perhaps more. Where did he find and hide her so long?

"How come ... we've never met?" I say stupidly.

"I go nowhere in public with Harold, especially parties. He refuses to have me 'decorate his presence' anywhere."

Which sounds like absolutist Lemming. Incredible, as if anyone couldn't benefit from such "decoration." There is no opinion in her voice, a mere fact which need not concern us since it seems to concern someone else. Our noses brush, stub a little.

"My wife is Liv and my daughter is Rebecca," I say steadily, studying the unreadable spaces between her eyes. "She's ten, and my mother Ruth lives in Vulcan."

"I know that," Gillian whispers.

"You do?"

"Yes."

"Well, I know a bit about Harold."

"I know. I've never been to Vulcan."

"How come, his parents still...."

"He won't take me. That has nothing to do with me."

16

"Surely a little."

"Absolutely nothing."

"Aren't you married, don't you live together?"

"Of course. But I'm me and he's he."

An incredible concept of marriage. As mine must be. To her now, we are kissing, in each other's arms, tentatively as children and tasting for the first time, really, to the contemplated texture of each other's mouths moving beyond the tip of sensation; that first a hasty gulp and these possibilities of feast abruptly enormous. I am staggered by her bending body, her slender softness that is against me and clasped like velvet steel since she does not, as Liv would put it, wear much underwear, o sweetest

"Easy, easy," she places between my lips, "there's no rush."

"Yes, there is, there —" and we are already coming unstuck, with a small sucking sound not at her words but at Liv's perception, sharp as struck steel in my head. For which I do and will love her, my wife, as for so much more presently unnameable since its language has nothing to do either with actions or sequential thought. Or instinctive secrecy. After fourteen years of marriage, fourteen to the month as it fell upon a Daye in the merrie Month of Maye, life together so settled and placidly complete that any memory of separateness, of being single and responsible only to myself — though I was that until the age of twenty-eight and everyone in the Mennonite world where I must necessarily touch it to see my mother thought I was either nose-in-the-air fussy or, perhaps more likely, unfortunately 'odd' — after all I had four older sisters and it was clear that someone with my looks and ability, as they told me so often, quickly before I disappeared again — how come I always disappeared like the Jew in the long night? — no man could really want to continue being a bachelor and cook and wash his own — any personal memory of singleness now like a micro-material discovery: a person so long vanished he can only be impersonally dead. Every cell in the body worn out and replaced three times — except the brain — that man is twice legally dead but surely, surely happily reborn to life together now, a personal landscape shifted into twos, threes since Rebecca. Tolstoi does not count. He is simply with us, his lolling happy face, black and tan body twisting around my legs, bumps me in the undiscourageable anticipation that I will tip him over and chase him barking and snarling just out of reach across the yard. I could come through the gate with hands dripping human blood and he would greet me in exactly the same way. But now to enter the house. I do not know how I will look at her. I drop my briefcase on the grass, roar and sprint after Tolstoi, a few spurts of energy which he evades in quick diagonals, taunting me with teeth slavering as though he would rip me open, and then I drop my hands and immediately he is against my leg, his long nose nudging upward for my palm, laughing at my fingers crumpling his ears. I do not know how I will look to her. At her.

I am tearing lettuce for the salad when she comes home. Everyone returns to his place differently; Liv shedding her light coat looks about, I know, with a clear eye: what has changed, anything, and how is it I can walk into this comfortable house, again, and know it belongs to me and mine? Her Swedish father came to Canada as a logger and sawed his way to fortune, money at any rate, but in her family everyone knew who owned everything, including Mama and all the blondly lovely children. Henk Neilson shared nothing with anyone. He might give you anything he had, and he sometimes did and then it was yours completely but until he did that it was his. "If you're sure of the ownership," he'd roar at me, "you'll never have trouble with the justice." Once I had the nerve to ask back, "But what about the love?" Twice actually, but that was long ago; he has not aged well. His daughter Liv has, and I hear her close the front closet door and she has seen my briefcase is not there so she knows I have come through the back, that is, walked the one and a half miles from the University Library on this overhung spring day threatening steamy showers.

"Hey," she calls, "smells good!"

"Borscht, salad and apple pie supper," I answer. The big knife slips aside on the Mexican tomato; that's all I need now, blood.

"The perfect freezer cook," she is in the doorway of the kitchen shuffling the handful of mail. So I can glance up at her, quickly.

I don't really need to. I have seen her just there so often the memory is like looking in the mirror when I shave: the short reddish blonde hair, the round face, crisp in profile, everything's the same. And any changing in her will be so gradual, and it will be taking place in me too so that relative to each other we remain precisely where we have been. Unmoved? No, the mediaevalists told us long ago that love first enters at the eye and no matter where it moves to from there it remains always in the eye, especially the unconscious eye of happy memory. Liv places the mail on the kitchen table coming towards me and I keep my head down, fanning sliced tomatoes into a spiral on their nest of lettuce. But sometimes things do change; if love is even possible, I suddenly know that I love her this instant as I never have before.

"Every woman needs a wife like you," she rubs her cheek against my stubble, her smell of office smoke but, deep down, of moss. Like always. Her smell, her size, the very weight of her tilted against me is as familiar as the worn sheepskin slippers on my feet: as I surely am to her. "I thought you took the rib roast out this morning."

"I did, but I got home too late to make it."

"You'll ruin your eyes reading that old stuff so long in that poor light."

"I take ... breaks. Quite often."

"Every day, at lunch," she grins. "And who else over there works nine hours a day at this time of year, who?"

"They say Lemming doesn't leave before midnight, I come home to make sup—"

"Harold Lemming is a minor pedant."

"But brilliant, no question there."

"Bah." Liv splashes water over her long hands in the sink, "What good is brilliance without discernment?" She dries her hands on the oven towel and bends to pull open the cupboards, narrowly missing my kneecap. "If he couldn't find a flush toilet, he wouldn't be able to take a leak."

19

"Death by retained urine poisoning," and I burst out laughing. "I should get Pete Ostruck to take him hunting, once in the bush —"

I realize I am laughing much, much too loudly; Liv straightens up, her eyebrow slightly arched at me, the bread-basket in her hand. I must come back at her fast.

"What's discernment got to do with one's habits of evacuation, huh?"

"Lots," with concentration, bending again. That's something else I loved in her at first, and now: her digging in, her not letting go until everything is resolved; which helps make her the excellent travel agent she is.

"What, what?"

"When you make a fuss about what you do five or six times every day, there's not much —"

"Does Harold Lemming fuss about finding a —"

"You ninny." Liv hips me aside, pulling out breadboard and breadknife in one motion. "It was supposed to be smart."

"O, it was." A great deal smarter than she knows.

"It's silly, a holdover I guess from our talking in the office, we finally got on something everybody has experience with."

"Men and toilets?"

"Yes!" she is laughing, slicing rye bread. "An old regular on his way now to Greece and he was asking about toilets — he and his wife travel all over the world and at some point in every long trip he says they are talking about nothing but toilets, what facilities, what smell, where are they, quick, quick, there?"

"Like Becca at the Duomo in Florence."

"Exactly. These people are old hands, they've been through everything and he's so polite he was just getting in a slightly tinted joke, I mean you can barely imagine him using one and we just carried on after he left."

"I know, I know," I say lightly, "every old man tries his risqué lines on you." Not lightly enough, o heavy.

"What about me in Florence?"

Becca framed by the hall doorway, her finger in a thick book as usual. 'Than whom the grasses so tall are not taller, my lovely daughter.' "I smell borscht," she says. "I'm hu-u-u-n-gry!"

I stir. "The last jar Gramma made, just about ready." My face in the beefy cabbage steam of it, my small round mother bent and shoving split poplar into a stove, memory like a sharp sudden flame. I am younger than Becca, I have lugged in an enormous armful of wood because I'm so lazy, always reading my mother complains gently, so lazy I'm sure to kill myself as the proverb says by carrying myself to death. Low German wisdom: *Awlle Fuelle drouge sich dowt.* You can't make a living reading she mutters to the open fire box, just because you're the youngest doesn't mean you can lie around and chew your fingernails all day reading.

"'Risqué lines'?" Liv materializes, nose to nose.

"What?" Momentarily lost. "You know, supposed to be funny, too."

"No old men sit there in my office, sigh deeply and casually cross their gorgeous legs."

I step aside; she has the soup ladle ready, which gives me the excuse. "They all wear jeans now."

"Oh, skirts are back when they need to be."

Not for some I could mention. Strong sandaled feet and warm calves, legs I have never seen but felt an instant inside their tough denim columns. When Becca bends to new shoots of spring grass above the creek bluff I see her sturdy child's leg outlined by her jeans, but also her ankles shaped tight in an adult vee of muscle and tendon. She is much closer to Becca's age than mine, dear god there is a sudden heavy doubleness in me that grasps at anything female as if I were once again awash with adolescence though I do not feel guilty, I do not, no, amazingly, not yet. I cannot understand that either, she was just there, this as it seems spaced awareness of female, even stunningly in my own daughter, soon I'll be examining the budding trees for stamen and pistil, the pistil must be male eh? – silly laughing, I could have said something, so, I'm so ludicrous a fool at forty is a fool indeed but at forty-two....

Past the edge of Becca's feet the bent cliffs that give Whitemud Creek its name are hacked out of the greening valley. But the stream directly below is curled tight, dirt grey with run-off, so much from this height like old rippled concrete that a person could easily step across or along it, the journey

21

home by water an endlessly repeated motif of all western literature which betrays man's implacable longing for change and new discovery, heroes are always travellers over water either leaving or returning home for or from adventure or new worlds, water the image of all prime matter containing all solid bodies before they acquire form and rigidity. I'm in the wrong occupation again; still. I should be pontificating on the mythology of literature where everything must always mean anything beyond what it most obviously is. My daughter's winter-white feet—to mythologize?—tiny in her worn Adidas, stand there solidly against the nothing of air and I reach for her shoulder because Liv has told me for ten years not to keep warning her of the fearfulness of height and speed and ice and the lightning quickness of fire. "Children have their own, natural, self-protecting fears," she says, "don't afflict them with your particular horrors." So my silent hand is a reminder of arms-length happiness and she glances about at me, her pink mouth forming that curve that will momentarily find a smile and Tolstoi's bark bursts in the brush behind me and I turn too fast, the clay crumbles under my left foot and for one instant the valley yawns gasp over eroded mud and Becca has turned and in that motion slammed my arm back and I thump down hard—thank God hard—on my buttocks as my feet flop out into space. Becca is kneeling beside me stretched on solid ground, the sky circling her golden hair.

"Hey," she says. "Be careful."

I pull her tight, kiss her natural honey with a whiff of borscht.

A long "hallo-o-o-o" carries from below. I ease up with Becca in my arms and we peer between my boots. Three hundred feet.

A man stands across the creek, a bluish dot gesticulating at the last roll of dirt clods I knocked loose pouring into the muddy water. The ripples from their fall spread, elongating downstream like concentric, growing eggs. The man waves more frantically, now that he has our attention, bellowing something; surely a decent middle-class yeller, you've disturbed my walk! If you fell I'd be forced to try and fish you out, be considerate or I'll carry around a neighbourhood petition about you! I wave down to him, as if friendly; I can't make a sound yet for my hammering heart and Becca and I withdraw cautiously, crawl back from the cliff. We stretch out together, the low bushes and grey grass of last year barely gesticulating in the air above us. Tolstoi's nose appears, snuffles nearer and he lengthens himself luxuriously along the hollow where our bodies touch. His nose in my armpit, breathing.

"Look," Becca says after a time, "there's heaven."

Through a rift wide as half the sky light sprays up between two layers of gilt-edged thunderheads; an immense halo crowning the evening edge of the earth. I move my hand under Tolstoi, who grumbles a little, and find her strong lithe hand in mine.

"I hope Gramma can see that glory," she adds then.

I'm about to remind her that Gramma's room over two hundred miles away faces north and though she might grasp the colour she could never distinguish that overwhelming detail, but saying it would be silly: those two have no useless logic between them. Born seventy-five years apart with perhaps fifty words of a common language and barely as much common culture – a nineteenth-century Mennonite peasant girl poor in Russia and an urban Canadian girl of the twentieth who has never needed anything more than to reach out and take it – yet the girl understands the old woman shrunk so tiny from living and who longs now only for the still unreachable glory of a literal heaven. Singing gently, her voice adrift in the hollows of her half-blind deafness now loud, now dropping two keys between syllables and thinning into an irreduceable thread, *"Dort ueber jenem Sternenmeer, dort ist ein schoenes Land...."*

"What's she singing, Daddy?"

And I swallow quickly, whisper, though she could not hear me unless I shouted into her ear, "'There over yonder sea of stars, there is a beauti – a better land.'"

"'Beautiful' is better," Becca whispers back.

"Yes, but the rhythm in English is...."

The rhythm here on the cliff above the valley slowly turning May green under a blazing, livid halo is the three of us breathing and the touchable warmth of our bodies and the tiny smell of new leaves and the unsoftened earth sheered away a little more by another spring run-off like every eroded parkland stream. There is being here, and memory: why can't the mind be empty, why always fingered by anticipation or hope or worry and always memory, what an infernal attribute to keep a human being restless and longing, angry without end. There is a white face rising into grey, there is memory to be slipped aside if possible, there are rivers cut sharply as rooting branching trees into the flat cardboard prairie *so that when he comes forward, quickly, the stewardess alone in the empty first class is contemplating the flawless face reflected in her nightcase mirror. He swings into the right seats. Already the plane has relentlessly droned itself over the river lying north and south here, over a blackish spiderwork of trees arranged by loops upon river loops into a wider valley — that has to be the Red Deer River — it is all so fast, too fast. He slides across to the left seats: that deep cut angling southwest must be the South Saskatchewan. He presses his forehead against the window; six miles below, between white prairie and white river, the fringes of brown cliff gradually straighten as if drawn freehand into mist. He presses harder, his forehead numb, but the raw valley below draws steadily away — the stupid pilot is flying dead-centre over where the rivers join their ice, it is already past and he has not so much as a memory of it.*

"Looks so cold down there, doesn't it!" The stewardess, her perfect face smiling.

Fury leaps in him, irrationally. "February," he mutters, "a Canadian...."

He is past her legs, she expects blooming bananas? back in his seat. Strong plastic trayback, strong plastic window. The Red Deer River loops across its shallow drift, swinging almost back to touch itself in shadows carved by the winter sun. The window hardens his face with cold, hardens the river out of curls into curves, then simply a bent line between the grey mushrooms of badlands. Soon that too has vanished in a long valley northwest, but now he has a memory to lay

*on the white land ordered by faint webs of fences, by squares,
oblongs of texture. The memory of that little man in a
summer day, white sleeves looped by gold links, a smooth
hand passing over his face and bulging eyes like a kiss and
suddenly holding … holding an unbelievable curve of white
teeth, teeth that have just emerged out of the man's own
manicured head. He must have seen that, he remembers
carefully, standing in front of their log house at Cold Lake
on the spot where his mother stood once, later, when a
greyish picture was being taken, she small in an apron like a
white yoke against the grey mudded logs and the even
smaller figures of two of his sisters already whitely aproned
on her right and himself a greyish smudge against her left. In
front of the screen doors where in summer he often stood
fearfully waiting to hear the cowbells return from the free-
range stretching west of their homestead, knowing his
mother would surely bring the cows if she could find them in
the mosquito-whining bush, knowing if she went too far she
must find them to guide her back home, the smudge-smoke
waiting, a blue flat cloud caught above the corral in a motionless net of poplar and spruce darkness. He had stared,
rigid, at the teeth separated with such inhuman precision out
of what he had supposed till then was a living face. The
man's blurred voice asks him if he can take his out too, and
he cannot so much as shake his head when he has never
thought it possible to try. And his mother's face beyond the
sheen of screen door, not laughing like the little grey man
when with a sudden jolt of terror he claws inside his own
mouth, tearing at his tiny, o blessed be the Lord Jesus immovable teeth.*

*"That's not for us, Bengelchi," she says, coming out and
nubbling his head. "We're not that advanced yet."*

*But she was soon advanced enough. The first in the family,
after she wrenched her left arm out of its socket falling between the split poles of the hayrack and after two years of
sporadic paralysis finally getting to a doctor who tells her she
should have been sewn together as soon as it happened, that
she will never heal straight now, not at her age and her teeth
draining poison like they are into her body. Her teeth then no*

more than broken black or yellowish stumps, destroyed systematically by chewing salt whenever their unending pain became more unbearable than the sharper, but briefer, agony of killing them.

The Bow River like a greyish crevasse laid into the Blackfoot Reserve; his tongue slides around his own teeth, capped, filled, so solid and strong the dentists always say, all those turnips and boiled cabbage grown in Alberta bush that destroyed his mother's ... he will soon be as old as she was then. She has always seemed so ... ancient? Venerable? Bits of pictures, touches, words will fall on him like rain as long as he lives and how will he ever recapture her? The feeling he knew when her eyes were still level with his and she would say a word straight to him, her hand firm then, unshaky on his own. "Die letzte Nacht im Eltern Haus." *To say that in English sounded merely silly, perhaps it was her lilt on "Eltern" that made the equivalent "parents" so bony: words she first said when he first ran and almost every time he returned, for a day, even the very short day he brought his wife through the door, married in an abrupt ceremony far across mountains and for which she had no more warning than to airmail a poem he never knew where she found. The poem was doddery though the feelings were right, for her; he could hear her voice sounding the words as her hand slowly moved copying them, perhaps out of her head:* "Wohl dir, du hast es gut ... " *Did she ever write poetry? Impossible.*

The Calgary airport is khaki metal walls and fans blowing through heaters hung from exposed pipes; after an L-1011 the rented car seems barely a basket. He folds and buckles himself in, it quivers, shudders on the streets and highways broken by a long winter. But the white mountains, the Bow River bridge rumbling and the air like ice sift him out of his jet-lag, out of the staggering weariness of walking momentarily on cement. Among the trees of this valley buffalo wintered with the Blackfeet, bedded in these folds. The voice of the long distance operator trying to hammer him awake, to make him understand. How had she found him at that Montreal hotel? Liv and IBS. How had she phoned and talked to

Liv? Finally. He had let her? He had nothing further to say about it. To say at all.

The memory has to be wrong, they could never have carried the tub up the steep pole stairs, leave alone the hot kettle, why would they have carried that up into the sleeping loft? Yet he remembers her bending across the tub in the angle of the rafters where he slept curled at night into wool on a straw sack, the house logs cracking fearfully in the cold when he rams himself up out of a nightmare or worse sleepwalking; the stovepipe stands erect into darkness at the edge of his mattress. And she leans forever at the angle of the rafters, clawing at the kettle from which his big sister Ruth has poured boiling water into the tin tub and thoughtlessly onto Eva squatting to bathe in the tepid water he has just been lifted from: that scream must have echoed in the kitchen below, and his mother's too, the kettle now in her hand with Ruth frozen in the soft steam of her pouring, her mouth fallen open and her hands still up, crooked as if still holding the blackened kettle which will suck up that steaming fall of water again, it will never have gouged at Eva's thigh, her tiny breast. Perhaps that did not happen in winter. Any more than it happened in the sleeping loft; it might have been summer when the gigantic bull stalked out of free-range, roaring, and shook his head and clawed dust about the yard all afternoon so that none of them dared open the door, not even his mother, and he actually prayed, prayed that his father appear, O lieber Jesu mach mich fromm help him to come, now from wherever he is, somewhere, help him to come big and strong enough home early for Sunday, help, and then there he is coming steadily down the wagon tracks with a thick poplar stick in his hand and going to the bull hoisting dust over himself, head down and roaring, and has hammered him across the nose and jammed the stick into his ring and forced him nose-high out of the yard; has smashed the poplar on the bull's swiftly fleeing rump. Smashing fear, there is nothing but happiness when the familiar appears, even his black father.

He cannot have been thinking in English then. How? In

27

the Low German she has always spoken to him, that he screams into the telephone to make her understand he will come, yoh, yoh he is coming! Yoh, as soon as a plane leaves for the west! Her perfect removable teeth as if carved from a marble picture filling her mouth, moving her jaw down out of the folds of her face into a strong chin again, the uneasy evenness of her quick smile which no longer depends only on her eyes and cheeks.

Only images are necessary to memory, the field snow sifted between stubble. She stands with her left arm crooked against the belly of a shaved, decapitated pig hung from a beam between two winter poplars, the long knife in her hand about to slice down the belly and spill guts into a tub already set below the cut neck in snow, guts she will clean and stuff with ground meat and boil in the fat cauldron that evening; which he will stir with a long pole, waiting not for the sausage but for the short chopped ribs to be crisp, stuffing wood underneath to keep the fire leaping and his feet warm. Or she herds chicks across a grass mat of farmyard to their log shelter away from the night coyotes. Or she tramps manure with him into the mud of a shallow pit and smears that between the crooked logs of the house. And once, when their black dog Carlo has torn the neighbour's dog apart and she has had to accept all the neighbour's obscenities because his father is not there—his father is never there, always away somewhere blackly working like a beast for someone who will just give him orders and a dollar not to be responsible—Carlo licking himself, easily content with his momentary defeat, his pink tongue cradled between teeth like shark fins—why can't you ever be home like other husbands, work here like you work for others? And his father stands so easily, arms ending limp in his overall pockets for the tears of a wife are simpler to forget than a neighbour who thinks him less of a fine fellow. And Carlo panting bloody in the corner shade of logs, the black fur splashed with white at his throat still perfect for almost one more year.

The water tower and eleven grain elevators of Vulcan. Roman god of the smithy, patron saint of all cuckolds. What he remembers here: white fields and distant white mountains

28

*like teeth, and always wind. Almost too much to climb home
against bent at right angles on a bicycle, snoring in the nostrils with slivers of a February spring. The elevators stand,
have grown larger it seems matronly flanking the highway.
Hiding the hockey arena. Words are too hard for certain
memory.*

*And she lies asleep. Her face held between her hands, her
mouth bunched hollow like delicate weathered rags. Despite
his all-day coming he has to lean against the curtain doorway; she is still in this remembered place under the water
tower, certainly. As if two-thirds of his life were not so much
as a sound swallowed by an empty room. The sound of her
songs, sad as he has always thought them, offering a faith
used as it seems for nothing but to long for 'the Home over
there,' though there were always edges of quick happiness in
her voice when she canned berries for winter, sweat running
down her uncreased cheeks, her left arm bent against her side
while the other moved swiftly for both, her high clear voice
glistening like a cobweb in the summer heat gathering black
with thunder over spruce. His stare must wake her; if she lies
like this when he pounds on the door, shouts her name in the
kitchen as he comes around into the living room, what could
not walk into the house when she sleeps? Alone, like this, just
the tiny shape half curled towards him; barely breathing. He
turns quickly, past the empty bed still standing in the corner
of the living room, out again, refusing caregana hedge and
water tower. Backs the car into the gravel street, away.*

*"He was so old, he really wanted to ... go," Lena is unable
to say the one word in her house. "And such a look, of peace,
just all of a sudden." She faces him, her legs folded sideways,
crossed at the ankles. "Always even when he was sleeping
with the pills, you know he breathed so loud, like gasping,
his face all—but there was this look, as if something just
beautiful ... as if he saw it all, all of a sudden, really beautiful."*

*For the first and only time he feels tears prickle along his
nose and behind his eyes. Lena leans forward on the chrome
table and tears slide on her cheeks, she does not move her
hands to wipe them away; she married the first man who*

asked her. The feeling does not return for him, not even when he comes through the door again and his mother is in his arms, when after a moment he lets her go so he can bend down and kiss her, he again feels only space. Not even grey.

Past her cheek he sees her hair pulled into that same bun she always made when she combed it out and he knew that either visitors were coming or they were driving somewhere, otherwise she would never have time to comb her waist-long hair. He is bent to her awkwardly, his back still kinked from the plane, as if trying to kiss a child without either lifting it in his arms or hunkering down — he cannot do that to bring his face level with his mother's — but she pulls back and his hands catch on her two shoulders, her bones fragile as willows.

"For a whole year he lay on that bed, in the corner, there," *she says in her gentle Low German. "And I cared for him."*

Her head is bent but she is peering up at him, out of the corner of her eyes, intensely like Titian's painting of the lacerated Saviour. Her teeth clack; he longs suddenly, desperately to pull her close against himself, out of sight and sound, to assert with one unconsidered overwhelming human gesture that really he loves, he has always loved, it isn't that he hasn't or doesn't love, or that he can't, no you cannot say that, no, you really ... but her voice circles him before he can declare anything.

"I haven't cried for twenty-two years. The Heavenly Father took my tears away. I cried too much then, you know, yoh?"

He pulls her tight; floundering for a murmur of understanding, the indiscriminate sounds of whatever language to get past her wavering right arm, her unwavering and certain intuition about him.

"Mam ... Mama, I wanted to ... I really...."

"Don't," she says thin and dry against his chest. "Don't lie. Not today."

Tolstoi licking my face. Becca says, "Is Gramma going to stay in her little house?"

Tolstoi really prefers feet, tongue so red, a tongue-washing of summer feet any adult will allow but with faces he must hesitate; only children bend easily. How many faces have I

30

dared ... wanted to touch with my tongue?

"Old Dad," Becca says. Immediately Tolstoi bowls her over, and she reaches, wrestles him to the grass.

"She doesn't want to leave Vulcan. As long as she can." As long as Olena lives just beyond the careganas, Olena who now bathes her once a week like a child. Who once held me when I was no longer a child.

The sky has lost its brilliance almost ominously; even in clouds heaven doesn't last. I hoist myself to my feet and my thighs ache strangely; as if someone were sitting on them.

"I always wondered, why did they name that place 'Vulcan'? Flat wheat country, cattle then, actually."

"Why did they?" Liv looks up from the small desk beside our bed where she is writing cheques. She does all the business in our house, everything down to having the cars serviced; I buy groceries. "And who's 'they'?"

"The CPR, who else. They'd long before run out of directors' names, on one line they got so desperate they started with Adam and went through to Zelma."

"This was for V?"

"No, that was Saskatchewan."

"It's hard to name a whole country."

"Maybe they used a classicist. In Vulcan at first they even named the streets Minerva, Apollo, Venus."

"Mars?" She sits in profile, signing something swiftly, frowning. I squeeze toothpaste on my brush.

"I don't know. They changed them all to numbers before we moved there."

"Numbers, numbers," she mutters.

"Haven't we got enough this month?" I mumble through fluoridated foam. I can't imagine why not, April was a low-cost month, certainly no class-ending parties, only one play and three movies, two of them stupid.

"Not these!" her exasperation somehow complete, I cannot clear my mouth noisily enough. "Street numbers! Millions of lovely names and there isn't a street name left in Alberta, just stupid numbers."

"It's just for efficiency —"

"We're *infected* with efficiency! All we can do is count!"

31

And she's standing, facing me, furious! I grope for the towel, wipe my face so she won't see my incredulous grin but she senses it of course and she's there at the door in one swift move, blocking me into the tiny bathroom with her strong hands high on the doorposts.

"There's not really millions of names," I say carefully. "In English."

"You can make them up!"

"Oh, I guess you —"

"You told us yourself, that town just south of Vulcan."

"Carmangay?"

"Yes, a man and his wife, and his name comes first of course."

"Gaycarman doesn't sound so hot, especially today," but she is glaring with set anger about to break, quickly: I just have to step aside for a minute. "At least she got in there."

"Not like Cardston and Lethbridge and Lloydminster and Lacombe and you name it, men."

I can never resist. "There's Burdette and Coutts, and Dorothy..." but she turns abruptly, her temper now refusing wit as it so often does not, happily.

"Don't snow me with your little facts," striding to her skirt's swing, "You know what it—anyway I was thinking of Vulcan. And Venus and Mars."

I'm glad suddenly to turn, fumble the towel over the rack. I hang it carefully even on my side and come out of the bathroom concentrating on unbuckling my belt. I have a certain routine at bedtime, I guess that's what happens as you approach your personal mid-century, soon it will fill my entire day? I notice that in Liv too.

"What about them?" I ask across the bed, over the slur of my trousers sliding down my legs. My voice is steady, I think,

"Mars lays Venus and Vulcan is humiliated."

Venus rising, rising.

"Vulcan's ugly," I say fast, "really ugly hunched over that forge all day."

"Uglier than that killer Mars?"

That certainly hasn't crossed my mind before. In the *Iliad* the Greek Mars whines, he's a coward, when he tramps across

32

the battlefield the earth groans, oozing blood. Why would Venus take such a brute for brilliant Vulcan, the immortal artificer? I fold my pants on their hanger, my shirt already in the laundry, 'Vulcan and his whole forge sweat to work out Achilles his armour, but flat and flexible truths are beat out by every hammer —'

"I don't know," I have to interrupt my tyrannical memory, "maybe old V had made too many of those golden maidens, they worked for him, did anything he wanted."

"Ancient R2D2s eh?"

I laugh aloud. That's better, much better.

"Sure, sweet science fiction automat —"

"They're better," she interrupts sarcastically, "they're *girls.*"

"Pure technology and empire," I shrug out of my under-shorts, toss them in the laundry. Liv pushes away from her desk and begins unbuttoning her blouse, her back to me. I want suddenly to do that, accept her intimacy of undressing but to move is impossible, into the tone of her earlier, inex-plicable anger. My head throbs like a signal.

"Vulcan makes a magic net," I say sombrely, "he can make anything and he catches them with it in the act and then he hoists them up and dangles them in front of the gods. He humiliates them with laughter."

Liv whirls, throws her blouse on the bed, the full satin gleam of her bra like polished armor. "I don't care about Venus or Mars, or Vulcan! What about Mars' wife?"

"Wife?"

"Yes! Was she sitting there too, laughing, like all those other voyeurs on Olympus?"

Who has ever given her a thought? "I ... I don't even know if Mars had a ... isn't Venus considered his wife?"

"So he steals her, great goddess of love and all beauty she," Liv's shoulders shift as they do when she abruptly decides it is no use. She turns away, her hands arch up behind her and unfasten her bra, drop it on the bed.

"That's all they were anyway, those classic gods. Voyeurs, and rapists. The almighty Zeus is an almighty rapist, that's all."

"Hey," I can talk quietly now. "Zeus was Greek, hey, what's the matter? Really?"

"Zeus is just a stupid old stock prod!"

She unzips her slacks abruptly no longer angry. The very curve of her hips, the bend of her back tells me what her face will not, since she holds it away from me. Disgust. Is this uncomprehended intuition, shapes rising in ashes?

"The women never have their own stories, they're the prizes in fights, or the whores, or jealous bitches like Hera, or earth mothers laid so easy, just oozing fruit. Crock."

"Athena," I say carefully quiet, "is born out of Zeus' head, perfect in form and wisdom."

Liv turns to me, her gaze as grey-eyed as though she were the virgin goddess herself implacable across the bed. Liv of the beautiful bones more in my eyes now than the first time I saw her naked, more beyond my reach for her 'I am suddenly trying to live / with a neutrality so great / I have nothing to think of, / just to sense / and kill it in the mind.'

"For the Greeks," she says, "perfect wisdom could only come into the world without the agency of woman."

"Then why did they make wisdom female?"

"Because they couldn't imagine anything male being pure forever."

Contradiction and brilliance. She groans, arching against me hard and gentle as a living rock to annihilate myself upon, a known warm country to lose.

"Men are so ... stupid, women are so ... stupid ... going in all directions...."

"O my beloved," is all I can breathe into her open mouth, our familiar bodies driving together on the edge of our o so familiar bed.

"We have too many numbers," she says after that. "We should be like the cannibals of Central America, count only one, two, and many."

"We're civilized, can't we add 'three'?"

"No," she says against my chest.

MAY
TWO

But I was thinking of her. In the arms of my wife this betrayal of the mind for a materialization in an ashen room while the body responds in time and place as it will and perhaps must — there is nothing 'must' in the mind; it is always betraying us for it is its own place and in itself can make a heaven of — hell? Did Milton write hell? He most certainly did, Gillian informs me. The mind can also make a Hell of Heaven; Milton wrote that too.

"That sounds more like him," I mutter. "Puritan."

"The poor man was blind," she says.

"So is my mother."

"He could live nowhere but in his mind."

"He could have tried the others, smell, or touch...."

"The best was gone."

"Hardly," at this moment I know the world needs nothing but the solitary tumescent graininess of touch. The world of seeing, no one but the archivist has ever seen me before in this indecipherable room and he, being functionary here, does not exist in the world where I eat and wash the car and worry occasionally about the bomb poised to disintegrate everyone everywhere in the world thirty-seven times over as if that were necessary, there trundles the world of seeing, let me be o well content with this present darkness when in light and I am sure I would not recognize her. Perhaps I would, far away between shoulders and heads at a party still, but I know I would be surprised beyond comprehension if I actually saw her now in daylight having felt her twice and smelling her, coming into this room again this morning as if I were simply going to work – he looked exactly the same as he did every morning, officer, his checked slacks and cream cotton jacket, it's really quite chilly in the archives bent over films all day – to work like I have always worked and seeing her cubicle already illuminated but as my step approaches – he never even went toward his reader, officer, where I'd stacked his files for him like usual – the light vanishes so that when I pass her pale hand emerges into the greyness without her head turning and touches, pulls my arms about her like an inevitability. From behind, down around her into intimacy in a simple motion, sitting on the university coldness of a wood and plastic chair. My mind has not betrayed me. Not me.

"Don't you ever leave here?" I say finally against her ear.

Her body moves between my arms, under my hands silently; chuckling.

"I can't, daylight is fatal."

"Aha, you too are a mere moiler in the pale darkness of archives."

"Like you. Only darkness becomes me."

"Clothed truly in bright darkness."

"Clothed truly in stygian darkness visible."

"Is that why you're doing this?"

"What?"

"Letting me, touch you?"

"Why are you doing it?"

"You want me to."

"Don't you want to too?"

"Yes."

"Like this?"

"Yes," I say, "yes."

Her lips widen under mine and I have lost all memory of kiss, an intimacy wimpling into a quick, moist depth that defies comprehension 8:45 on a Wednesday May morning what is there to remember? My body is hard, lean as a tree and she an ache along my roots, she gasps suddenly I am fastened upon her so hard; a tinge of blood between my teeth – this is impossible.

36

Slowly one must let go, loosen. I fumble and find a chair shoved under the next reader, there seem to be legs of things in unexpected places, the whole room trapped and clanging with them metalically wall unto wall uttering very loud speech but I finally manoeuvre the chair into silence and sit and nothing collapses under me either. Amazing – he was just going around banging into stuff, officer, like he didn't have no co-ordination you know, motor moron – after a moment of breathing I can tilt forward into the reader and flick on the light switch without crashing to the floor. In the ugly yellow light her profile seems to tremble and my heart jolts, but immediately I know she is laughing.

"I'm sorry to be so ..." my voice croaks as the room echoes, "quietly discreet." I get up, "I better go to my reader, Eddie Dalrymple will think I had a coronary and bring an ambulance."

Her hand brushes mine as I move past. "I'm here till noon," her voice says.

"History too?"

"No no, English. Graduate research assistant."

"Oh."

"It pays better than practising piano."

"Do you get paid something for that."

"Not enough to live."

Which sounds practical. Don't you live with a husband? spins once around my mind and then I'm very happy I didn't ask that, her head gone inside the world of her reader and her slender body bent I could take between my hands, no, the reels I have been plodding through wait for me, stacked; perhaps Dalrymple has gone for a very early coffee, perhaps he has a very private friend he cannot wait to – and there is what I've ordered, a Scot Sir George Simpson so small and pushy he made himself "the Little Emperor" of a land three times the size of Europe. His world available for the twirling in celluloid shadows: *Narrative of a Journey Round the World during the Years 1841 and 1842.* The year he was created Knight Bachelor and travelled via Halifax, Boston, Montreal, Edmonton and the Sandwich (now Hawaiian) Islands and Sitka (now Alaska) across Siberia to Moscow and so back to London. Published London 1847, and by Lea and Blanchard of Philadelphia, for even then the Americans wanted everything from the Mexican Gulf to the Arctic and they got a very large piece when they bought Russian America as it is labelled vaguely above Sitka on Simpson's map, in 1867, Seward's Folly, $65,000,000. People always wanting what is not theirs, never content, feeling one thing and wanting the brush of something else along the grain of their fingertips, a touch like silk thread sliding on their skin: nothing so simple and impersonal as simply ruling a territory Sir Simp-son.

I thrust my head inside my reader tunnel and I run, fast, on the words flying and gradually I disappear. I become aware of elementary ambitions; I do not want to control the British Empire through politics but I am simpleton Sir George money-hungry, my right hand cranking slowly and my eyes sliding down the centre of the grey pages with the periphery always there – when I get old enough to need bifocals I won't be able to do this, that will be soon, very soon, how – my mind poised to hook at anything that has to do with Indians and "Broken" or "Arm" or "Maski ..." something, "Mone-guh-banow" in particular or anything with "Eyes" or with peace treaties between tribes, and I find myself at a peace treaty on the prairie that ends as always in even more gruesome bloody battles but only Indians in general and no names in particular are given, why would I-Simpson notice Indian names anyway? I am dragging a Highland piper across the prairie so that at every Hudson Bay post I can be piped through the gates, Indians in general – to me they are never anything but general no matter if their tribes are as different as Germans from Hungarians – in general they adore ceremony, and something nags me about a recurrent meeting with a group of Metis emigrants from Red River on their way to the Columbia – 'natives of Red River settlement ... twenty-three families with all their carts and horses and cattle and dogs' – and I also utter occasional lyric rhapsodies on the steamship and the sad lack of clean "inexpressibles" as I must of course label underwear, in the summer dust. This is all very interesting, though my nineteenth-century prose style is not as elegant as Butler's (is it possible I am too stingy to pay for an exceptional ghost writer?) but when you're looking for one vague thing only (you are not sure exactly what) or faint allusions to what you are not sure of and avoiding something absolutely certain just behind you and look and look steadily ahead, your thoughts get sprayed with occasional small shot when you want only the sufficient mercy of one silent, massive bullet. The image of my slate-and-spider world barely swims by like a stunned fish, I am surrendering to what is cranking around the back of my most recent memory when something solidifies on page 126, the emigrants again, trying to get through the Rocky Mountains and

> having been treacherously deserted at Bow River by their guide, they providentially met an Indian of the name of Bras Croche, who, being better acquainted with the mountains than their own guide, carried them through a little to the southward by a pass infinitely superior to ours....

"Bras Croche"! On his journeys again! She has led me like light in this garish yellow tunnel; what I have found before only in English and Cree and Blackfoot now suddenly stares at me in French. No, in George Catlin too, in yet more unreadable anglicized French, Bro-cas-sie. The words spring out sharp, precise as needles and in another hundred pages I have discovered the gem, the slash of character that declares this is the chief I want for certain, this indelible man I have heard of in whispers only while sifting through fifty years of occasional-travel braggarts:

> After the arrival of the emigrants from Red River at Puget Sound, I gave their guide, a Cree of the name of Bras Croche, a short trip on my ship, the Beaver. When I asked him what he thought of her, "Don't ask me," was his reply; "I cannot speak; my friends will say that I tell lies when I let them know what I have seen; Indians are fools and know nothing; I can see that the iron machinery makes the ship to go, but I cannot see what makes the iron machinery itself to go." Bras Croche, though very intelligent, and like all the Crees, partially civilized, was never-

39

theless so full of doubt and wonder, that he would not leave the vessel till he got a certificate to the effect that he had been on board of a ship which needed neither sails nor paddlers. Though not one of his countrymen would understand a word of what was written, yet the most skeptical among them would not dare to question the truth of a story which had a document in its favour. A savage stands nearly as much in awe of paper, pen and ink as of steam itself; and if he once puts his cross to any writing, he has rarely been known to violate the agreement which such writing is supposed to embody or sanction. To him the very look of black and white is a powerful 'medicine'.

The power of words written down, the absolute word made visible. And me wrapped in this enormous condescension regarding savage 'medicine,' in quotes. Who indeed was here partially civilized once he has closed his hand to make such words. The historians' fact beyond fact coming to me like a *coup d'état.*

"Would a prairie Cree travel so much? All the way to the Pacific?"

"Listen, that man travelled – over mountains and rivers, his home was in the Beaver Hills just east of here, but sometimes he traded on the Yellowstone River seven hundred miles south, and John Sanford of the American Fur Company probably took him to Washington in 1831, he rode wherever he —"

"Washington, D.C.?"

"Yes, all of 18,000 people there. And Baltimore and New York too."

"Why would they haul prairie Indians that far?"

"To impress them."

"Look at all the stuff we make?"

"Yes, look, don't try to fight us in your wilderness. Be smart, just knuckle under."

"Was your Mas – ka – whatever impressed?"

"He had very good eyes. Maximilian, Prince of Wied says he met 'The Broken Arm' hunting near St. Louis in 1833 and he had a medal of Andrew Jackson hanging around his neck."

"Old Hickory. He was impressed."

"Yes."

"You Prince of Weed," Gillian says. The noon sunlight on the quadrangle between the university science buildings droning with air conditioners is too intense to look at her directly. 'I knew a woman lovely in her bones, when small birds sighed she would sigh back at ...' I do not know, at all. In light, in any one of its possible meanings. Behind her seated long on the clipped grass a yellow frisbee is floating up and sinking between pastel clusters of people.

"Wied," I say, pronouncing the German 'V.' "Wied. He was out in de vilds, killing tings vildly, but not Indians because for dem dey vere de *noble* savages."

Her smile widens between the incredible fall of her black hair. "What's funny?" I ask her. Her nose as pale and straight as any Egyptian's; I don't know her well enough in daylight and beyond touch to surmise what she is thinking. Profile elegant.

"You," she says after a moment, looks at me. "You don't just answer, you lecture more or less," and I realize her smile is a kind of joy at what I have said, me still the prof or likely elementary teacher.

"People talk, I haven't even said anything about all the things I know about Old Indian Killer Jackson with two bullets in his gut, it's a nice thing people can do, talk."

"Some talk nicer than others."

"The oral tradition, not the literary —" the yellow frisbee angling, rotating easily over us as a muscular young man shirtless in shorts rushes past, reaching, the air tinged with his passing, "I have to talk to you, I guess fast, whatever I know – or I'll be reaching for you."

She studies me seriously. Her eyes are ... I can't see them, the air is too bright, but they seem flecked with gold. Her teeth perfect. "Sunlight," she says, "is for words only."

"Sorry!" The muscular bumpkin charges past me, snatches the settling frisbee away as it seems from her ear with one expert swipe of his enormous hand. And then he hesitates above her, of course; stares. His stupidly handsome face oozes admiration and I hate him, he's a liar, sorry my ass

41

his little trick wouldn't fool a frog, "I'm sorry," he repeats and actually arches himself all bulging above her, staring, "it slipped, my hand's getting a bit sweaty, sorry."

She flicks a glance up. He might be a thick lamppost swaying slightly in a breeze for all the expression she bothers with. He wouldn't dare stand there naked Neanderthal if I didn't look so silly middle-aged professor and she so obviously young graduate student and I can hardly control the fury that leaps in my chest because he doesn't care what she thinks of him, I should chop his hamstrings right there in his naked knees or wherever they are, stare, she's sure a body worth picking up, stare meathead.

"If your hands get so sweaty," she is all gentle sincerity, "just wipe them on your jock strap."

"I shoulda let it bang you," he says as gently, and muscles off bulging.

She swings her brown legs around easily, folds them with her bare sandled feet tucked under and faces me directly while keeping her distance as is proper in the centre of the campus, spring dresses passing on sidewalks, a student having lunch with her adviser and the brown bags fallen over, open. I often sit here eating alfalfa sprouts and Vulcan Mennonite sausage between rye. Grass and cliffs of trees hold back regimented, featureless cinderblock and glass and brick, the sky blue despite the drone from chemistry exhausts. I feel so heavy now, I am ludicrous, God in Heaven, mindlessly middleagedly ludicrous to let this settle in my lap.

Her head tilts, her brilliant eyes catch me from under her brows. No plucking thin and painting in, one glance and you understand she is a person with ineffable class, the body a mirror of the character, the sharp, precise quality of marble. She has lived twenty or twenty-four years and been hounded since puberty by pimple-faced lechers and her mother slapped her baby bottom I desire like a gasp suddenly to feel under my fingers, no jeans only skin against tipped exploring skin and she's made love to (with? allowed him?) her husband hundreds of times probably and even wanted it? She had to or she wouldn't have married him or remained so, she cannot nor ever will be an enduring Griselda and she sits before me with her strong thighs that have held a man (men?) pulling those jeans vivid over her knees and what am I, she is crazy and I am even crazier because I'm twenty years older and know better than she a man can say anything, if I tell her five words she'll go, she—a chasm of decades. I've lived two of her lives already and don't know one minute of what she has ever been, is, wants to be, what is it she does, turning to me, what is she rising in a strange ashen place? Touchable where only shadows of words ran by me and the remembrance of worlds dreaming themselves past and to come in the probable memories of dinosaurs, nothing more, and she looks at me after slitting a jock as easily as she could flabby me, oh I'm in fair shape for forty-two, one sixty-six and five eleven, she can as easily slit and slice me thin as pink succulent ham. This is banal. The white stitching of her jeans tucks down so tight between her thighs.

"Listen," she says motionlessly. "The University of Calgary has a collection of Canadian literary manuscripts. Dr. Wipf wants me to go there tomorrow."

"Oh."

"I'll be in Calgary Thursday and Friday," without emphasis.

Her calm face contemplates the trees behind me; she may be seeing the battlements of Athabasca Hall through them as if driven up by a wash of May green. There is something I should be saying, surely, 'drink to me only with thine eyes and I—' but that's certainly not it, idiot. Silence stretches. It's been exciting but good-bye. The right man for the moment must accept the daring of the moment. Surely.

"Why are you interested in Broken Arm?"

"The ... the problem is, writing prairie Indian history."

"There are few records?"

"Well, if you could even find out something about their more recent leaders, but even that's hard, a matter of factuality, except stories still told by the old people on the reserves but I don't speak Cree, I should to do this properly but I don't, in the oral tradition remembering the past date by date is no Indian tradition, how can a white man find any fact beyond the story memory of a language he doesn't talk unless

43

he tries to trace say one name of one person through all the white documents he can find, letters, diaries, notes, travel books, white gossip in the unlikeliest places you can dig from the nineteenth century? 'Mas-ke-pe-toon' in Cree means 'broken' or 'deformed arm,' and that's distinctive enough but he had other names too, every Indian had several at the same time or at different stages of his life and he was called "Eyes on Each Side" too and 'He Who Has Eyes Behind Him' and the Blackfeet called him —"

I dribble to a stop, more or less humiliated. As a scholar I cannot of course be absolutely definite on my humiliation, but since I am not the purest possible scholar (I really don't speak Cree), personally I can be fairly certain. She considers me unblinkingly; the massed clouds pile up over her like white towers and she offers a smile, a warmth of easy happiness that brushes aside my clutter like a full body rising o fumbling old Prince of Weed indeed.

"You choose one important man with a physical oddity and try to trace him?"

"That's it ... part of it, yes. He was also a pacifist."

"Pacifist? A Cree chief?"

"Yes. And later a Christian."

It is past one o'clock. Were I a typist I should now be uncovering my typewriter; or a travel agent my computer terminal. I didn't tell her the whole truth either, not even a poor scholar can in one burst because the oral Blackfeet did keep a very precise annual memory of events with their individual winter counts; neither their official memories nor those of the Crees were unsystematic but they were systems adapted to memory and of course they vanished at the first full gap in the tribal memory. How can I explain when after years of work I know little enough – Gillian is peering at me intently – "Christian?" her lips parted.

"He changed, you know, Maskepetoon. He was a ferocious Cree warrior, a spring and summer horror against the Blackfeet and then he changed, it seems...."

"People change," Gillian says.

Momentarily the sunlight seems not so bright. "Sometimes, yes," she says. "It could be like standing on your head in order to see the world clearer."

I do not even see her for staring.

She continues, the mouth that has kissed me offering sweet, terrifying words: "If one morning you began walking on your hands, the whole world would be hanging. The trees, these ugly brick and tile buildings wouldn't be fixed here so solid and reassuring, they'd be pendent. The more safe and reliable they seem now the more helpless they'd be then, dependent."

In the ashen depthlessness of the Micro-materials Reading Room shadows over my eyelids come and go, pass unsystematically. She has pushed me, perhaps I have fallen into that perfect white between what few words I have found into another world—drink me, eat me, all you have to do is taste me, come, drink ye all of it—I cannot even grasp for, float on those doubtful old words of prayers I discovered in myself Saturday evening, *Lieber Heiland mach mich fromm* her tone is here, her turning words and her shape before me like any immortal Cree; but for her skin which I have never seen she is one of them seated there among the poplars above the banks of the North Saskatchewan River waiting no doubt for the signal scream of attack at the ford below where the Blackfeet have crossed to trade behind the spruce walls of Edmonton House. A hundred and fifty years ago, to be touched by anyone who dares to find her. A simple world opening in this same air, all I have to do is follow where she is already, walking it always seemed to me a simple world. Because I knew so little of it; follow; when one knew exactly that these are my friends and these are my enemies because life without ambiguity is built on set clan, loyalty, hero, enemy, it may be comic or tragic but never ironic and I prove my manhood upon the body and blood of those my forefathers here long before me identified as enemy and I can have as many women as want me and I can satisfy. Follow her. In those days so long ago *when the Mountain and River Cree were never sick because there were always enough buffalo to keep us strong, when we had a great chief called Mas-ke-pe-toon, The Broken Arm.*

No one knows now where he got that name. Perhaps as

some say it was from fighting a grizzly, or in battle, or per-
haps from a vision he had on the Medicine Lodge Hills above
the Blindman River when he was young. At that time the
Blackfeet already knew him as The Young Chief, but even
before that he was called The-One-With-Eyes-In-The-Back-
Of-His-Head and one spring he left his women and he and
his Young Men rode as far as they pleased from their country
on the North Saskatchewan, south through the lands of their
fierce enemies the Blackfeet and the Bloods and the Piegans
and the Assiniboines and the Crows, all the way to the Mis-
souri River where they traded at the mouth of the Yellow-
stone. There they also met white soldiers whose guns ended
in long bright knives. The soldiers took him with some other
chiefs down that river for many days and up another and
another and over mountains until finally they showed him
what they said was their Big White Father in an unbelievable
place called Washington who hung a large silver medal
around his neck. But when after three years he came back to
the North Saskatchewan with all his Young Men still alive
and more horses and rifles than the Mountain and River
People had ever seen, he would not say one word about it.

"If I told you everything I saw by that Stinking Water," he
said, "you would only call me a liar."

He stayed with his People then for eight years. His wives
gave him sons and daughters, he hunted buffalo and killed
Blackfeet as any man of the People must, and everyone might
have forgotten his journey if he had not kept rubbing the
silver medal which he had never removed from around his
neck. It was worn so smooth now that the profile of the man
on it, the man who gave it to him, could barely be seen even
when it was held flat to the light. Once he told his wife Ma-
tono-wacap that while he was on the boat going down the
river a white man had made an exact likeness of his face with
paint on a piece of leather, but she clapped her hand over her
mouth in astonishment and quick terror that he had not
killed such a devil immediately. After that every morning
when he awoke she was bent over him, staring into his face,
for she knew that just as he was wiping away that White
Chief with his fingers, so that painter would one day destroy

him; and paint on leather cannot last as long as silver. So he smiled at her every morning, his face more powerful and sharper than ever, and said nothing about the boat that had brought them back against the current of the river without either sail or paddle.

In those days when the Mountain and River People traded at Fort Edmonton or Rocky Mountain House the Hudson's Bay Company mounted cannon at the corners of the forts and locked the gates and opened nothing but one small door with an armed man standing there who allowed no more than one man at a time to enter. Maskepetoon traded hides and pemmican there sometimes for tobacco or tea, or a rifle if they let him, but during those eight years when he rode against the Blackfeet every spring, what he had seen fasting as a youth on the Medicine Lodge Hills kept coming back to him. One day when his second wife, Susewik, enraged him, he drew his knife and with one swift, brutal motion scalped her. She did not, however, die of that. Gradually the top of her skull healed white and dry like a buffalo-skull at the Thirst Dance and she protected it with a small cap she sewed of fur, but sometimes when she lay in his arms, laughing or crying with him, he again saw the Blindman River valley open below him, the high mountains at his back and Gull Lake a silver coin among the trees where the earth flattened away. And then the rainstorm would come up from the south again, from the Red Deer River canyons there and he would see his Mountain and River People riding south and the Blackfoot and Blood and Piegan warriors galloping north to meet them with war cries shrilling high above the thunder and his People screaming in turn and his left arm would reach out between them, would grow huge until it split the prairies, a giant swelling log laid between his People and their endless enemies. "What does it mean?" he would whisper in Susewik's ear. And his left arm which could bend a bow or pull the largest horse to its knees in one easy, unstoppable motion, would cramp around her in agony and she would laugh at first, happily, and then recognise the pain in his face. "What is it?" she said then. "What is it?"

His father had told him something, though he really did

47

not want to hear what the old man said. Every time he rode out against the Blackfeet his father, who could no longer walk and lay between robes all day long and thought, would say, "Is a man's true greatness to be sung in the scalp dance? What do your powerful eyes, what do your travels to unnameable places help if you see only what everyone sees, that war is glory, that killing is revenge? You have always seen different, why can't you see different about being a great man?"

But there were always so many mothers in camp wailing for sons and daughters lost forever to the Blackfeet, or fathers for sons and grandsons and brothers for brothers and nephews for uncles and young men for their blood friends and sweethearts and little boys growing slowly older on hate for their fathers' killers, that Maskepetoon could not listen. The Blackfeet had named him The Young Chief after his first raid when he killed three of them with two arrows and an axe, and often now they avoided his camp as if the very sight of his long shadow on the lodge-hides were enough to terrify them. There were always so many Blackfeet that needed killing.

"There is truth and there is lie," his father continued to say. "Hate and love, war and peace, goodness and evil. What do you want? What do you see?"

Then seven years after he had come back from his first long journey, in the spring when the first grass is green and beautiful for horses, Maskepetoon and eight warriors rode south as usual out of the parkland to the prairies. They swam their horses across the Red Deer River and two days later as they came up between The Three Hills he heard birds chirping. At his signal the riders stopped, listened; it seemed the wide prairie about them was dancing with meadowlarks. "That is the enemy," he said and thrust his rifle, the only one they had, back into its scabbard. "We will ride slowly towards that low hill." They did that, and suddenly from the west a man appeared, coming towards them. The man rode very tall, blurred huge in the heat that shimmered over the plain. "Form a line behind me facing him," said Maskepetoon. "And no one touches a weapon unless I give the signal." So the warriors moved into line and Maskepetoon rode forward a little from them on the hill. He was peering into the mirage, the immense rider slowly, slowly floating closer and after a moment he said, "That's not a Blackfoot, that's a Blood." One of the eight Mountain People kicked his horse to run from the most magnificent and terrifying warriors of the plains, but Maskepetoon wheeled and seized the horse's bridle and hurled them both back into line. "Sit still," he said. "They are all around us."

The Blood on a beautiful bay stallion rode a wide half-circle about the base of their hill. The Mountain People sat motionless facing westward as he slowly rode up the hill behind them, then between them in the line. That horse carried that big Blood through them it seemed without so much as a thud of a hoof on stone, up behind Maskepetoon sitting rock-like on his horse and then past and a hand reached out, drew the rifle up from the scabbard against Maskepetoon's left knee as smoothly as if it were plucking a berry. Maskepetoon did not move. The Blood rode on, his back towards them all, then suddenly whirled his stallion and faced them. He held the rifle he had taken flat across his horse's withers.

You are a brave man, he signalled with one hand.

"All those birds sing so beautifully," Maskepetoon said in the Blood language.

"And you are very wise too," the Blood said after a moment. "Come."

He turned and raised his hand, and it seemed the earth all around them grew warriors like grass, none of them had ever seen so many Bloods, not even Maskepetoon on the Missouri. So they rode into that huge camp in a bend of Kneehill Creek and the buffalo started coming south then so they helped the Bloods hunt and feast for sixteen days and then rode north again driving a herd of gift horses loaded down with presents, including meat and four better rifles than the Company had ever traded them, and they easily avoided a large circle of Blackfeet and galloped out of the trees into home camp beside Battle River Lake whooping their triumph. But there was no one to greet them. The bright green trees by the lake were black with funeral platforms. The Blackfeet had come and killed over half the camp, men, women, dogs, everything including Matono-wacap with all their children. And Maskepetoon's father under his robes.

"I cannot wail any more," Susewik told him. "Your two oldest sons are alive. I think they will heal by fall."

She had been up early that morning, the two boys getting water with her from the lake. She had dragged the boys into the rushes but she had been unable to hold them back as long as it took the Blackfeet to destroy the camp and when they got loose from her the warriors were already so full of killing they casually cut down the two little boys charging them with hands full of gravel from the beach and left them for dead. Who needed to bother with children's scalps on such a morning?

Four of the men could find no one of their families alive to mourn with them, so they came to Maskepetoon that same evening. "There are only fourteen warriors left now," they told him. "Come, we have to ride south again." But he did not go with them. Two days later seven of the thirteen came back and showed him their Blackfoot scalps. "We know who killed your father," they said, and before he could stop them they told him that name. "We left him for you."

Not even that stirred his terrible rage; he refused to fight but took his people north and east to the Beaver Hills beside the shallow lake where geese nested white as snow all year and there they healed that summer and fall and winter. The buffalo came very easily to their autumn pounds and in the spring when so many birds came north they could barely see the water, the eighth spring since he had come back, he heard of a new white man in Fort Edmonton who spoke for The Great Spirit. The Cree who told him this said the Blackfeet were so impressed they were giving the God-man the hand nearest their heart to shake because they thought he had floated down from the sky in a small piece of paper which Factor Rowand at Fort Edmonton opened and he became big enough to step out of it.

Maskepetoon laughed aloud at that. When the man came to his camp shortly after he saw exactly what he had expected: one of those white men with a fringe of beard and *white collar he had seen often on his first journey and to whom he had never spoken. But this man whose white name, Rundle, as usual meant nothing, was very gentle; he carried a small cat on his arm so the camp dogs would not tear it apart and he prayed every morning and evening lying on his knees with his black book in his hands and so Maskepetoon let him touch Susewik's new son with water and give him his child's name, Jo-seph. A very strong name, Rundle said through the interpreter, a name to save his people.*

For Maskepetoon now knew two things certainly: though the Young Men looked at him every day, he could not ride against the Blackfeet that spring, and he had not seen the Medicine Lodge Hills vision since his father was killed. And a third thing was fixed also: his left arm, which looked as thick and powerful as ever, sometimes hurt so much at night he had to talk to it. When he went outside then to look for the dawn it seemed the light was rising in the west, that the world had been turned inside out. And when he faced the sun there growing large above the Beaver Hills, praying as he always had with his eyes wide open, he saw the crimson light gradually darken into another colour through his tears.

That summer, eight since he had returned, Maskepetoon heard that Governor Simpson of the Hudson's Bay Company needed a guide through the mountains to the western ocean. Though he had never travelled in that direction, he said he would take the Governor there, and he did. He left Susewik and her baby with his band and took his two oldest sons with him. The mountain passes with their terrible roaring rivers frightened them, and the smell of the bitter, undrinkable sea clenched between hills covered by trees as monstrous as the rivers and vines crawling everywhere alarmed Maskepetoon in a way he could not remember of himself eight years before; though he knew now he was more and more aware of powers beyond things. The Governor went onto the boat waiting there for him. They called it Amisk, The Beaver *and invited Maskepetoon aboard to sail around the harbour, so he went and the boat moved slowly on the water without sails or paddles, shuddering deep within itself as it did so. This time he insisted they take him into it. There below deck he saw a*

51

stinking fire and machinery turning which they said made the ship go, but he could not see what made the machinery turn. Fire they said. So he had the Governor write on a piece of paper that he had been on such a ship and when he stood on land again beside his two sons he took the now featureless silver medal off from around his neck and threw it into the western ocean. When they got back to the Beaver Hills again, the paper with its incomprehensible marking was all he would show the People. And his two sons would tell them nothing either.

He would not kill our traditional enemies now. He said it was useless to fight, peace was the way people had to live and after a year he heard Rundle talk again. This time the white man spoke of a "Prince of Peace" and so Maskepetoon invited him to sleep two nights in his lodge. The story of Jesus who finally died hammered up high on a tree was worse than anything he had ever heard but the story of creation and fall stung him with happiness. He told Rundle the Mountain People were like young birds reaching up with their mouths open, waiting for food. And that summer for the first time Maskepetoon rode with his two sons into a Blackfoot camp carrying only a peace pipe and talked out a truce between the Blackfeet and our people that lasted all summer. The Company Factor at Rocky Mountain House was very happy for that. He offered to teach Maskepetoon how to read his own language and in a few days the chief had learned the syllabics and could pronounce anything written in Cree, though it took a little longer for him to learn to write it. His sons learned the writing even more easily than he and a summer later Rundle touched them both with water and named them: Benjamin and Joshua. Benjamin went to Fort Edmonton and started to learn English from Rundle.

The next Easter Maskepetoon went with twenty men to trade hides at Fort Edmonton above the river bluffs. That evening they drank whisky at Whitemud Creek and suddenly his terrible rage overcame him again and he took a man in his hands and very nearly killed him. He left then, south, without talking to Benjamin, and so met another white God-man called Father Thibault coming north who said

Rundle did not really know the right way about Jesus, The Prince of Peace. For three years Maskepetoon thought about what these white men said again and again and again. He made another, longer, truce between his people and the Blackfeet and one entire summer made another journey, guiding a fat English lord east past Fort Carlton to The Pas. There he met another white man named Reverend Hunter who said both Rundle and Thibault were wrong; he alone knew the way to heaven because he had a building with a bell which he rang when it was time to pray. Maskepetoon looked in his black book; it looked just like Rundle's but he could read nothing there, it was all English. So he returned the two-month journey back to Fort Edmonton. Rundle told him immediately that Hunter was of the Church of England and it did not matter what he said, no more than the Roman Catholic Thibault, but Maskepetoon told him Benjamin was now coming back with him to the Beaver Hills.

"Each of you three," he said, "say you know the only way to heaven. Who can tell what you know? You should call a council among yourselves to agree on what you do not know. Then I would go with all of you."

Rundle gave him parts of the black book transcribed in Cree syllabics and Maskepetoon promised to read it, perhaps every day if he could, but said it was time for Benjamin to return. That spring Joshua and a young man with six fingers stole Sarcee horses; the young man was killed doing it so Joseph gave all the horses to his family. Later that summer Rundle and his cat went east with the brigade down the river to return to his home over the Stinking Water. And that fall, eight years after Maskepetoon had first laughed to hear that Rundle had come from the sky in a folded piece of paper, the Blackfeet passed the camp of the people in the Beaver Hills on their way to Fort Edmonton. Maskepetoon with Benjamin and four other men rode to them to pledge a truce with them so they could trade for winter in peace. The Blackfeet gladly accepted these words from the man they still called The Young Chief and that evening their leading men came to eat meat with the People. As they rode into camp without paint or feathers, our women and children welcoming them

with dancing and laughter, one of the warriors who had rid-
den with Maskepetoon when they faced the Bloods nine
summers before came close to chief and, pointing to a grey
haired man among the Blackfeet, shouted the name of Maskepetoon's father's killer. The welcoming shouts died. The
chief stood motionless, a dreadful blackness hardening in his
hard face. The Blackfeet looked about at the Cree warriors
suddenly surrounding them, bristling weapons; they could
not deny either the name or the deed which had been sung
long ago in so many of their dances.

"Bring him to my lodge," Maskepetoon said at last.

The Blackfoot stood alone in front of the lodge with the
small group of his friends behind him and the People surrounding them, all of us waiting to see what weapon Maskepetoon would bring out. But our chief emerged with
nothing but his embroidered ceremonial suit in his hands,
the old suit of beads and quills and scalps he had not worn
for years. "Put it on," he said in Blackfoot, and very slowly
the old warrior did that. "Bring my horse," Maskepetoon
said then, and when it was brought he gestured, "Get on."
The Blackfoot looked at his friends without hope, then
mounted in one swift movement and waited, his face
clenched to accept whatever hit him first. Maskepetoon
looked up at him.

"Both my hands are empty," he said then. "You took my
father from me, so now I ask you to be my father. Wear my
clothes, ride my horse, and when your people ask you how it
is you are still alive, tell them it is because The Young Chief
has taken his revenge."

Slowly the old Blackfoot slid from the horse and faced
Maskepetoon empty-handed. Then he took him in his arms
and held him hard against his heart.

"My son," he said, "you have killed me."

That night Maskepetoon had a vision again. It was not a
dream because he was not sleeping. He saw one of the
Mountain and River People who had walked in the way of
Jesus and been good, doing more than it was possible for a
man to do. This man died and was taken up into the white

heaven. There the man found everything beautiful, and numberless white men all happy and singing among their friends for there was everything that could be desired, and more. But for the man it was all strange. He knew no one, there was no welcome for him, he met none of the spirits of his ancestors, there was no riding or hunting and no feasts around the fire; and finally he grew very sad. At last God heard of it and called to him, "Come here," and he went. God asked, "Why are you sad in this place I made for your joy and happiness?" So the man told him. And God looked at him sadly. "I can't send you to the Indian heaven," he said. "You chose this one. But you were a very good man so I will send you back to earth again. I will give you one more chance."

Maskepetoon lay under his buffalo robes staring into the pointed darkness of the lodge above him. He could hear his wives and sons and daughters and grandchildren breathing in sleep all around him. His left arm throbbed faintly, a drum beating perhaps or a bell ringing, he could not tell which. His long journeys spread like bright rivers, searching across the mountains and plains of his life. I will give you one more chance.

"What does it mean?" he said aloud. "What does it mean?" he whispered.

To see the whole world pendent, hung on nothing. On a hair of the mercy of God. A cold vision of the world right way up at last, how had it come?

"I'll have to go to Calgary tomorrow." I'm setting the supper table around Becca tossing a vegetable salad so high that an occasional inch of green onion—she knows I love green onions and will fish every bit out of her bowl for myself—rolls across the table.

"Please carve the roast," Liv says at the stove. "Vulcan too?"

"Hey!" Becca bounces around, "take me along, see Gramma."

"Business, sweets, business," I snatch a slice of cauliflower and wheel before she can rap my fingers with her wooden spoon. "The elusive fact," I chant, "the loneliness of the long-buried manuscript, the razzle-dazzle of —"

"Cut it, Old Dad," Becca says, "you just don't *want* to take me."

— the wilful body, the unimaginable vision.

"Not for two school days," I say, "or three. I'll have to stay overnight twice or thrice."

"School shmool, I always know everything in shmool school, why can't I, huh?"

"Glenbow Archives?" Liv asks.

"Yeah." I'm getting out the knife and sharpening stone, past her round hip; she stirs cream and flour into the roasting pan for gravy. "I found some great new stuff on Maskepetoon in George Simpson, of all places, so I have to go through Rundle's journal again, I must have missed something."

"I thought they'd printed that, you've got the book."

"Oh sure ... but it's edited, the manuscript always tells you more things, things the learned editor didn't think important or couldn't list everything – it's always a matter of choices – and the McDougall papers probably have something too, I have to sift all through that stuff, and there's —"

"Again?"

"Simpson," I hastily stroke the knife to a ring of steel, "gives me a new connection between Maskepetoon and both the fur trade and missionaries of the 1840s, there's sure to be things there I didn't notice, not knowing the Simpson connection, it's a whole new way, of seeing it."

I'm breathless repeating myself, my tone edged with manic and for an instant she catches me with a sideways glance, why am I talking to her like a grade five teacher?

"But I need the car Friday."

"Sure, sure, I'll take the bus."

And she grins suddenly, her forehead agleam from the bubbly gravy that wafts beef through the room.

"It's like IBS," she says. "Only now you're doing it to yourself. By bus."

"Always something old, something new if you're alive."

Liv breathes moist in my ear, then I feel her quick tongue. "Hey," I am concentrating absolutely on roast slices, "not fair, I'm trying to make this edible."

56

"Quit smooching!" Becca calls.

"We're not," Liv twists the burner off. "I'm just telling him he'll never change no matter what, we were silly to expect it."

"I've changed, really, and I can change more if you want me —"

"Yeah," Becca interrupts, and I'm glad to shut my mouth there, "he's changed, remember all he ever made for supper was rice fried with onions?"

"Before you existed, smallcreep," I tell her, feeling marvelous suddenly with trust in me like a flame of adrenalin and I manipulate the meat as easily as a conversation, "and you forgot the eggs, I always made a real meal of it by mixing in eggs so it had everything, protein, carbohydrates, vegetables, everything, what more could you want?"

Want, want our lovely child stands between us, her hazel eyes peering up. Her voice is too maturely innocent for a ten-year-old — the precocious problems of an only child —

"A whole meal in one frying pan?"

"It saves pots."

Liv says, fast, "But not stomachs."

We all laugh; I'm carving roast like manicured flakes.

"That's enough sliced, really," Liv is pouring gravy. "He's okay, Becca, he turned out a lot better than anyone could have hoped with such a marvelous Mennonite mamma."

"Don't you malign my Mam."

"I'm not, I'm saying she was too good! To her little *Jasch*, cooking everything he liked every minute and he just had to come in and sit down and shovel in, and polishing his shoes for him and cleaning up his room and his bathtub ring and washing all his —"

"Ironing his socks," Becca inserts quickly. Her favourite incredible line, child of the automatic washer and dryer.

"... peace and comfort, give him what he wants, nothing's too good for *mien Jasch*."

"She knew how to treat a man, none of this female mockery." Till I ran away from her; him: the memory jerks through me as Becca is chanting,

"Mien Jasch!" in her hilarious travesty of Low German,

57

around me like a small swirling bacchante as I carry the roast to the table, *"Mien Jasch, dit es mien Jasch mien Jasch."*

So of course there is an accident. Her head jolts my crucial elbow and the half-sliced roast angles off the plate, away, with me lunging desperately after and I do catch it between my arm and thigh and the fridge door; almost; most of it sliced at my feet.

"Give it to Tolstoi," Becca says crouching helpfully with me, picking up with fingertips. "He likes eating off the floor."

"He'll even lick the floor."

"He will not," Liv declares. "You'll wash it."

So Tolstoi gets the three bottom slices: one gulp and a pathetic, long-nosed pleading for more; it is impossible that he ever have enough. Becca and I examine the yard trees as we do on alternate nights for leaf caterpillars. We seem to have found and cut off all their egg rings in April and so have hatched none of our own, but we now discover a thin parade of them trundling across the gravel alley, a vanguard of the distant army already devastating Whitemud Valley. We trample them as far as they extend while Tolstoi considers this massacre fastidiously, refusing to add a paw, but after leaving that squitchy spoor across the alley we retreat indoors to the beginnings of a gentle rain. The sky looms massively. I enjoy spring rain; it turns that endless suburban yard grubbing into a soft winter evening with a book in the armchair, but today I cannot read, there are no words I dare consider, there's nothing I want to think or fix in the house, certainly not the loose towelrack in the bathroom or the faucet more or less dripping since February and the rubber washers Liv bought lying like an accusation beside it for four months now. 'There is / my fear / of no words of / falling with words / over and over of / mouthing the silence..../ to the perfect white between the words,' I have started a trail far beyond words. I re-hang tools unnecessarily in my basement workshop and push jars of nails and screws around and want tomorrow and tomorrow and tomorrow to be here now, one thoughtless plunge through sleep and I am in a bus and the highway black and white stripes south to prairies where

58

space sits without limit on every visible edge and a glimpse of Liv's feet bare to ankles passes at the top of the basement stairs. Do research assistants travel on buses too? Why didn't I ask, stupid? Her narrow feet, on a crowded bus leaning east through the Rockies one winter night I lay in the aisle with my head on my sheepskin and the foot of a girl seated above me in my hand. A foot unsheathed of its boot in the warm cocoon of breathing people hurtling through darkness, a foot slender like some delicate sensuality fitted into the hollow of my hand, curving, almost arching, I was gradually certain it did arch to my fingers sliding down the instep, the softness of veiled muscle arching beneath woollen socks and I felt a surge like water through me, I rolled over in the aisle to get my face closer as if in unconscious sleep and above the ankle broadening into warm calf my exploring hand found skin, incredible sensation I could taste it, and slipped down under wool, the limits of my skin against that smooth tight boundary of skin so alive it seemed to push back wherever I touched it, I was reaching down inside all warmth and mystery. I cupped the heel, the total bend of the foot and its tensile intensity of muscles, finally toes. And they touched me back, strange, so nakedly different; one by one they searched me out as if I had been slit top to bottom and spread open while I lay rigid, my facing asking for touch dented against the metal floor bar of the seat, it was impossible, unnecessary to breathe as they toed along my fingertips tenderly into the palm of my hand longing for something and in the darkness I could not open my eyes, I heard nothing of the taut whine of gears on a grade, my sensation locked upon those soft, blunt touches in my hand. If I were touched close anywhere else I would disintegrate. I look at the palm of my hand in wonder: twenty years, these blunt fingers, there is a callous beginning out of a burst blister against the ring from digging up the garden, eight feet by twenty-three. A ring that is rolling, it has no end. Liv slipping it on my finger for ever.

She is rummaging in the washer. I go around the furnace and brush her round back and begin to sort laundry, darks, whites, inbetweens. I feel her glance at me thoughtfully; I make thoughtful decisions.

"Athena is pure patriarch invention," she stuffs the washer. "Every man's deepest dream of being able to bear offspring and they'd be male perfect of course, beautiful and forever virginal, pure reason, just head."

"Offspring without the necessary messiness of woman," I elaborate jocularly.

But she will not be joculed. "Of course, and the fertile body mystery."

"Nobody ever said man could do it by himself."

"There's nothing so inexpressibly *creative* a man can do as begin a life and that —"

"Hold it, hold it, woman alone can't do it either."

"Mary didn't need a man."

"Mary?"

"You've forgotten her?"

"She was 'found with child of the Holy Spirit,'" I say with precisely remembered logic. Two simple little prepositions 'with,' 'of' kept every question at bay – memorize, just memorize, some day you'll be old enough to know what it means. I don't seem to be old enough yet.

"Immaculate you say, but not spontaneous conception."

"Of course," I continue logically, "there had to be the male principle in there somewhere, even for Mary."

"And since for Jews God is strictly masculine, it's obvious a female was needed to produce 'a Son' for Father."

"Of course."

"How curious," she pours soap into the washer container. "God can get along without man but not without woman. He had to 'come upon' a woman, ha!"

"King James didn't mean 'come' that way."

"How curious," among soiled clothes she is unruffable.

"Yep," I say too carelessly. When I cross my eyes the shades coalesce and it's easier to decide on inbetweens. "And that little Christian statement has dignified woman forever. The reason you can talk —"

"Why does woman need to be dignified? She's got as much dignity as God: he's as helpless as any man to give birth without her."

"Come on, he could've made Jesus just poof! any way he wanted to."

"Then why didn't he?"

"He didn't want to, obviously."

"So why didn't he want to?" adamant.

"Who knows? The inscrutable ways of —"

"Inscrutable ways of God!" a derisive echo stopping, scooping and flinging my incomplete heap of whites into the maw of the washer. "Oh sure, 'inscrutable,' you know perfectly well that's piss-poor theology."

I am standing upright, which is the only reason my jaw doesn't hit the floor. She never uses language like that, not in seventeen years; the world totters.

"In the Bible," she bores at me, "everything God does means something – well?"

"Does everything he *doesn't* do mean something too?"

"Don't weasel around – to get his precious son into the world he uses woman but not man – come on yourself."

My mind is blank; spray-painted with ignorance.

"Push your theology a little," she says. "On the analogy of God being the Father and Jesus the Son, the Holy Spirit must be the Mother, right?"

The Bible verses I saw underlined in red since I was a child betray me immediately. "'That which is born of the flesh is flesh, that which is born of the Spirit is spirit.'"

"God as Mother, yes!"

"Well then how can the Spirit impregnate Mary? Woman to woman?"

"Don't ever underestimate Christianity," Liv claps down the washer lid, still intense. "The Jewish-Christian way of talking about God and humanity is far more profound than any Greek. There's no simple divine body appearing out of thin air, no magical busting out of anyone's head, plop, there's your wisdom or salvation or whatever. Woman is essential to life but God doesn't go around bulging with lust and rape Mary like Zeus would have, or turn her into a heifer to hide her from his jealous wife always glaring after him when he runs around on earth. There's something both male and female about the Holy Spirit, something mysteriously dual."

"God as androgyne?"

"Or un-sexual altogether. That's maybe one reason why Christianity went farther than Judaism, which stopped at God as one, indivisible and forever male. For Christianity God can both impregnate and give birth, he's complete unto himself." She grins at me suddenly in the glaring light of the basement bulb; she seems to be swaying slightly in the rhythm of the thumping washer. "How's that for a Christian apologia?"

"I didn't know you cared."

"I don't much. Papa's male Lutheranism was worse than nothing."

"As bad as my dad's fundamentalism?"

"Not that bad!" She turns quickly then, contrite, almost laughing. "I didn't mean that so hard, sweetheart, really."

"You can mean it as hard as you want, you knew him too, long enough."

"As you read more, the Jesus stories just make more sense."

"What are you reading?" I have her nose to nose, her breasts touching mine and her long thighs; she will not retreat an inch.

"I'll never tell. You'll anticipate and beat me to my arguments."

"I'll find my Sunday school Bible, I'll show you!"

"Oh," she throws three of my whites on the inbetweens, "it's so beastly long, you'd have to read yourself silly to find one useful feminine point. The Jews were so male hung up. You better go and get Becca to bed."

We haven't talked Bible in years, and Liv's practicality can short circuit any word at the stroke of a clock. She'd make a hopeless man—and I realize that thought is profoundly sexist. Too. I turn from her reluctantly, the force of her so vivid now I could almost forget that noon shape leading from the grass into poplars. Not quite however, o no.

She says after me, "Do you really think man can change?"

I echo words I have lived through today, several times.

62

"People change, if they were hanged by their heels forever, yes."

"What, hanged?"

"No no, never mind, I was ... being silly. Yes, sometimes they change."

"I don't mean just 'change' you know, I mean ... like 'basically different.'"

"Like 'ye must be born again' like my dad always said?"

"Not guilt, more like moving into a new place ... without hopeless guilt, yes."

"'Conversion' theologically doesn't mean guilt anyway, it just means 'seeing truly different.'"

"And then acting it?"

"Yes. 'The old things have passed away, behold all things have become new.'"

"Yes, like that."

"No feminist should ever trust Paul."

"What?"

"Nothing, nothing ... I'm just smartass again, nothing." St. Peter spread-eagled and crucified head down; and praising God he still had not dropped the pendent world to be shattered like crystal.

And I flee. The wicked flee, even up household stairs from Jesus stories. Strangely, Becca is not reading. She lies on her bed with her hands behind her head and still dressed, staring at the stippled ceiling. The eighteen stuffed animals she sleeps with in an unalterable arrangement of squirrel, frogman, whale, pooh-bear, beaver above others buried against the inner wall lie and stare up fixedly with her. In the long evening light the room seems poured full of gold, floating, and I push into it, across to draw the curtains. Outside is rain still: straight down, one luminous cloud settled above the house and across the schoolyard on the roof-angled horizon the gigantic sun shines through bright water like long strings of hanging, constantly disintegrating glass. Truly now the rain rises, so it must converge.

"Dad," Becca says behind me, "when did I begin?"

The curtains should not be closed. I sit on the edge of her

narrow bed. "Why do you ask?" Stalling, my washed golden girl.

"You said, before I existed."

"Yes ..." very long ago, "I did, when I cooked mostly in a frying pan."

"Well, when did I begin?"

A memory that cannot forget seeing, words rise like air through the drab water of willed forgetfulness and longing, face it, longing the words to come again and I follow their visible trail as I follow an intuition, hoping; hesitant at first and in gaps, but they are there, solid, solid good like the fundamental rocks, nothing to trip and fall between.

"'In the beginning ... God created ... the heavens and the earth. And the earth was ... without form and void, and darkness was upon the face of the deep; and the Spirit of God moved upon the face of the waters, and ... God said, Let there be light, and there was light, and God saw the light, that it was good, and God said, Let the dry land appear, and it was so, and God said, Let every living creature appear, and it was so, and God said, Let us make man in our own image, and it was so; in the image of God created he him, male and female created he them, so God formed man of the dust of the ground. And he breathed into his nostrils the breath of life, and man became a living soul.'"

In Becca's motionless face, her eyes are enormous.

"When he breathed?" she says.

It is easier to nod.

"Not when your sperm united with mommy's egg."

Some course-compelled teacher, 'unite' indeed! I avoid laughter, barely.

"I doubt it." The golden light in the room is so livid and extraordinary we sink in it as effortlessly as through water. "That's a different way of talking about beginning, what I said was like poetry about where human life started, there's something particular about man that isn't there in anything else God made. When you talk about eggs and sperms you talk about bodies beginning; not human life, your life."

"Where did my body begin?"

"Oh, that's different. In mommy's body, for sure, on a hot

summer day in a coulee above the Tramping Lakes, in Saskatchewan."

Liv had just said, 'If I never see another alkali-crusted slough I'll thank you sweetly and fervently forever and evermore, I want the rain forest of B.C. don't you understand that you idiot?' But the Tramping Lakes have no alkali; they are a lake chain folded narrow down the ancient bed of a river and if you have been given the ears, beneath them at night you can still hear the buffalo running there as Big Bear declared in a vision, 1876, and in 1969 Liv said to me, 'But it's only three o'clock, what in God's name can we do here, it'll be barely dark at midnight,' and I took her to the ravine purple with saskatoons and at midnight by the lap of the black water we heard the buffalo where the Giver of All runs them still, heard them running the true curve of the earth in their kept place under the lakes until he can give them back again to the land and to the people for whom they were his gift from the beginning.

"That's a really good place to start," I say to Becca. "One of the best in the world."

She swings her bare feet past me, gets up and begins to remove her clothes. "I'd like to see that place, soon," she says thoughtfully.

"Okay, but it might not look very particular to you."

"Maybe a little particular."

"Why?"

"Because I'd be looking at it," she says. She steps out of her panties and turns, pulls the nightgown from under her pillow and funnels it down over her head. Her body before it vanishes in long red and yellow-flowered flannel is slender, angularly straight like any angel's. That's what they should remain, innocent slender angels, when they grow curves they materialize in grey rooms and become tempting, another step and they're whores, angels or whores, what else can a man see, why can't he see different, why can't he see all women like daughters, like lovely sisters, if I look past Becca as daughter she becomes a sex thing, her perfect skin something to rub myself stiff on fast, the fold between her legs a hole that makes her enterable, brutally violable. Horrible ugly words. Acts even more horrible momentarily smear the bright image of her head emerging, my daughter and so I cannot will not think of her that way, mine, why should I ruin what is mine, someday I may have to give her away in marriage ... why? Have I ever owned her? One unforgettable afternoon, one 'shudder in the loins engenders there,' how could that establish ... Liv at least gave her blood and flesh and milk, maybe she should give her ... fathers always give daughters away at Canadian marriages, a male transfer of ownership but that's certainly not the way Mennonite families used to do it. Liv's father never had the chance to give her away. We told him by phone after the fact, silence at the other end of the line more searing than any curse.

"Where does that come from, what you told me? Hey."

"What?"

Becca is shaking me, "That 'in the beginning God made man.'"

She belongs to no one except God as any ancient Jew and certainly Maskepetoon would say. I pray never to violate her because she is herself and good, dear God help me I will try with all I am not to. I cannot give her away because I have never owned her.

"Old Dad! You're not listening."

"I am ... listen, I will always be your father."

Her dark eyes meet mine, startled.

"No matter what happens, remember that."

"You couldn't stop ..." she asks slowly.

"Never."

And immediately she is reassured about something she has not sensed until this instant; she merely understands I have said that.

"Where does it come from?" she asks then.

"What?"

"The 'in the beginning!'"

"O, that's Hebrew poetry. The first words in the Bible, roughly. How the whole earth was made and then everything in it."

"I want to read it all," she says. "Buy me a Bible."

"No, you get allowance for books you want."

Her eyes narrow a little as she stretches up and kisses me rather more deeply than usual; though perhaps I am merely triggered finer. "You buy the educational books," she argues, "you bought me *An Illustrated History of the World.*"

"And you bought *Alligator Pie.*"

"And you bought *Growing Girls.*"

"Which you've never read because you're always reading *Mad*. I won't buy you any more books, you want them, you buy them."

"Then you have to raise my allowance."

"What? How much do you get now?"

"Four seventy-five."

"A month?"

"How about a week?" she says quickly, flipping into bed.

"A month," I say firmly. "Okay, a raise to five dollars and you buy yourself —"

"Five twenty-five. Books are getting more expensive every day you know."

"I know," I lean down to her, "the enormous increase in paper production costs, high printers' wage settlements, the price squeeze from OPEC oil . . . ."

She is laughing, a small girl lying there she could laugh Yasser Arafat away from his machine gun.

"One fifty a week?" she deals.

"Five fifty a month," I decree sternly. "And you buy your own Bible."

"I will, Sweety Pops." She clinches her eyes shut, still smiling, and folds her hands under her chin and repeats in that quick reversion to the two-year-old which I cannot understand, some ritual our attempt at pressureless child-raising has made her cling to, who can tell when she will suddenly discard it like her stuffed animals; if ever:

"Now I lay me down to sleep, guide me through the starry night, wake me when the sun shines bright amen."

There is a line missing. I don't know if she ever knew it, why didn't I teach her that too, didn't it . . . no Lord, no soul keeping; just the starry night to traverse and the implication of another life there, perhaps we live another long, complicated journey of a life when we sleep, a life as real and separate as the one we live now while ostensibly awake and with characters as different as we are from ... dream? Please don't let me stay there, or be lost there, that life in the starry night have mercy upon us the grey one I have no memory of in this... guide me through night the grey one ... 'night is related to the passive principle, the unconscious, the feminine (only Greeks or Jews and we their unthinking heirs would assume those three belonged together) so Hesiod named night The Mother of the Gods and held that it preceded the creation of āll things,' chaos and old night, guide me through all that existed before male was conceived, the dark night of the soul – why starry? 'She walkes in beauty, like the night / Of cloudless climes and starry skies....' No clouds there, ever.

Tolstoi barks, too long and I descend into evening crimson glistening wet, the world burns in water at the horizon. He is quiet at my call, having declared his territory once more by urinating at the corner post as the shadow of my neighbour (I say, "Great evening," and his deep voice answers, "Beautiful") is led along the alley by his dachshund and then Tolstoi trots up and sits licking my hand selectively as I hook him into his collar. Poor beast, thankful every brilliant evening for a chain. The last vestige of chores: a dog to fasten to his kennel under the bushes against the house; of a May evening when the pasture was still poor my father would throw hay to the cows in the corral, huge forkfuls heaved over the fence, the air thick with hay and spruce and smudge-smoke, mosquitoes whining in the darkness under the roof where I lie listening, knowing every sound to the creak of the house settling in upon itself and the call of hunting coyotes lonesome, somewhere. Did my father ever lie with another woman; contemplate, in a recess of himself he had not noticed before, long so to lie? He must surely have thought of it, it is impossible that any man never ... but I cannot believe that, not of him. No shapes rising from the musk of old summer caught in winter hay, from the heat of cattle breathing in darkness. Breath passing upward there for him never more than that: unhurried breath.

I sit on the toilet and reach down between my legs, shift my limp penis slightly so that my passing water will not splash. There is no one to hear. Innocuous dangling flesh, all social silence, to pretend no one actually does this or if they do they never think about it, clean thoughts clear as urine ha! So when the city builds a special can for $50,000 under Commonwealth Stadium just so the Queen of England will have her own place to "go" during her one-day visit to the games, there is a sudden fume in the papers because I suppose it strikes everyone good gracious the Queen does this too, she pulls down her underpants and – we must be sick to avoid – 'but love has pitched his mansion in the place of excrement'... prudery. If love were not pitched there maybe we would talk and watch and make as many small and large ceremonies out of excreting as we do out of ingesting. There isn't a good short word for that: 'eat' is fine, but 'shit' is *verboten* to all but the cursers. 'Live in a heavenly mansion, not in some foul sty,' says the old Bishop to Crazy Jane. That is a very heavy comment on his understanding of love.

Liv comes in, glances briefly at my hairy thighs, pants around my ankles and my socially sanitary silence, then turns to the sink. She begins her ritual of contacts. As a child removable teeth terrified me; I might have died of an encounter with removable eyes. What other part of the body will have been improved a generation from now? The cancer-prone breast? The uncontrollable penis? If yours has untoward longings just remove and have yourself fit with one of scrubbable germ-resistant plastic, removable at will, if it's short-sighted then ... what is a short-sighted penis? Myopic, unable to see distance; love enters at the eye, and exits there too I think, the penis is connected to the eye by one direct four-lane extra-sensitive nerve, head eye to penis eye and its activating genius is not light but desire, desire to see deeper and deeper up into that endless mystery. 'If thy right eye offend thee, pluck it out and cast it from thee: for it is profitable for thee that one of thy members [any one?] should perish, and not that thy whole body should be cast into hell.' Which eye, Jesus pray tell, should one pluck and pitch to avoid casting, which eye pray pray tell should I pluck and pitch for profit gladly?

"You are so quiet doing that," Liv sprays lens solution into her hand. Her voicing my thoughts no longer surprises me. It seems to me sometimes she is herself particularly noisy on those mornings, rare, when she gets up before me; she knows her splashing hits me like a diuretic.

"Men have external directional controls," I run my hand down her right thigh, slim and taut for all her years. Not that member.

"That's why men invented the beastly toilet."

"Men again, what's beastly about this toilet?"

"It's physically easier for women to squat, you know that."

"I always assumed squatting went out with the homestead."

"Well, it is. And a hole in the floor like they have in Europe would be better for you too. Sitting so high strains the wrong muscles, you lose all benefit of gravity. Lots of doctors say our toilets cause most modern constipation and backache."

"That's it, the modern toilet as Male-Ex-lax conspiracy."

She moves her fine rear from my hand. I get up, step out of my pants altogether, reach both arms around her bent to washing.

"Patriarchy and private enterprise combine again to shaft you!"

"I got it the first time, smarty," she reaches for the towel and with that shift nudges me out of the fold of her body. "Go away and sleep," she says. "I'm starting to bleed."

"So?"

"So?"

"Bleeding? You like it then."

"Not tonight."

"Oh, tonight you have a headache too."

"Yes!" She turns laughing, takes my head between her warm hands and kisses me fast. "You know as well as I," she says into my teeth, "that's the best cure for headaches. If I want one."

I pick up my toothbrush, feeling her two hands and the air on my body, always so totally covered by cloth or leather, always hidden by something, if her hands were always there.

70

"Just you sleep," she says, steadily and takes herself into the bedroom.

"You keep kissing me and I'll really wake up." Her familiarity with my body turns my thought. "Did you ever see your father's penis?"

"Huhh. I don't remember."

"Then you didn't."

"For all I know he didn't have one. Did you ever see your mother's sex?"

"Are you kidding? How would a Mennonite kid ... did you?"

She answers, hard, "I doubtless had my eyes shut and mouth open when I was passing through."

I burst out laughing; I can only avoid choking on my Crest by spraying it against the mirror. The shadow of my laughter has gobbed up the shadow of my face, sweet William.

Hey, what's the matter, really? I asked her last night and she did not answer and I should ask her now more than ever but I do not. Perhaps tonight she would answer me. If she wanted to. She might leave me with answers to questions I have not asked. She might ask me. There are answers wives and husbands should not offer each other until after they are no longer important.

I have not thought of that before, either. I stare up into the darkness and I am not dreaming; neither am I having a vision. I am circling on apprehension, almost presentiment; and hope. That has to be faced. For if hope in the heart of man lives on lean pasture, how will it not flourish on rich? Dreadfully.

MAY
THREE

I have sometimes longed for exploration and unimagined discovery in the recesses of an archive or an ancient paper horde. I have no interest in deep digging the soil or the few unseen places perhaps left somewhere on earth, or the moon for that matter; these are beyond me and uninteresting as probable facts, but I have dreamt of discovery in the causalities and events of a possible people's past, in the jungles and sundreamed gardens of the human condition.

I now realize that was always one of the latent lures of the computer for me: somewhere, someday that massive spinning information could just possibly reassemble itself beyond the control of any programmer and all that complex data would reconstitute itself in a truly inventive explosion and mother forth a treasure no one had dared imagine before: like Columbus, sailing for China or at worst the edge of the world, in warm October moonlight suddenly encountering the gentle Arawaks smoking tobacco on the Bahamas. But for a computer, such an explosion of fantastic new world would of course not be discovery; it would be mistake, and the whole purpose of computers, as for all technology, is to eliminate mistake. That is how to control a world: to make the unexpected impossible. Bah.

Such control, the very possibility of it, is humanly hallucinogenic. The entire known world becomes more and more a grid of ever more complex and tiny electrical connections. There came a time when I was shatteringly thankful I could give up trying, even in my small business world, to construct

72

it, but most North Americans in business and science and especially government are already well beyond the mercy of halt. It came to me that by exploring human history I could experience both data and chance; there the mountains of character landscape are explorable, the misfit terrains of personality endless and various even though no one but I cares to unearth them. Perhaps, for example, somewhere sometime there existed a race of people whose males bore the children (beyond any couvade) and the females were what we would consider the fathers, or perhaps they alternated doing what we think are birth-determined functions and perhaps somewhere there is still a trace of such people. It was of course eliminated from the patristic human record as too confusing, too disorderly for the dominance-driving male ego to acknowledge, but somewhere there might be such an island as Cheju off the coast of Korea where to this day oceans part to prayers once a year and only women work away from the home as "breadwinners" while the men stay there to cook and nurture the children. I wonder, do the women also go out in the evening to drink at the pubs?

Granted, my more drastic example would require a certain biological and not only social change, but presumably if it is imaginable it is also possible — as the concept of pouch reproduction, marvelously strange, flowered with the marsupial discovery of Australia. Or the male fishes that at least carry the eggs and later the attached young. Pehaps my male and female fathers (alliteration is some consanguinity!) existed in Uqbar: I already have the mirror, but sadly no misprinted encyclopaedia. Or a matriarchal society like the Lengua Indians in desert Paraguay, which uses infanticide for birth control because to them no body is human before it has been looked upon and named. When the time of birth arrives the mother decides whether she wants a child at all and what gender it is to be while she retreats into the privacy of the thorny bush. She digs a hole in the sand and births over it (dust to dust), avoiding any possibility of seeing the face, and if it is the wrong gender she covers what she has never so much as induced to take one breath and never thought of naming, covers it as simply as she would whatever

73

else her body expelled by natural process: excrement, sweat, urine, festering thorn.

These possibilities surface in the new Glenbow Archives; I do not remember them so insistent in the old. Originally the archives were housed in the first Calgary Public Library building, weathered sandstone of Carnegie dignity from the turn of the century soaked in the slow breath and memory of people reading, thinking, bumbling after the great and banal thoughts stumbled upon by their predecessors. Now everything is glass, sandblasted concrete slabs and blue humming computer screens, there is a kind of technological insistency in the air; the world here is rushing after the racial and religious and sexual equality of the computer terminal. But how can men and women ever be even roughly equal having been dealt such different hands? Not reproduction – not even idiots argue about that – but attitude, security, decisions, powers of the mind – when we moved to Edmonton it was because IBS transferred me, Liv had to find the new travel agency to work for, she had to move into the indelible smell of pastlessness emitted from every fresh-painted wall like words you have to keep learning the meaning of again and again, and I feel here instinctively, sitting in this immeasurably efficient building where data arrives swimming on microfiche and screen, that soon no actual original documents nor even grainy pictures of anything will ever again be visible to the eye of researchers like me; every known fact, every bit of datum recorded anywhere in any archival or word horde will already have been pre-digested into electrical impulses that must be rearranged and regurgitated by machines before humans can assimilate them, and research will be nothing but the imaginative playing of computer consoles, the twiddling of banks of buttons like space-rocket panels where everything possible is already known and programmed for, all places screenable, all mystery and discovery and visible difference vanished, every word ever written or picture painted or diagram drawn or thought thought now looking as if it has been made by an IBS typewriter, there is nothing left but the electrically stimulated twitch, who cares what female or male or neuter manipulates the buttons. Chance is impossible.

74

"That's not imaginatively rational," Gillian says.

"One failure in the power grid, one errant magnet and it's worse than the destruction of the library at Alexandria. Three-quarters of man's accumulated knowledge, of his history and stories, wiped out, kaput, finish Can-á-da."

"'Can-á-da?'"

"We had a free-enterprise pessimist at Cold Lake when I was a kid, always waiting for the Communist hordes to bust in with machine guns and take over his miserable little store, he always said, 'Germany kaput, now finish Can-á-da,' meaning Canada was already done for."

"He wanted Hitler to win?"

"Hitler was fighting Stalin, wasn't he?"

Gillian shakes her head, black hair flaking light. "Someone would have to feed it all into the computers in the first place, that would take forever."

"Not necessarily, it could just be an automated camera, flick through the archives of the world coded to some scheme or other—name, symbol—every "y" ever written could be flashed on the screen before you, take you years to see every "y" if that was what you wanted but there it would be and—"

"A machine transforming all words into magnetic particles, without a single human standing by?"

"Not just words, pictures too, anything, the very shapes of artifacts statistically collated, the anatomic particles of paper or cloth, do you know how many possible facts the world contains? Devour the Glenbow in half a day, the entire National Archives chewed into magnetic squiggles in less than a week, a mere matter of material arrangement, the unleafing of paper and clay at the speed of light, the machine tracking through stacks and electronically ingesting every fragment and dust blot and homogenizing it all into one —"

"Absolutely and totally boring," Gillian says and rises easily as a flame, she may teach me touch, that undulent white skin, and steps into the dark bathroom closing half the door. I remain on the couch as she has left me, my marvelous rhetoric a sudden hole in the air I thought I was breathing. I am untouched. A vari-coloured and vari-limbed excrescence on the overstuffed burgundy plush, lamp light from over my

shoulder shining straight down the length of me like anticipation. I hear a rush of water, the room drifts beyond my
fingertips in something not air, what pattern does hair lay
along the inside of her thigh? My shoed foot lies sideways on
the carpet, most large and familiar and suddenly ugly.
'What's freedom for? To know eternity.' The door swings, she
is barelegged when she emerges at the dark with her hands at
her waistband and she drops her skirt on the floor and walks
through it towards me straight as the arrow that flieth by day.
A body moves more ways than one, that total length of leg,
an inside flush with a shadowy drift I cannot quite register.
The May evening light is still at the window.

"What is this?"

"Shut up," she says soft as stones against my teeth.

And of course if I don't know I can simply wait to find out.
Her hands and the long, round insides of her legs both
touching my sharply pressed trousers uncrumpled till now.
Her face tilts.

"I want to know, what can you do besides think and talk so
marvelously."

"I can ... kiss," especially when I have – want – no choice.

"Okay ... anything else?"

Her dark eyes bunching up at the corners, she is about to
burst out laughing! This naked-legged girl astride me
clothed, the vee of her briefs notched blue below the edge of
her shirt, her lips gleaming from mine, the roots of a tree
grapple through my body like claws, if I could now breathe I
would certainly be gasping. I lean forward, my hands come
up under her shirt on her smooth muscle-folded back, skin,
my fingers can't spread wide enough for skin and she tilts
away, laughs easily. I know her so little I don't remember
hearing her laugh, the round weight of her pendent at my
locked hands, swaying.

"Why do you stare like that?"

I shake my head. Tears raze but laughter can annihilate,
legs and thighs veed over me.

"Swallowed your tongue? Already?"

"You said, 'Shut up.'"

"O that was your theorizing, I mean now, at me."

76

"We're supposed to be ... at a most crucial moment, laughter seems like, I donno, slightly inna ... inappropriate?"

"Violins," she sways back, body a springing bow with throat arched, "the audience leans forward, tense, 'How much will we see? What?' Not 'crucial' moment, it's the most sacred moment in the greatest voyeur art ever invented, the North American movie, what, what *exactly* will I see?"

"Not as sacred as the confessional when the man tells his wife, 'I'm really sorry dear, but I love her.'"

"That's it, the wife explodes!"

"Or if *she* says those three little words, the husband explodes."

"Always be sure about your most sacred explosions!"

"The match of the four-letter word, too often profaned...."

"For me to disdain it," she contradicts me.

The small word that masters and enfolds the act. I am too enmeshed here to know truly what I have said, 'wife' recalls nothing, she tilts me back, her breasts loose under cotton brush my cheeks as the light clicks off and we are in our lovely grey, she is all grey upon me with her weighted warmth deep seven-stranded colour. My hands slide around her buttocks and along her legs which lift to me, bending, her full thighs now round and heavy like the heavier warmth of breasts swinging free of my two hands and I can only tip her back, the skin of her neck suddenly grained between my teeth and her black hair against my face, her long legs pressing my chest, I am clasping her doubled against me and I feel her strength pound inside me and she clasps, pulls me even tighter, we may disappear into each other out of this barely bearable straining of curled skin. If we could satisfy ourselves like this we would, all the strength and sweetness we have bumbled about with ignorantly throughout our lives suddenly here rolled into one huge grey ball about to batter down every livid red citadel we've been ignorant of for this cannot be anything except beginning, all things they say are pure to the uncontaminated, some say, and an inevitability like a door smashes open in my head and I sense an abrupt loosening I have known only a few times in my life: why not?

what if this keeps on happening? didn't we want exactly this? when we came here and sat down deliberately alone in a numbered lamp-lit room? don't we? would I destroy something forever? what is that something which could be so destroyed? will the round world roll wrong?

"Yes," in my ear, "yes," and the moist pointed warmth of her contradictory tongue speaks to me there. The ripple of her overpowering laughter in her throat. "Hey old man, this is no computer."

She fills me round and full as a suckable grape.

There is a pattern of closet doors in the darkness. Wrong. They should be over there but they float ... and a smell smudged with purple movement like a reptile leaning over me as I run, frantically without motion but in terror and the light line from the street lamp far below dusts the curtains: in the Palliser Hotel, Calgary, old with sandy bricks like stone from the quarry once cut above the Bow River where the Crowchild Trail is now hacked through the bluffs. Sometime in the night I am awake. Listening. The sound of footsteps, someone walking, somewhere I hear them move steadily like a house settling when snow folds down winter stillness. In a hotel bed, to the single sound of feet. 'Is there anyone there? said the Traveller, / Knocking on the moonlit door.'

And looking across the bed. Down at me. In the locked and door-chained I am certain grey darkness of the sleeping Palliser. A man stands between the bed and the wall, the wall against which the bed is tight. I am certain, beyond her mound of shoulder and sprawled hair I see sombre eyes as if I saw them in a sunlit mirror, dazzled in light this is no dream I am not sleeping. His face gaunt, long, so close even with the bed between us that his awareness controls all my reaction, there can be no surprise that he is here in contemplation of the closed sleeping face of the woman who has lain between my hands, I between her knees all this time; whom I have not yet dared tell I love. If ever. A faintness like eyes shining.

"How can a human being live the good life?" I ask in the grey night.

His face must be half the meaning of whatever will be said. Words alone cannot answer a question only words can conceive. But it is inevitable that he will speak, as inevitable as his still, level voice,

"You ask like that, and it can't be answered."

"Philosophers throughout history have asked —"

"But I'm no philosopher," he says, "and neither are you."

"I'm not?"

"You have too little rigour of thought, no necessary inevitability of logic." He clears his throat scratchily, as if from long disuse, "And you imagine too much."

"Plato was the greatest philosopher ever, and also the most imaginative."

"True. And the last he imagined for Socrates was that cup."

"Hardly better than you."

He laughs aloud; fundamentally amused. "Wasn't I at least symbolically more impressive, all spread out?"

"We all die, symbolically or not."

"In a manner of speaking yes, we die," and he comes silently around and sits down on my side of the bed. Beside my feet bent back from the back of Gillian's knees; whom he has not yet looked at. I have to twist to see him, I have to untouch her shoulder. She stirs, snuggles down warmer, sleeps on, o palpable rounded snuggler. "You aren't concerned with dying," he says. "You're in bed with a woman."

"Actually I often think about that in bed, afterwards. Death."

"Especially in this one?"

"The 'small death.'"

"In this one?" he insists.

"I know, I know, she's another man's wife."

"Does that bother you?"

He says it quite expressionlessly, gently; as in fact he has said everything so far. Almost as if he hasn't thought anything about this until he says it, each sentence both discovery and statement. Hardly, who no doubt has thought of everything, finally and forever and from the beginning and all time.

"Well," I manage finally, "I presume it bothers you."

"Why should it?"

"If you go around at night just ignoring locked doors," I flip a gesture, "you must run into —" my heart jolts. What am I saying!

But he ignores my thrust, is suddenly relentless, "Is that what really bothers you, that you're handling 'another man's goods'?"

"She's nobody's goods!"

"But you said, 'she's another man's wife' when you could have said, 'I'm not her husband.'"

"By implication it means exactly the same thing."

"Not exactly," he says. "Especially not by implication."

I feel his weight at my feet shift, the light from the street far below shines through the bathroom door, still half open and it cuts through the seeming dark solidity of his head and shoulders. He is there, both weight and voice.

"If your right eye offends you," he says, "tear it out and throw it away."

"That still leaves the left."

"Tear it out and throw it away."

"I can still hear, I can still smell for god's sake!"

"If you want to live by the law," he says in a voice so cold it shivers me into fury, "you must destroy *all* your senses."

"So go ahead, mutilate yourself, I won't!"

"I do not live by the law."

"It's easy for you to talk, did you ever love a woman completely?"

"What do you mean, 'completely'?"

"In every way!"

"You mean genitally."

"Okay, okay, spiritually, genitally, orally whatever you want, penisly!"

"I lived with women all my life, as much as men. To love genitally is a kind of beginning."

"How would you know!" I'm upright in bed, yelling at this steady response, the utter gall of this so conveniently arranged immaculate conception! "It's me and this beautiful woman, here, we're the ones born between the faeces and the urine, 'beginning' my ass, how come it overwhelms us like this, runs us down like a herd of horses, why such a power in the mind and between the legs that it rams us into some body space where there's nothing but spinning overwhelming sensation, huh? Anybody would have to be 95% dead not to want this, to tear down buildings to get this *once* once you know how good it is! Did you ever feel that, better than you ever *felt* anything? We just know your perfect remembered words of ambiguous wisdom, dropped here and there to all those ordinary people suffering the usual stupid events of their usual stupid lives, tralala, words words — where are the stories of you standing somewhere pissing like I suppose even you had to and suddenly your mind spins aside and this big schlong here in your hand is hard as a pipe hammering you for attention? Do you know how that feels, huh?"

"Yes."

"Yes!"

"To love genitally is a beginning, also an end."

"Always ambiguous, ambiguous, can't you ever say anything straight out?"

"You have fallen in love?" almost sardonic.

"Yes, yes, we have, you know that as well as — did you?"

"What?"

"Ever feel a hard-on push against your pants, or whatever it was you wore?"

"I said yes."

"Well 'yes' isn't an answer, it just begs —"

"Yes," he is back to the dry, steady tone that sits on the edge of something but never quite commits itself. Almost like laughter. "That happened to me, yes."

"'Yes' is no answer!"

"Of course it is. And I was circumcised too, so my penis rubbed against the nice cotton undergarment my mother always kept so crisp and clean."

I stare in the pale darkness; my anger is sudden and gone and I wish I could see him plain, he has been pulling my leg, dear God would he pull my leg?

He is laughing. "Of course I would," he says.

"You have all the advantages."

He shakes his head. "Not as much as you think. But I like your passion."

"Passion's a meaning that goes two ways."

"Don't I know it," he says grimly, then grins. "But it's odd. Why must love be a fall?"

"It's just the way it's said in English, just a semantic ... how did you say it in Hebrew?"

"In Aramaic you just love someone."

"'Falling in love' doesn't mean anything literally."

"And you've done it twice now, which is less than some but twice more than many."

Twice. The ocean lapping against logs and barnacled stones with Vancouver lights arranging themselves in and out of a possible far city to the circle of Liv's full body inside my arms and a gull squawking, stupidly, staring down at us from the concrete gun emplacement. Gaping black at the base of the sand cliffs as if a cannon had exploded in its belly. I felt then, incredibly, a giant spike had driven through my skull and backbones down into the stone beach between my feet, my arms around Liv as if banded and she gasped, not resisting. Twice. Can you begin and then begin again only with the end of the first beginning?

"What do you want to begin?" Tight in my ear, like a caress.

She is there, the evening lights are moving over the water and I cannot talk past this ugly concretion, immovable human excrement not even natural enough to rot in the salty air. "They made these, would you believe it, to try and keep out the Japanese, would you belie...."

"It's a lovely wide inlet," she says. "It should be protected."

"A bulletin board for permanent obscenities, Oliver L fs Jane B, that's all."

"No," her hands search under my shirt, "invasion terror, in a war people suffer invasion terror."

"I believe you're wrong literally," he says seated on my bed. "Why in English is passionate love a 'fall'? Why not 'soaring into love,' why not 'leap,' 'blossom'?"

"It has to be said somehow."

"Because," he continues relentless propositional again, "the image is right, you really do think you can't control yourself, you are overwhelmed, helpless off an edge as if pushed, pulled by a force out there somewhere, right? That's what you *want* to think."

He's right, that's what I have been thinking. Overcome. Rolled along in an inevitability materializing in a grey room of grey past patterns, like a shadow of a story I could not anticipate, a sickness that both debilitates and lines my spirit with iron at the same time as it convulses and hardens my body, suddenly off the far edge of my flat world, but his tone … it isn't sardonic, no, it is not biting, or mocking. More a gentle irony that understands and at the same time refuses to accept so platitudinously easy a response, fall, helpless it isn't that easy! I am contradicting what I have lived in self-conscious happiness most of my adult life!

"You think in a very ancient tradition," he says gently now. "The wise of this world have always treated love as a contradictory, somehow mindless abnormality. 'A frenzy,' says Plutarch. 'I have so much joy in my pain that I am sick with delight,' sings Chretien de Troyes."

"What did you do with physical love?" I am sitting so upright I could touch him, his smell like faint sweat in my nostrils. "Tell me."

His eyes bright and hard and grey in that grey hotel room I have rented for the night as any traveller or pick-me-up will rent after me, the CPR blanket rough as shingle under my elbow. Somewhere a radiator hisses, begins to percolate. Humanity exists; my feet cold as stones.

"To love is to be," he says finally. "Love is exquisite health. Being human is not body and spirit the way the Greeks thought, to be human is to be dust living by God's breath. That breath, spirit gives our body substance, otherwise we're only dust."

"Which is also a metaphor, of course," I do not try to check my sarcasm.

"Story perhaps?" so gently.

"Okay, story."

"How else can we truly talk?"

"It's sometimes nice for a rock just to be a rock!"

"Of course. Until you put your foot through it."

"What?"

"Well, if you must be the philosopher, rock is poor analogy for life since in your formulation it has only one dimension – substance. Life has a few more than that, dimensions."

"I know, I know it's too simple but —"

"My story of breath and dust is too simple too."

"O don't worry, it's tangled enough, so you say to love spiritually you have to love bodily?"

"There is no breath without dust, there is no body without spirit."

"Can you answer my question!"

"Can you stop thinking them so stupidly?"

"It's the only way I can think them!"

"Then think different!"

"I'm trying!"

"Try a little harder. The story we live is not so flat. It is in God we live, and move, and have our being. You limit God's breath too much, to one custom's way of doing and thinking."

"It's more or less all we have to live by, everyone, by some accepted order. It holds our worlds together."

"And fine worlds they have been and are, aren't they." He is sardonic now beyond all irony. I can barely see him in the lightening dawn of the room, the brightness of the bathroom door suddenly as if transparent through his shape.

"Why are you so afraid to discover your body? The truth of the spirit is your body."

"Another ambiguity."

"No. If you love God you can do what you please."

"You just said God is a spirit."

"Yes."

"Then I suppose one must love God genitally too, huh?"

"If he has a body then why is that impossible?"

"Well, you just said he was in every body!"

"I know."

"So he is ... *em*bodied?"

"He must be. Do you think he would make bodies and not have some himself?"

"Did you ever love anyone with your body?"

"Do you think God gave you passion without having any himself?"

"Did you?"

"What kind of an eviscerated human being do you think me?"

"Weren't you a virgin?"

"Virgin?" I have jolted him at last thank God into actual surprise. "Heavenly Father, what does 'virgin' have to do with anything!"

"Purity, you always talked —"

"How are virgins 'pure'?"

"Well, they have kept themselves un …" the word tangles me suddenly, so mediaeval I can hear the recorders high, bodiless as thread stretched to breaking, I sing of a maiden that is makeless.

"Yes, 'unsullied,' yes, yes, go ahead, 'clean'?"

"…from the opposite sex, they…" well may such a lady—

"Exactly!" The word roars, it is one with his roaring laughter, "As if another human being could dirty you!" The entire hotel reverberates like a massive train thundering through, blasting a hole out of the very bowels of this room, the iron tracks of it hammering along my bones long after its rush has shivered into silence. The high ceilings eventually vacant as an astral whisper. Dirt. Purity. Only the dead are frozen antiseptic clean.

Gillian is awake in bright sunlight; awake but not yet awake she burrows down against me and when I turn an instant to her she is suddenly aware, her head rises and stares at me large eyed. Flecks of gold now in basic black. Surprised perhaps, though her warm soft length so fitted along my body aching at points under the sharp sheets she might have been awakening there like sunrise for years.

"It is you." Perhaps she had dreamed, dreaded someone else. She bends again, hides her face against ribs. The momentary gleam of her shoulder and upper arm seems so narrow, child-like, little broader than Becca's but I do not dare

85

admit that, push that away over an edge, away, 'The smiling mouth and laughing eyes gray, / The breastes round and long small armes twain,' and there is an aloneness between us and we do not know each other though she barely touches my right length; I am suddenly, we are both, afraid. My body empty, drained.

And words rise in me, hard, bright grey, making a path I follow like light. "You are a Cree woman in a clearing among small poplars, the sky piled up blue between summer clouds, and you are singing in the wind a story someone must hear and I come to you riding a black horse, though you have never seen either a white man nor any horse, and we appear to you as one between the small trees and you stand up, coming, the song from your mouth weaving me and the horse like cloth out of the air flickering between the poplars turning the underside of their leaves pale to your song. And you come ... to me, there...."

Silence. Momentarily the path goes nowhere, wherever it began; she says against my skin,

"What do I do, I am beside you on the black horse."

"You kiss me."

"And you ... turn to stone. Both of you."

"Oh."

"Because rock is eternal, and centaurs everlasting."

That story is ended; there is perhaps ritual left and that will grow when the place and the shape and even the words are forgotten, when the trees have been chopped down. Her hand shifts under the sheet, the edge of a possible axe; gradually her fingertips become individual small footsteps over me as if I were braille and she stone blind.

"Does that feel good?"

"Lovely." She will surely suck blossoms from flesh.

And she is curious. Explores undersides, folds, spheres ... why can't I think 'balls,' they are as much me as the cheeks, lips anyone can stare at if they want and I assume everyone knows I have them wherever I walk by, she is gently fingering my testicles and the spaces between—but even that sounds coarse and she so delicate, Chaucer would have written her a motion of 'swete gentilesse.' A lovely word, why is it now gone, forgotten?

"You have a foreskin."

"Midwives on prairie farms don't carry knives," I tell the high ceiling.

She senses my self-deprecation; bitterness perhaps. "A foreskin is lovely," touching it. "It's barbaric to cut it off."

"Necessary sanitary, they say."

"Barbarism, Jewish barbarism."

"Every day, remember my bush beginnings."

"Every day?"

"Sanitary you know, above all."

"It makes you nice and pointed."

Fingers reading me, a coming to my senses like sunlight searching in folds, along edges and strangely the small worm of my daily life curls warmer and without a dream of volition, only limpness. Unpredictably stupid body, unfathomable when it should be obvious, I certainly cannot look at her curved sideways to me, certainly breathing up now to find my eye. Is this overwhelming ... romance or an annual conversation with myself in my doctor's office, no, I don't have to get up at night, no, I'm monotonously regular, yes, a glass of juice every morning, now the pads of her fingers are round and smooth ... my head tilts to her face classical as Nefertiti, black eyes now unwinking and dilated in the brilliant light. Her eyelashes flicker to my sudden small surge.

There is another conversation we are not having. I see words run across her inconceivable cheekbones, a finger writing   the morning sunlight   where have you been   never anywhere before   are you alone   yes will you dare see me in daylight   will you let me try   whom did you bring with you   no one either   really   yes if words were wrens they would be written on the air   like spider roads yes   blazing threads of sunlight.

Her hand leaves, in silence. "Excuse me," with a sudden long movement she is over me and walking across light to the bathroom. I will not think. Poster wisdom has it love is never having to say you're sorry, the CPR should plaster that on

87

ceilings, presumably the beloved enjoys crushing, desires
needles through the gut, presumably no lover would inflict
that, imbecilic presumption, who the more easily can? Love
is not love that alters when it alteration finds, o no it is an
ever-fixed mark, o no it is a flat-footed morning bathroom
necessity, o yes it is a short-sighted blur sprayed about by radiance, a shining between legs while a toilet rushes somewhere scissoring closer, separate as devastating nightmares.
'All lovers live by longing, and endure: / Summon a vision
and declare it pure.' She lifts back sheet and blanket and forks
herself astride naked me, kneeling wide-kneed with her
strong thighs faintly fuzzed, blondish there not black, the
look down her long nose steadily deliberate. Lips open.

I take her between my two hands I think; but she is decid-
ing all this. As if she created my feeling at each instant before
she does not touch me. There is no need even to turn my face
from the ceiling, she intercepts that bending forward, her
arms straight braced on the pillow beside my head, my face
between her hanging breasts. On teeth and tongue I taste the
circle of her limbs, her warm weight enters me inside the
black curtain of hair, her look bends mine without a gasp to
soften this unwinking act. I will be rooted out no matter
where my burial, and she will come there with me.

And then she speaks; I am instantly furious, keep quiet!
This is more than enough, shut up! screams in my head, my
twisting mouth closed with her mouth even while her impeccable words slit my anger and my scream and carry us in
the rhythms of our bodies farther and farther from the flat
base of our beginning upward, as if we were converging to a
lacerating flame, her words more than body,

"Hey old man, hey, when will you be, come an histor, ian
you're a fact, *mon*gerer, fact-mongerer, history isn't *facts*, it's
perso*na*lit, y the whole *world*, the universe, is personality,
when will you, everything is, perso*na*li...."

Her words force me, my body me, as if I were tightening
upward through a pressure point, forcing ... her words

"... the world is under, con*struct*ion, do you feel, that?
always every world, is being made is conscious, ness not only
faaaaaacts! do you feel, that!"

88

My body is a groan drawing thinner and thinner "... yes ...
yes ... ssss...."

As if the bed, the room were burning with someone. What
does virgin have to do with anything, did someone say that?
I am kissed beyond thought.

The gravel streets cross at right angles under the green water
tower; I see all that again as ever again the instant the highway rises over the long hill from the north and there the rail-
road and the eleven grain elevators still cut their diagonal
between fields and town. Each detail unchangeable in my
memory as it has been since memory, wanted or not, the arena too in all seasons though I am aware of every repaired
roof, each renovated house corner where a picture window
has suddenly effaced small panes. On the corner under massive cottonwoods, in the leg shadows of the water tower our
tiny house seems marinated with age, the yellow edges sag,
even the rich brown asphalt of the roof Becca and I nailed on
last summer, she in short shorts hammering carefully on the
slope between her bent brown legs, seems to droop as if afraid
the certain twice-weekly hearses driving by from Pioneer
Haven at the end of the street will suddenly turn into this
driveway and stop facing the double doors of what was once
our barn. Wooden doors I once cut through the end walls,
saw clamping.

There are logs of memory stacked here for the burning but
I will not begin to pick up any of them, I will not so much as
glance at Olena's cottage visible of course through the spring
careganas. May your house be safe from dry rot.

"Mam, I'm here!" knock on the back door always unlocked
and barge in, remorselessly cheerful. "Mam!"

By the window of course facing the street where she cannot
have recognized my car passing at the corner, nor hear my
fast steps through the kitchen except as a smudgy black distance out of which my voice comes, the creeping silence that
is now joining her long blindness like a relentless companion sprinting to catch up. "Mam!"

"Heh?" Head lifting in the spring light. *"Weh es daut?"*

"Mam, I'm here!" I needn't shout. Deafness is gradually destroying her sense of words but she recognizes my voice by any sound it can make, even on the telephone two hundred miles away as if she were still keyed to my every murmur, in sleep intuited by nightmares and came and shook them off me still like rain without a ripple to my awakening.

"Jasch. *Na oba Jasch.* Is that you?"

I can hold her seated easily if I kneel, her knitting fallen in her lap and her soft face against mine but the texture is quite her own, both grainy and polished warm like cushioned glass. She will hold me there bent and kneeling until I age enough to understand, she was the first and she is the last and she will live me into the meaning of all the others, three now and maybe four and who can tell who will materialize in the next ashen country I enter: if so much arises in the grey, what mystery must a daylit prairie hold? I will not think.

"You didn't phone, you'd come."

Her two hands are seeing my head and she smells like old dried apple, nudging me away a little to find my hair, my broadening forehead, the length of my nose. Blindness has taught her understanding touch, well, perhaps me also; she probably always knew what I couldn't endure, the assault of it; I'd leap on my bike and charge into the Vulcan wind, sweating corners into the schoolyard but momentarily sand-blasted clean, her eyes not even a memory but her passing touch a stain to be ground away before it soaked through me everywhere.

"Every time you're thinner. Doesn't she still feed you enough?"

"Just feel here," I shout, moving one hand from cheek to waist. "That's thick, eh?"

"Not so much either," chuckling and her eyes, still as darkly beautiful as when they followed me into the darkest corners of my child's mind, tell me her Mennonite peasant wisdom more easily than words: the heftier the healthier. "Na, if you didn't just sit behind that desk, reading and scribbling. You don't have cancer, heh? Stomach?"

"No! That I don't have, cancer!"

"You're so thin."

"That's good! I'm not farming, I don't need to be wide as a barn door to turn a ... handle ... for ... a reader," I cannot say 'micro-reader' in Low German, there is no word, "I don't need...."

She can't hear anyway. Every time I come she feels me gaunt, every time it seems a completely new discovery as if she has forgotten in the month or two, or weeks I haven't been here. She is both teasing and serious; that her own once powerful peasant body has fallen to a tiny looseness of bones knitting in a chair escapes her, though perhaps she would remember if I roared it in her ear, felt completely over the cloth-like drapery of her flesh till she understood that, there. But my changing life is impossible to explain, it would have been so even when she still saw clear as light and heard the faintest sound of a child crying: if I had been building houses or sewing up accidents or preaching, yes, and teaching school of course but why leave one good job when you have it, inside where it's warm all winter and it feeds your family, to go into risky business and then leave even that when they still want you and spend years of so much good money at almost forty going to university again to do nothing but snoop after old stories? If they had happened to you or your family you knew them anyway and why would anyone else care? Whom did stories help? Explain that in a peasant language like Low German which has no abstract vocabulary beyond 'sin' and 'decent,' my God even love could barely keep you trying to explain.

"How long will you stay and then you have to run again, somewhere?"

"Oh, half an hour," I roar quickly, "an hour, I'll come back again tomorrow, I have to ... visit someone ... in the country, I'll stay half an hour!"

Her face is motionless, concentrating, trying to fathom the hollow whisper of my bellow and after a moment nods; she may not understand so I draw 1 over 2 with my finger in her palm, twice, and she nods again.

"That doesn't pay, from Edmonton."

"I have to, go this afternoon, here on the land … a farm here…."

"It's alright," she says in her small uninflected voice, then her usual: "You always have it so busy."

"No, no, I have time, I have!"

"*So druck*," shaking her head, and then oddly as if she understood my clumsy half-truth, the very tone of my denial: "You can have all my time too. Right now, all, I want nothing of it anymore."

After a moment I can laugh; bend and kiss her so close she will feel the pulse of my laughter against her face soft as rags. "No, no! You keep every minute! You have to keep it, yes!"

"You can have it all," she says inside the prison where she must live now. Time. She knits by feel and watches the dark shapes of cars pass outside now in a greyness. The smaller shadows of people she can barely distinguish, what does she do inside her small head day after endless day, does she have enough memories for all that thickening black silence? My half hours holding her hand for the next year all piled together will barely fill one waking day and what are they to remember? Skin and felt bone, a short apprehension of love. I should have brought Gillian to her and explained in monosyllables, 'This is my good friend, I met her at work, she is working …' what? All she would know was touch and smell and a stranger's voice like mice skittering in an empty house and even if she could hear perfectly—especially if she could see perfectly—she would say staring at me, 'Na, what have you done with Liv?' The subtle possibilities of 'friend' more impossible to explain in Low German to that face than modern existentialism. Certain memories she does not need, she has enough of me.

Her left hand finds the drawer of the end table beside her. Glasses and hearing aid. It gives her more headache than hearing, but if the atmosphere is right or her psychosomatic state or some other such uncontrollable factor fits it may bring my voice a little closer: not any unfamiliar voice but mine perhaps, for a few minutes. It shrieks painful as an electric needle and her face hunches as she fumbles it to ground inside her ear, still shrieking, but I do not move; she will do this in her way, as she can.

Her face becomes ancient madonna again, though glassed and wired. Thank God he died before she lost sight and sound; but perhaps he would have died quicker then, of apoplexy yelling at her to come and change his urine bag, it was going to run over! though all he ever called it was 'water,' the terrible 'water' he would never again control after all the pills and the operation and so used it to confirm the domineering helplessness he had wanted to achieve all his life and which his children had refused him as soon as they had any perception of it, which was at birth, how could even a mewling infant miss that in him? He was doubtless actually thankful, though I sure as hell was never around to see and accuse him of it, that he now had sufficient reason at last to be what he had always wanted, hadn't the doctor cut that out of him, he couldn't help it could he? Sufficient at last to lie or sit in one spot all day while her duty ran her for him, some days he would barely lift his arm to blow his nose, waiting for her to bring his very breath from the kitchen and breathe it for him because her duty could not let him just kick off – that's a precise Low German word, *kripea*, used only of beasts or in human derision – kick off if he was too goddamn lazy to inflate his obscenely healthy lungs ... I haven't thought like this in years, years. She must feel the heat of my red shame, my face so close to hers. But I cannot for the moment help it.

"...actually that was the next summer," speaking of some place in her memory as if she can still momentarily hear her own voice, the resonance that led her above every voice in church like a clear searchlight among candles, "the summer of the black blizzard. He drove north then, by Cold Lake, with Jakob Poetker and that one with the short crooked leg, that Wiens ... and found the homestead by Cold Lake there and we were living in my uncle's granary by Sunnynook, loading – *Krumma* Wiens, that *Krumma* Wiens came on the yard with his truck to load a little of our stuff that he had room for and that's when...."

Her voice fades inward, Crooked Wiens our neighbour be-

93

fore my memory, and I shout quickly, "Didn't you drive? On the wagon, all the way?"

"Heh?"

"With the horses and wagon, to Cold Lake!"

"Yes," she says quietly, "of course we did. The two brown ones were so bad when we got further north where the grass was we had to stop almost half the day for them and the cow and two heifers to graze, we had no money to ship them on the train like *Krumma* Wiens did his, ours walked every step over two hundred miles and so weak grazing just at night wasn't enough, it was by those Indians near Lloydminster before there was any grass. You could count every rib, and other bones too, huh ..." she is shaking her head, the gaunt animals carved like skeletons by the morning sun and her girls around her in the hayrack piled with every piece of stuff they own, faces pudgy from too many potatoes. Me in her lap. Strong and plump from six months eating her; perhaps her blindness, certainly her destroyed teeth began there.

"He wanted to go to Peace River, that was the best place where they were all moving there by the thousands, but Wiens said it was too far and it's all north, it rains at Cold Lake too and four hundred miles closer, I'm not driving four hundred miles farther for the same bush, you can pound your hollow nags all the way there and if you find grass maybe you'll get to Peace River the year after next, and on the way you can practice making those snow piles like the Eskimos for winter too. He had a truck, *Krumma* Wiens, a big one all full of his stuff, he had so much. So we went to Cold Lake."

And who could call that the mistake of their lives? It wasn't as bad as the Russian Revolution and the anarchy and Stalin's collectivization; but for Canada it was bad enough. He made one brilliant move: somehow he got himself and family out of Russia. What loudmouth was living beside him then to tell him what to do? Maybe if he had five sons he could have sent them one after the other into the Drumheller coal mines near Sunnynook blazing under the prairie sun (he wouldn't go near those mines himself) as soon as they turned fifteen and hung on through Depression and Second World War and maybe owned five sections of grain land when the rain started again in 1950 – such business sense was as likely for him as walking on the moon. The perfect excuse: what can you do with just six girls living after two boys born dead in the anarchy and then finally one *bengel* born in Canada? As if he ever needed an excuse from the minute he was born tenth of eleven surviving children in Russia where you could not divide an inheritance no matter how big.

Her hand is against my face. "He was forty when he came to Canada," as if she is explaining everything; again. Her transparent hand like a beam of light into the past.

"You were thirty-five!"

"Another country is different for a man. He was taking the seed drill back to Sunnynook, to the elevator man, and he took Lena along, she could drive so good then and *Krumma* Wiens came just when he was gone [that was his kind of timing all right] and said we had to load on whatever we wanted to send with him because they were leaving that afternoon whether the wind blew something more up or not, it was just another reason *to leave the godforsaken country, if it wasn't snow it was mosquitoes, if not heat then sure grasshoppers. The extra horse, the grey, was in what had been the pasture beside the granary trying to paw a mouthful of dead grass out of the sand. Beside the levelled dugout the mound of stones had been blasted clear, but the fence was down all the way to the road allowance because the Russian thistle piled against it and the drifting weight of sand broke the posts off. Not even topsoil – grey sand, west of them to the mountains nothing else was left to blow here and bury them.*

"Well," Krumma *Wiens shifted a little as if he wanted to scratch himself, staring at her button up the front of her dress where Jaschchi still nudged but there was nothing left for his mouth there,* "what do you want to send along with me?"

She was suddenly happy like a pang in the ferocious, gritty heat that her husband was on his way to town with the seed drill they had paid on year after year but never owned. Wiens' truckbox was stacked high with things under canvas.

"What have you got room for?" she said, knowing him as surely as those clouds coming up from the west.

"Your oldest girl."

95

The ground was cracked wide open by drought, like glass smashed. The crack at her feet was so deep that despite the intense sunlight she could see no bottom, only the restless sand granulating down into shafts of light that seemed to widen dreadfully as they deepened. Where he had driven his truck onto the yard he had carefully straddled one.

"Got room for our cow?" she asked as if she hadn't heard. "I don't think she'll get to Cold Lake if she has to walk."

"How about you?" he said, still staring. His huge eyes bulged out of their eyeholes as if without moving he saw around her back, under her, under her clothes where between her heavy breasts her needle had neatly written the only word she would ever have for him: no.

"The cow gives good milk," she insisted impossibly.

"Your young one too, bring him too, it'll save you three weeks of hayrack on those bush trails through the Indians."

"And your Lensch?"

"Don't you bother about my Lensch," his gaunt wife enormous with another son no doubt, wordless as a bearing tree.

"No," she said. And looked past him and the truck and the corner of the granary where they had tried to live for eight years for the benefit of her uncle to the field where the clouds were piling up black as sand-dunes in a final bronzing of sky, "I don't bother about her. You'd just tell her to go lie under some bush and I'd lay Jaschchi away under some other bush and then you'd show me how long your crooked leg is."

Slowly red seeped into his beaked face. No Mennonite woman ever talked like that to a man. Silence, dumb obedience, he stared directly into her as if she were already stripped.

"Anything I've wanted to do," he said, "it's always been long enough."

"Maybe till now," she said turning. Behind her Ruth ran out of the barnshed dragging little Eva by the arm.

"The calf bumped her," the older girl shouted. "In the stomach, that dumb calf!"

And suddenly the wind hit them like a gasp, and stagger. Twelve feet away her daughters vanished as if the earth had

*exploded into sand, she clutched her baby and Wiens seized
her from behind or she would have fallen backwards, broken
her leg in that crack.*

"Into the truck!" he yelled in her ear, "quick!"

"The girls—"

*"In there!" His hand rammed her skirt up between her
legs, he was heaving her up, in, violent as the black blizzard
and she was screaming,*

"Ruth! Eva!"

*but she was forced inside the temporary breathing eddy of the
truck cab and through a torn space in the storm saw the small
shapes of her girls already being drifted over like stones even
as they crawled, their faces clenched shut and yearning
ghostly toward her and she hammered her fist in Wiens' face,
pounding him,*

"The girls, there! there!"

*and he turned, took a step towards them and disappeared.
She dropped Jaschchi squawling on the seat and leaped to
the ground, still screaming but the storm rammed sand down
her mouth, there was nothing to see or hear, she was blind
and deaf and choked in the fist of the black blizzard, she could
only reach out, her one hand on the open truck door and
stretch into the roar so loud it seemed to be nothing so much
as silence, her straining body slammed about she could not
even guide them on the thin string of a scream because she
was choking.*

*But then when her fingers found something, she held it.
She would never let go even as she drowned, was buried, and
that was Wiens crawling up her body and without breathing
they gradually wrestled up through sand into the truck cab
and clawed the door shut and could begin coughing, vomit-
ing, racking dry dust out of themselves in small tearing explosions. And there was Ruth heaving dust between their
feet, Eva hung on Krumma Wiens' left arm like braid-haired
fruit, they were both there. Wiens placed his veined hand
around the little girl's neck and unhooked the jaw, the small
teeth out of his sleeve. Mouth and eyes opened to her at the
same time as from some gentle hibernation.*

In the suspended grey truck interior she heard breathing:

97

they were all breathing in what was now silence. The truck shuddered, lunged sideways, they were hurtling north down that track through Indian bush toward Cold Lake, she heard the barnshed splinter as it seemed above them, perhaps crash and vanish as they left such surface stuff behind and slowly they were moulded together downward into the intense vacuum of the storm: one small huddle, the girls under her skirts, her tiny silent son in one arm and in the other the man's face against her breast still moist from her baby's mouth. As if she alone could confront this journey into this suddenly whirling, so silently screaming earth; as if whoever needed her need only find her and bury themselves in her, and she would carry them all on this dreadful descent beyond roots groping in the dark for sustenance, beyond warm comfort down into the boiling centre of the molten earth. There has never been nor will be an end to her motherness. And when the black blizzard had passed and she waded through its drifts to the tipped granary where nine-year-old Suzanne shrieked drily, without pause, and her youngest daughter Katja lay half-charred under the knocked-over wood stove, mercifully dead of a broken neck but her lips frozen back on her teeth in a final snarl of scorched agony, certainly when her husband and Lena came plowing back in the wagon from town and found her wrapping Katja in her Sunday dress, she had this feel of mouths about her forever open, in hunger perhaps, or astonishment, or suffering and terror, or all of those. Her husband groaned,

"We stayed too long in this devil's place," but she was beginning to understand the ultimate intimacy of open mouths; attached to her glowing, 'a pure acetylene / Virgin / attended by . . .' to leave the prairie. But he didn't really have any room, all that Wiens' stuff was piled up under his canvas already on that truck, so we just drove the whole way in the wagon leading the cow and the two heifers and the grey horse, Lena sometimes rode it, it was too weak for pulling."

"I've read in the papers," I shout in her ear. "Over twenty thousand people made the trek north, till 1938."

"Heh!"

"Over twenty thousand, going north!"

98

"Not just to Cold Lake."

"I know, I know, north, lots to Grande Prairie and to Meadow Lake in Saskatchewan too."

"We should have been paying all that travel debt we still owed the Canadian Pacific Railway for bringing us from Russia, and we didn't even have enough to eat, we had to move."

"Seven hundred and sixteen dollars," I tell her, knowing that story of the Moscow rescue so well, one of two hundred families, man and woman and three girls with another born on the Moscow train (that was his kind of timing, all right) and that baby Suzanne at least carried free from Bremen to Didsbury, Alberta. *Die liebe Reiseshuld,* a considered business act by the CPR, an inconceivable mercy to the Mennonites dropping as the gentle rain from the boundless Canadian heaven of Montreal.

"The first year," she says the way she has so often, inwardly as though this particular memory came to her for the first time in years, "1931 when Papa earned fifty cents a day and we paid the CPR one dollar in January and two dollars in February and three ..."

"All the way to twelve dollars in December," I shout, laughing, "no presents for Christmas!"

"No presents for Christmas," as her toothless mouth folds into such loving gentleness, her blue eyes wavering, groping like her hand at my face; and I know again as I have known for years why I can never finally be rid of him: she loved him.

"You weren't there yet to notice," she smiles. "We were still waiting for you."

A shaft through my chest, what am I doing here while Gillian drinks coffee at the New Moon Cafe on Main Street where Harold forever ashamed of his clodhopper beginnings has never taken her praises be, and I will park the rental car there momentarily and pretend to see no one I know on the street or peering from a window when she comes out and slides long-legged into the car as if we were both strangers in town, a woman so young and beautiful getting into a car with that Jasch Dyck with salt in his beard already, what's he doing now, where's his own wife and daughter? He sure

99

didn't take her to see his mother either, what was *dien Jasch* doing with that young one sitting alone with her fingernails in the cafe behind a map like she's never seen a wheat field before? What are you saying? *Mien Jasch*? I am such an ass, but I couldn't leave her sitting in a highway ditch between all those open fields roaring with spring tractors, one person alone is ten miles visible on the prairies … and of course farther than that in a prairie town full of eyes adjusted to known faces and distance what a totally stupid ass!

But she is standing on the bank corner – how long, so exposed, did I keep the time exactly? – improbable class against stucco cradling a paper bag in her brown bare arms and with one glance she recognizes my pastel Dodge approach and turns as if making up her mind, walks down the cross street past two galoots in dented cowboy hats who slowly pivot and smell after her like curs in perpetual heat, I should pretend a middle-aged heart attack and run the car onto the sidewalk and quite accidentally break both their goddamn craning necks, slowly, circle four blocks, she comes towards me under the budding May maples of Oma Thiessen's yard, the sharpest eyes in Vulcan dear god and I do not slow any more than I am though she hesitates and I turn right one short corner from our house and right again, one more long oblong, will I ever dare stop, will she have to walk forever down the streets of Vulcan while I slowly wind and rewind around blocks until I run out of gas or the one town cop finally blocks me off at an intersection and all the starers come from behind their windows to surround us while he says quietly down to my head hung in limp exhaustion across the wheel, 'What is it Jasch, why are you wearing out our gravel streets?' At the blank side of the high school auditorium she slips through the door I stretch to fling open, her skirt hiked above her bare knees and she drops the paper bag hard and wipes dust out of her eyes; laughing.

"The wicked flee," I am laying a very fast cloud of dust straight into the country, "and no man pursueth."

Her head lolls back on the seat in uncontrollable laughter like any teen-ager. After about a mile she manages to ask, "What direction are we tearing?"

"Away, just ... away, I'm an absolute idiot."

She touches my sweating arm. "No one saw us together, it's okay. Okay?"

"I'm so stupid at this I ... how come you didn't stay in the cafe? How'd you know I'd ... all of a sudden get worried?"

"You hadn't thought of it," quite naturally; it's obvious her job is to think if I don't. "You were so excited showing me this big country, the town I've wanted to see for so long, and I didn't think there'd be all those men with their Massey-Ferguson and Wheat Pool caps coming in for coffee and staring at me."

"You're unbelievable sitting there, those stubblejumpers what else could they do."

"Oh, a few were quite handsome with their hair cut so high above their ears. I'm going to kill Harold for never taking me here."

"Haven't you ever met his family?"

"We meet in Calgary," and she looks at me with her black eyes. This is not part of where we talk; not now, perhaps never though we're begging it by coming here.

"It just hit me," I say quickly, "talking to Mam, anybody sees me with you they'll ask her, they'll sure ask Liv the next time we're here, on the off chance they could be catty, somebody sure would."

"You're so well known?"

"Notorious. At sixteen I was Vulcan's one NHL hope but I ran away and wrecked the hockey team."

"Because of hockey?"

"No. My father."

I spray rocks around the corner north through the dipping intersection at Conliffe's farm. Before the new highway was paved, this was the quickest road to High River and the manic screaming fans of the High River Rustlers. Clean, bloody hockey, you weren't safe there even standing at attention to sing O Canada; the night I scored six goals both my wingers feeding me pucks out of the corners got their noses smashed by high sticks.

"You were really a hockey star?"

"Not after sixteen."

101

"Why'd you quit?"

"Because if I'd played they'd have found out where I was and I was just sixteen, they'd have sent me back to Vulcan."

"Because of your father?" She is inviting me, Harold is *verboten* but my useless father ... well. Maybe not entirely.

"I'll tell you," I turn right again, east, the noon sun on her bare shoulder and the dust clouds of tractors spiralling up higher in the heat like wind devils reaching here and there. "Sometime. A long miserable story."

"Everybody has some miserable story," she says.

"Yes." The gravel drumming under the car, the road folding itself up over hills and hills into the sky fifteen miles ahead. "Why are we doing this?"

She says nothing; she too must be staring ahead into black splotches of noon heat flat like thick harrowed fields, boiling slowly. After a time she reaches a long arm into the paper bag and peels a can she finds there open. Orange juice, beaded cold.

"I had a perfect childhood," she says, voice level as the fields. "Father manager of the local Eaton's store, always enough money, you know so one never noticed it, my mother always cooking well-balanced meals in a tasteful kitchen. My only brother a bit younger than I thought me the most beautiful girl in the world and arranged mirrors in the hall between our bedrooms to watch me undress. The second night I noticed him in my dresser mirror so I told him if it mattered that much he better come in and look for whatever he wanted because he wouldn't see it again. So he did and after that I shut the door. He's a happy geologist now, smashing rocks every summer all over the eastern Arctic." She offers me the can, tipped right, and I gulp one mouthful to a sing of teeth. "Even the captain of the basketball team, six-foot-five asked before he dared kiss me. My mother always said she was so happy I was such a sensible girl and didn't let my looks go to my head like my aunt Sylvie who was a silly fibbertigibbet and ended up just wrinkled."

"Just so you could finally see Vulcan?" I answer my own question and she stares at me again, quickly.

"I had no idea you'd want to come here."

"He didn't tell you I was from here?"

"We've never ever talked about you."

"You're so independent, why didn't you come and look, on your own. If nobody controls you."

She is looking at the pointed road skim under the hood of the car.

"My father worked thirteen years for that farmer," I nod after a while at a shelter belt and red roofs a mile north. "That's where he got a job so we could move back from Cold Lake, just after the war."

"If you insist," she says almost woodenly, "I married Harold because he's perfectly methodical. He quite possibly schedules his erections."

"Is that why you're doing this?"

"No."

"Then why?"

"Why are you?"

Why are we quarrelling at arm's length? Because I like the way my wife feels in my arms after fifteen years and I like the way you feel after two days ... but I will not speak such contradictories. Perhaps she would if she felt them; what does she feel? If she does, why would she reach for me again? The first time I saw Harold Lemming enter our History Seminar Room, the perfectly groomed candidate, I knew out of nowhere, it was just a crazy flash out of nowhere, I knew if that man had a wife or a girl-friend or a mistress I could take her away from him if I wanted to, I knew that ... and it was self-deluding. Really? Or overwhelming universally invidious jealous because young as he was his professional credentials were better than mine would ever be. I had never before thought that about any man or woman even when I was responsible for all hiring at IBS, can the longing subconscious anticipate, actually remember the unhappened future? Perhaps, even as it already prays to anticipate the past, the beloved familiar and the beloved new now a landspace the same and different in their sameness, a total psychic and physical terrain subtly new because the one is so thoroughly known it makes the understanding of minute difference possible. And that justifies this desperate anonymous tearing through the

103

landscape of my childhood? Lemming's landscape too, which he has rejected more sensibly than I: as an adult when he can more completely control it. A modern literately technological man. If she were simply a research assistant as we agreed to pretend if necessary, I would certainly have introduced her to my mother no matter what her looks in peasant skirt and off-shoulder red blouse, to Olena at very least who insists I send every monograph I write to her so she can mess about in it a little with love and no comprehension; when Mam tells her I was there and didn't so much as wave to her – one more secret tears up an entire childhood; again.

And here the land rises for us in waves, crest upon crest eastward. 'Clay lies still, but blood's a rover; / Breath's a ware that will not keep. / Who'll beyond the hills away?'

"One person can't be everything to another," she says quietly beside me, and in our short, vivid silence we seem to have left certain words behind. "Especially like marriage pretends they should, forever."

"I know that." The rush of the car is like a nail driven relentlessly into the rising land, and I add stupidly, "I have lots of friends, who are lots of things for me."

"Close friends?"

"Not very, actually more acquaintances really, lots of them."

"But your women friends don't touch you."

"How do you know?"

"Do they?"

"Not much," laughing a little.

"Here?" she reaches across; those words are definitely far behind, there is no seeping dust here but touch, touch.

"Never there."

"Why?"

"It's not their territory."

"Why not?"

"It's not necessary."

"Why?"

"I never thought it was."

"But maybe it is."

"No, I never thought it was."

104

"Do you think so now?" Her hand tightens slightly as the car lifts us over the last spine of hills and the land falls away as it rose before us breaking wave on wave down to the Bow River prairie in the enormous indistinguishable distance. There is no farming here, grey winter grass warming for spring and cattle to a distant shimmer all around us streaking away into marginless away, in this open we seem to sit motionlessly high on the curl of surf; despite our terrific, rock-spraying speed. Higher.

"I think so ... when you do it."

"Just me?"

"I've never felt much, there, even when others obviously did. A very few others, not many," and I don't add that sometimes I wanted someone to, recently, but that someone didn't. Once while I was teaching there was a woman who could not seem to matter to me at all, though she wanted that desperately. But this is very different.

"Why me?"

I finally look at her, cover her left hand with my right. She is leaning towards me, her eyes unwinking in her face so beautiful it is like a spasm the length of my body, this tension of sudden, possible doubleness. And I am stunned happy we are in a rental car, that Liv has never sat there, never exactly there and I do not have to nor dare think of her.

"I can't say, why you. Yet. But it is."

And she devastates me suddenly, as if she has not heard me and we had not left a quarrel in ten miles of dust."

"Harold is quite satisfying to me," as dully as if she were announcing breakfast, "that way. I'm not highly sexual."

"What?"

"That's true," the stiff, sober prairie turning around us, rolling its hummocks down. "I get along just fine without sex. It's not the sex."

I'm so angry I want to hit her.

"Are you lying?"

"Why should I?"

I am stupidly destroyed. Feeling flushes through me and I know I should be thinking differently but I can't, hadn't we agreed unspoken to avoid some things what did I think, I

105

mean for heaven's sake I'm forty-two, well I did, somewhere, the secret virility stupendously disclosed to only —

"I guess, for me," and even to myself I sound petulant, "you're sure highly sexed enough."

"Hey," she says quickly. She has unsnapped her seatbelt and slides behind my shoulder. "You are for me too," against my ear.

"I thought you enjoyed it." Her moans hammering her slim body out against mine, her face fantastically clenched and yearning I was almost alarmed, so piecemeal the body dies, yes ... yes yes!

"It is marvelous," and she means it. "I wouldn't have done it again if it hadn't been."

"Simple as that, no good no go?"

"Who needs it if it's no good?"

"Sometimes it's not too good, at first, but good enough to tell —"

"It will be a lot better."

Her tongue finds forgotten whorls in my ear, 'I met her as a blossom on a stem / Before she ever breathed,' and like a possible invitation we pass a clutch of white-faced cattle staring from a trampled waterhole, all heads turned and the spring calves leaping about their motionless mothers; her liquid sound is as devastatingly intimate as her touch.

"It will be even better," she says.

"Out here on the prairie?"

"Just stop."

"We'll get tromped by jealous cows."

"We'll never notice, come on," her body coiling on the seat.

"Wait a bit, just a bit, wait," as the car shudders over rails between posts. "That's the second Texas gate, right, where are the directions?"

"You don't need directions!"

"The site, that's why we're dri—"

"Sight, you're looking for a sight?"

"Shush. Sight too, you'll see something you've never seen before," blind and one-handed I fumble in my briefcase as she snickers in my ear, "Not that, silly!" driving and getting

106

hugged hard impedes me a little but I finally feel the relevant folder. "Here, research assistant, do something, read. You can read?"

"Not in a moving car. I get nauseous."

"So get nauseous," I order grandiloquently, "here."

"Upchuck all over, you don't mind upchuck?"

"Yours will be lovely, read!"

"Okay okay," she straightens elaborately, raises the paper clutched in both hands. "Alberta Archeological Site Inventory Data Borden No. EdPc-1 Culture Return to Cross Ref—"

"Not the letterhead you loony! 'Location,' there, right there 'Location/approach' item number 8."

"'Number 8 Location/Approach Site on south bank of the Bow River (site is 1 1/2 miles west) on the highest hill for many miles around, overlooking the river with a remarkable view. Access road right to cairn. Approach: east of Crowboy corner past second gate (Texas), turn right (south) at first trail, south to corral, through gate (east)—'"

"Have we passed a trail south yet, since that second Texas gate?"

"Where's Crowboy corner?"

"The empty school you didn't notice, have we passed a trail south?"

"I didn't notice," cattishly. "I was doing enforced reading."

"Nauseously ... no, I think we'll have to get down more, to the flats."

"This is already 'a remarkable view,'" her voice changing as she turns her head. It is indeed, even for an archeologist; we are swimming down the last long incline to the enormous hollow of prairie spotted by random clumps of cattle or bright spring water holes like bits of fallen sky, hollow as it seems in the immense circle of horizon washed to a shimmer of green under the blazing noon sun, the delicate sprayed silvergreen of sage or wolf willow. The white road eases down straight east, and five miles ahead or perhaps ten is a quick slash of trees and bright roofs.

"We won't have to go to that ranch, not that far."

"Have you been here?"

"No, but it would say so there if we did."

"If it's his land shouldn't we report?"

"Then it would say that too."

"Oh." She studies the sheet. "First trail south ... past second gate, why is it called 'Texas'?"

"Probably where they developed it, rails or pipes spaced over a ditch so a cow can't walk across but you can drive."

"It wouldn't work if you were riding, would it?"

"No, but I'd bet that rancher doesn't even own a —" and we lift over a small rise, the car on gravel like blown ash settling in air and four massive cows sprawl comfortably on the warm road right across our path. Their calves spring away at our rush and noise, tails erect and white rears flying, but the cows do not move as I slam brakes and slide desperately, wheels locked in the slurring gravel so close—I cannot steer to avoid them, they are like massive headed tank barriers staggered directly across the road and the ditch is mud punched out by hoof prints—so nightmarishly close that one cow partially disappears under the line of the hood and I gasp in horror for the Thud! as Gillian screams.

"Jim, Jim!"

clawing at me. But nothing happens. The car has stopped, and the cow heaves herself up, front and shit-slimed rear molting red, if we had hit her at our speed unbelted Gillian would have joined her in a spray of windshield and smashed body dear God am I insane. The other beasts do not deign to hoist themselves up; simply turn their heads with their stupid bulging eyes spaced across their empty foreheads and stare, the flies settling back at their corners. Finally I allow the car to move again, bend very slowly between them.

"An inch is as good as a mile," she offers a little shakily.

"If it was an inch. 'I heard a fly buzz when I died.'"

"Almost," and continues in her singing voice,

"'The difference between Despair
And Fear—is like the One
Between the instant of a Wreck—
And when the Wreck has been.'"

"Is that all of it?"

"No."

The car seems to have stopped in the middle of the road

that goes over an easement into sky. There on my right is the trail south. A pair of tracks worn into grass beginning at a ramp and culvert across the muddy ditch. Does she really want to come with me? Her face lifts, she is laughing at my hesitation after having come so far and I turn in, straddle the tracks for a distance and then trundle into them to avoid erratic rocks. Up dry and hard, around a curved hillock and the road behind us and the ranch have vanished, we are alone where the trail loops down past a full slough. Slowed to a walk away from the straight manufactured gravel, the landscape changes immediately like a page flipped into an unknown country; I look at Gillian again and her eyes reflect that too.

"We are with the buffalo," she nods to the scattered cattle. "They're grazing south now, out of the northern bush where they've spent the winter."

"Nobody knows for sure if buffalo really migrated," I tell her. Her bare arm against my cheek is soft, tangy at her shoulder.

"Pedant."

"Imagination necessitates accuracy."

"Imagination necessitates only horizonless freedom."

"Which is impossible."

"Which is why it is imagination."

"Imagination is impossible?"

"It is the only personally meaningful possible, away, away from all necessary."

Do I so love to contradict her because she is uncontradictable? I can only talk the factuality of stomach.

"You have some juice left?"

The one can she opened has spilled into the carpet; that's why we pay rental. She clicks open another, feeds me and then herself. We lower windows to the heat of this slow ululating plain so huge to be in it seems minuscule; a drift of sage enters, bounces.

"How would you have explained that, me smashed up out here, with you?"

"Maybe I'd have been smashed too, if I was lucky."

"Then what would they think?"

109

"They'd think pretty clearly."

"Yes."

"My pants all moist because of you."

"Me too."

I stop the car and in one movement she slides out with me. To clasp her is like a single tree on prairie, arms and shoulders and trunk and legs holding sky and earth apart, holding space together. Surrounded in this sudden blue light my head feels so shriven I cannot encompass this, I have to imagine it and cannot, I am too small and hemmed in, I must destroy limits I have not yet been able to trust when her body rises, her legs twine up about my waist as I lift her, cotton skirt bunched and long naked legs circling me like her arms and her lips and eyes laughing with me. I lock my hands beneath her bare buttocks, o we could swing each other wild.

"Wait, it's not far now."

And she slips down, wanders away into bright noon; her shape between low sage and silver grass. There she is moving, bent to smelling things, particular as a wilful fauna up the tilted earth until she is outlined against sky and distant as it seems, but really no farther than fingertips if I leaned after her. We are here together who had not met a week ago and we will never have been here except together, where this particularity of silence is caught and held in one hand, wind from grass and warmth heard in a singing string. The car clicks steadily behind me, technology overheated. I should go away, walk easily after her through hollows and around sloughs and over the mounds and hills of this prairie until she leads me beyond tectonics and the medicine wheel emerges above us on the river height and points us in undreamt directions, the great stone wheel which guides everywhere from its centre and eternally inward to itself, 'I should have let you lay me in the ... snow / then lift me back / so that my body's trace / might / still be there / come spring / a power in the grass.' Our days not merely, sufficiently, grass.

"It's been pretty messed up," I call to Gillian, and a shift of warm wind sifts my words away. "There may have been twenty, twenty-eight spokes radiating from this centre hub, but it's been pretty messed up, you can't really see them any more."

"The outer rim is still fine," she calls back, walking around the thin line of head-sized rocks as if she were laying that stone circle – she is – about me on the crest of this round hill. I stand balanced at the centre up on the great mound of larger rocks. The hill, fuzzed spring green below the old grass, is bare except for this marred wheel and a few small heaps of rocks scattered outside it. South is prairie to the smudged horizon, far west the dented hills we crossed, north eventually the folds of the Bow River turning in one gigantic bend south, and east across the river ravines the glint of a roof, perhaps a human habitation too far away to distinguish, signalling momentarily in the sun.

"One hundred and thirty steps all around," she says pacing up one of the disarranged spokes, stopping below me at the edge of the wheel's hub. She hefts one loose rock, and drops it. "This must have taken years to make."

"Maybe centuries. Maybe they each brought a stone every time they came."

"Why did they make it?"

"Or who?"

"Didn't the Indians?"

"They don't know any more."

"Was there anyone here before Indians?"

Gillian turns below me held by air on the mound, her arms level as if she were lifting a spell from the horizon with her lifted skirt. The car is a small lump like tinsel where the prairie is folded down to the river. Wind tosses her hair into a long black flag. The stillness about her small movement is so massive, unendurable I must lecture space, fill it somehow with facts, I can always bristle facts.

"There is ... one of these, wheels, just like it on Moose Mountain in Saskatchewan, and one almost undisturbed ten thousand feet up in the Bighorn Mountains in Wyoming. The Cheyenne there say the sun built it to show them how to make a tepee."

She does not listen. Still turning below me she transfigures the wheel into chant, "This is our centre fire."

"The fire in the centre, always burning."

"Burn fire, give me life, burn, burn."

"Where you came from is the door flap, always east so the people can sit here," I clamber down the west side and turn to face her over the mound, her vivid head and shoulders and breast, "always look toward sunrise through the fire."

Turning she faces me again. "Where do I sit?"

"Here, my left. The honoured guest always on my right."

"Maskepetoon, the Broken Arm is here."

"Yes ... of course."

"I serve you both," she comes left around the mound, "that's what I do, here."

"Yes, you do. Here on the side of my heart."

Our arms are circles about each other before the great fire of prairie stones built here so carefully by an unremembered people, and a sudden cold breathes over us like pain. Gillian shivers.

"I can smell him."

"Whom?"

"Maskepetoon did ride here," she whispers.

"In this country of his fierce enemies the Blackfeet. And thought of all these ancestors who no longer live in paradise because there is no one left on earth to remember them."

"Is that what they believed?"

"Yes ... what does one do with ancestors?"

"You remember them?"

"You try."

She accepts this personally. "That doesn't bother me so much."

"Oh?"

"More what to do with myself."

"The twentieth century, maybe I'm still in the nineteenth. I don't think that bothered Indians much, then."

Her arms tighten slightly as she says, "Maybe this wasn't Indians."

"It must have been their ancestors."

"Maybe not. Maybe this was made by goat people, or

mound folk that still live in Sweden, maybe it was giane that eat mens' toes for midnight lunch and won't sing unless you nibble their ear."

"Where do they do all that?"

"In Sardinia. A giane is always tall and beautiful, with such long, long breasts she throws them back over her shoulder."

"Could she lift a stone then?"

"Of course, and think how warm it would be."

"I'm a leg man myself."

"Is that all?"

"No." I'm kissing between the tops of her breasts and then sideways, "Everything, I want everything."

"Was this place for cairn burial?"

I lift my head; her dark eye — there is the faintest dust of freckles across her nose — pushes me back to stones. "If it was, there's nothing left to show it."

"We should be here at night, when the stars are shining."

"Why?"

"Starlight is so old, some of it began thousands of years ago."

"And then we would ... see?"

"Then we would see them here in the old light of stars, the ancestors bringing their stones."

"How come you know so much?"

"I read, there's endless books lying around our place."

"Come on," I say abruptly, "you're all goosepimples."

And with a quick glance she turns from me, bending her head; but walks with me west, very close body along body through a scatter of stones which the ground has already half swallowed; outside the wheel a huge rock bulges out of the brow of the hill and we squat in its hollow against the sun side. Heat radiates through us, the west wind here in small swirls of prairie grass and the faint song of its bending.

"They must have found ... something," she says quietly.

"Just a few arrowheads among the stones, chips, bits of carved pipe, that's all."

"How old, do they think?"

"About four, five thousand years."

113

"What?"

"Someone was here when the Egyptians started their pyramids."

She laughs suddenly, a ripple along her ribs under my fingers. "And Earle Birney writes it's by our lack of ghosts we're haunted."

"That's silly, I think."

"We're haunted by ignorance."

"Nothing ever happens, the Indians say, but what has been already foretold."

She tilts her head back against the rock's smooth flank. "Whitey and his ignorance was foretold?"

"The Cree had stories about white men long before they ever saw one. They called them 'those who drift ashore,' maybe drowned sailors and they knew they were white as peeled logs."

"Let me peel you," Gillian says quickly.

We both do, standing up and unleafing each other's clothes onto the warm rock. We can stand side by side easily, touching anywhere in its granite shelter but when we are slightly apart a strange feeling moves through me, I look at Gillian and her eyes waver aside also. To the sun and the rock, the wind, the enormous grey and silver prairie centring us pale on its highest hill at the rim of the primordial wheel, open surrounds us in this light breathing everywhere, lifts us up as if we must be at last permitted to see forever in every direction with only the impossible limits of light to limit us. See ... and be seen. I have never been so fearfully, fathomlessly, naked.

And then I comprehend something. This rock is a buffalo rubbing stone, the hollow under it the trench worn by thousands of buffalo tramping here, rubbing and scratching and throwing dust over their insect-plagued hides. I hoist myself gingerly up its smooth side and of course directly across the centre mound is one of the smaller rock piles outside the opposite rim: the rubbing stone and the hub of the medicine wheel and the small cairn lie in one exact line, pointing northeast.

"Hey," I reach down to Gillian, "look at this."

She comes up beside me light and shivering; pulls my arms about her.

"See," we stretch on tiptoe, the centre burns grey so high in the sunlight, "the three line up, straight as a gunsight to the horizon."

We press together, pushed up so tremendously between earth and sky.

"What ... what's it aiming at?"

"Sunrise. That's where the sun will rise as far north as it goes, the summer solstice sunrise."

And the rubbing stone on which we stand front to front is the base of the cosmic gunsight; we are together being aimed into the ceaseless ritual movement of the universe.

"They have to bring the sun back," she says against my cheek. "Before it vanishes north and they freeze."

"Can you throw these over your shoulder?"

"They're not long enough."

"I could kiss you from behind then."

She turns inside my circle. "Do it anyway."

We have to get down quickly, back into the warm hollow of earth against the rubbing stone; the length of it no longer than we need lying down. Mare's-tails fray into the sky above us, flaring out quickly, whipped by some stratospheric wind and then we mould ourselves together, trembling as gently, finally we know we have given ourselves over to this relentless rush into space. The mind knows only what lies near the heart. Such awesome presence surrounds us, we have to close our eyes.

MAY
FOUR

"We went to church yesterday," Becca says into her orange juice on Monday morning. "I took my Bible."

"Church!" my voice more or less squeaks in astonishment. The only church we have ever entered with her is All Saints for choral concerts; and once the Vulcan Mennonite Church for her grandfather's funeral. I look at Liv silently stirring oatmeal, flicking off a switch. "What church?"

"The one you said you always had to go to, Mennonite."

Liv taking our daughter into a Mennonite church? I can only stare. She comes with the heavy porridge-pot, face too Monday austere to proffer me a glance.

"But the man there didn't talk about beginning at all," Becca fishes orange residue from her glass with her long finger, licks it so lengthily she might be a cat. "I thought maybe, but he didn't."

"What ... did he talk about?"

"Love, just a really long thing about love."

Liv dollops out my oatmeal. "His text was The Song of Solomon," she says abruptly.

'O let him kiss me with the kisses of his mouth, for thy love is better than wine.' Certainly than orange juice and porridge on Monday. No one forced me to remember that; I can't believe what I'm hearing.

"You heard a Mennonite preaching on The Song of Solomon?"

"It was a good sermon," Liv turns to the sink. "It would have explained a few little things to D.H. Lawrence."

Becca giggles. "'Thy breasts are like two fawns that are twins.'"

"The minister read that!"

"No, he skipped around, but there's lots of it in—"

"'Fawns, they feed among the lilies, thy neck is like the tower of David builded for an armoury, thy teeth like a flock—'"

"You memorized the whole Bible, every word?" Becca laughs with me.

"He's afflicted with total recall," Liv's voice flat over water hissing into the pot, "anything he's ever read."

"One of my more devastating characteristics."

"Everything just off by heart."

She has her teeth locked into the beginning of a week all right, solidly. Becca glances at me and I wipe my face easy. Liv was asleep last night when I got home from the last Calgary Airbus, warm and folded as usual snuggling into my bend without even an automatic glance at the clock, O blessed be church and sermons of love and I wanted her then like a rediscovery of a known land, the reconstructed texture of the weekend that had exploded into being out of nothing and anticipation and I fondled her until she accepted anything on her breasts and between her legs but squirmed about for mere comfort and slept on, "James, I'm sleeping!" Now she steps around me deliberately into the hall, the closet slides open. I should be there; before her swift coat, through that dress against the hall window I would see the quick space between her tall straight legs.

"Come on," I say to Becca, getting up, "do your scales."

"See you!" Liv calls, and the door bangs.

At least it wasn't just 'bye.' Becca will be standing at the living room window, waving. Everything off by heart, why call exact memory that? Though I know exactly what I did yesterday, and maybe Liv senses it too, driving that distance back Saturday evening from the prairie through the brief May dark to Calgary and the Palliser Hotel again all night and morning—while they were at church here—and driving seventy miles back to Vulcan Sunday afternoon alone to sit in that small house again with its tinct of old age and remorseless memory, my mother not able to knit of course because it is Sunday and quiet as a bird by the bright window as I read Psalms to her, roaring Luther's ancient rhythmic German into her whorled ear until she smiles, knowing them off by heart and feeling them with her fingers in the palms of my hand more than from my voice braying what I have long despaired to ever forget, the words branded upon me in not only one but two archaic languages, O Lord thou hast searched me and known me, *ich sitze oder stehe auf, so weist du es, O Herr Gott,* to whom vengeance belongeth, show thyself. Heaven forbid. Her long prayer following almost like a song, hypnotic and variably high or low, loud and quiet because she cannot hear herself, almost singing in the tuneless song of the deaf that changes key in the middle of words and jerks me about with all the slow torture of hearing my mother pray for me inside the soundless, impenetrable walls of her immeasurable and overwhelming love, *ich fleh zu dir mein Herr und Gott, aus meiner tiefen Suendennot,* clasping my hands.

In the living room the scales stop. "Old Dad," Becca calls. "Are you coming?"

"Yes." I shove the milk into the fridge and go to her, my half of the piano bench. She is playing young Mozart now and I watch her lithe hands move over the bright melody arching like small happiness and settling full in chords, triplets and syncopation flashing. When she was seven she already played her own 'compositions,' never the same way twice of course and she fully believed she could match Mozart's prodigious childhood and I'd tease her, 'No, no, please, you'll die too young and starving!' the house clanging with two-handed chords. Memorize, comes from memory, comes from knowing things completely by heart. 'I had the rented car and I was going to Vulcan anyway, which is halfway there, and I came across these references to the wheel/cairn again so I thought what the heck, it's pre-Blackfoot and pre-Cree, pre-everything but it's part of the world no one knows anything about, the parallels to Stonehenge and Avebury and the Mayan pyramids no one thinks the buffalo prairie has, evidence of a civilization here before memory in a careful piling of stones mostly disturbed but at least not plowed through, cultivated and sowed to wheat so I drove there and got hooked on the ... space and I ended up in the dark in a little village hotel, a beer parlor full of Saturday night cowboy hats and three empty rooms upstairs – if I'd had a sleeping bag I'd have preferred a bushy ravine above the Bow River, I was just out there with nothing white visible except a powerline I could ignore and I felt so ... naked, so....' I have said some of this to Liv in passing this morning and may get a chance to say more; if she wants to hear it. She knew I was staying till Sunday, I phoned from Calgary, what is the matter what does she know? Nothing, there cannot be anything.

"You're not listening," Becca says an inch from my face. "You're not, what'd you do on your trip?"

A kiss with closed eyes is much the same, though the body's different. And smell. If I were blind and deaf I would not be 'of three minds, / Like a tree / In which there are three blackbirds.' Or four.

"Olena said to kiss you for her," and I kiss Becca again, wanting the breath of skin. "She'd have sent you some coconut wrinkles, but she didn't know I was coming."

"She could've given me something else."

"You goose."

"Did you bring me something?"

"Only a stone, come on, I'll show you."

"A stone!"

"'Or what man is there of you, whom if his son ... daughter ask bread, will he give her a stone?'"

"I don't want bread either."

"Go wrinkle your coconuts."

She leaps onto me, all arms and powerful legs and like a slash I hate that unknown stranger who will someday lie between them, brutishly taking, and she certainly wanting him, and I jog her up the stairs pounding me. I stubbed against the fist-sized stone when I opened the car door but to Becca it seems just a chunk of granite sitting in my palm, a faint line of earth all around it and a whiff of prairie crunching winter-dry as crumbs. A band of white cuts through it; a wishing stone.

"Right there," she says doubtfully, "I can smell it."

"That's the kind of stone they gathered in their medicine wheel, for centuries everyone who came there picked up a stone laid it in the circle. An offering."

'Bring thee now, something for thee' aiming at the summer dawn, 'I love the dawn with the half-risen sun rosy like the head of God's phallus,' o to be a poet and woo the round earth till it rolls roaring in adamantine throes, riotously. Olena offered me coffee thick with cream from the copper urn at her elbow, her smile widening the room as she reads my face, laughing: I did come to see her, if not Saturday then Sunday, the breasts that once appeared in my nightmares like the unattainable Big Rock Candy Mountains still moving with her enormous laughter. I close my eyes in her house so strangely dim even in the brightest daylight and afloat in my forties she will certainly seduce me behind my eyelids as easily as in my boy dreams with my body so hard and violently quick from hockey, the welfare children she cared for then hanging about her like thick fruit, always three or four of them pinkly mewling out of round mouths moist with milk which once I had imagined hers I could never again unimagine, her laden woman's shape moving in the shadowed house with great hands warm enough to enfold any body, any longing. Olena Rostick, *di Russische*. The year the town council gave her a plaque and fifty dollars for "Service to the Community," she hired workmen to jack up her small house and put a foundation under it. Beneath the careganas I lay and watched the men dull as labouring oxen spade a trench for footings, begin to mortar cinder blocks along a white string; when they plodded away that evening still stupid of where they were working, I crawled under the hedge and though I had not moved all day I still wasn't prepared to find myself looking beneath her house, along pale rough joists which had never seen the sun and I saw that cellar hole black and gleaming faintly with jars of golden apricots, purple plums or saskatoons, and I lay on my stomach in the dirt, staring, I could not have endured anyone seeing me there longing for a personal intimacy that was almost lust, a secret voyeurism though I knew neither word then. 'Lust' in German means happiness, joy, *'Ich habe lust in dem Herrn,'* that's what I feel again when I see the narrow cinder foundation like a fringe of old skirt woven in oblongs, a heat washes over me, the boy breathing hollow in that mystery hidden there, that thick opening of desire no simple lifetime I know now will satisfy.

"How long can she stay in her house yet?" I jolt myself into practicality, monosyllabics. "It's too hard for you, all this work."

"Where you put her?" Olena asks.

"We'll take her to Calgary."

Olena laughs, unbelieving, "You think with Lena or Susan?"

"No no, they can't take care of her, a nursing home."

"They lay her in one bed and she never get up."

"But she can't hear, even with that terrible hearing-aid, she can barely make out shapes moving."

"She knit, she walk around her house, she make meals. She know where it is, what she want."

"There's nothing in her fridge."

"She eat bread and oatmeal and drink postum and every day I bring her the soup."

"That's what I mean, it's too much for you. We agreed you would clean the house and wash her clothes and help bathe her once a week, and maybe look in every day to make sure, if she can't manage with that we'll have to ... there's too much, Lena hardly ever gets down here, when was she here, eh?"

"Oh, four or five weeks maybe, they—"

"The end of February, wasn't it? Don't protect her, she told me! She's so mixed up with her silly kids she has no time for Mam, she—"

"Jascha listen," she clasps my right hand tight between both hers, her round Russian peasant face stippled with brown age but her eyes bright without a trace of cobwebs, "I have it the babies here all my life, hundreds and I don't know where one is now, why should I, and they say I can't have

121

them anymore. Your Mam, poor Mr. Querengressor in his little place, they good for me, good." She laughs again leaning back, there seems such a waste of love here, she could thaw an army. "What do I do here, heh, just rot on my little pension?"

"There's nothing little about you!" I am dancing around in front of her, her hands in mine and she rises to me, the linoleum squeaking like hard snow under her bast slippers and for a moment she is in polka rhythm, her hips and arms lifting like feathers but then she drops to a stop, gasping.

"Jascha, you crazy, you give me a heart attack!"

How I would have loved to attack her heart, I did then, a boy hemmed in by rare, small happiness and steady, steady guilts while this love-rich woman lived beside us; I could focus every longing on her, all the desire I forced away from the vivid femaleness I knew lurked in my older sisters who could never wear a short-sleeved dress much less a bra until they left home, my father standing rigid inspection for sin at the door every Sunday morning. And Olena breathing beyond a gangly hedge, unconscious as sun and rain that falls on the just and the unjust. Not so untouchable really; she once held me crying hard against her, just tall enough then to anchor my face between her breasts. If I could have cried more often.

"We got over the dog," my mother said after his funeral in her drifty, seemingly bottomless voice, "now we still have to get over the tail."

Alone, strangely she aged so fast none of us was prepared for it, least of all Lena whose husband Aaron finally declared they had to move to Calgary now, there was no carpentry left in Vulcan and he had to have a few good years or they'd have nothing to retire on. Ruth and her family had of course been in Penticton, Susan in Calgary and Maria in Pincher Creek all their married lives; Eva died in Cold Lake, Katie in Sunnynook on the day before we moved north. So Olena *di Russische* was our only hope; or Pioneer Lodge. But Mam is beyond that now and if she ever stumbles against anything or turns sharply, her leg breaks and she will not stand again. Olena was our only hope then, and is still.

"It's too hard for you," and I'm so scrambled with thought

122

I don't realize what stupidity I'm saying, "you're getting so old yourself one of these days...."

She thumps herself back into the rocker, "I die just like that," she claps her hands together hard, almost as if she were cheering on mazurka dancers, "like Oncle Hildebrandt, in the middle of Sunday, just dead."

"Old Hildebrandt died?" The pastor who was my father's final ultimate and immovable authority; they fitted together like a fist and an eye. Sermons a blast of thunderstorm, you didn't know what had hit you but you were shaking.

"One Sunday he just preached," Olena is smiling, "and he pray a long prayer and sit down and we will sing the last song when just like that he jerk up stiff and fall off the bench, on the floor like a log, just crash, and the doctor and nurse run there and work on him till the ambulance come and take him to the hospital but he's dead already, I could see it, all the time they try to start his heart, dead."

"In the ... in front of the church?"

"It was all full, Sunday, and he die in front of us on the floor, by the pulpit."

"The whole church just sat there," my mother says when I ask her. "What could they do? The doctor was doing it, and the whole church quiet for twenty minutes till the ambulance came, watching him breathe and die."

When I first saw him he was no older than I am now, but he seemed so ancient and powerful I mistook him for God, Ancient of Days, his enormous prayers often more effective than his sermons because of their fierce drama: he worshipped the Creator directly then (while fortunately being overheard by Sinners), explaining again and again the Evil of mankind, a power of planned Evil more black than God in His incomprehensible Elevated Otherness could perhaps quite grasp but as long as He did not grow weary of meting out Judgement, did not permit the One Sure Hand of Punishments to slacken why he himself would faithfully report all—

"He was a very good man," my mother intones. "He always knew right and wrong. It's like a white shirt he said, is it clean or not? If you have to ask, it's dirty."

The living room is stifling in May heat but she sits with
her back against the gas heater; knowing my long silence and
its reasons.

"You still think Pa was like that because of him?"

"He wasn't like that so much in Cold Lake," I roar at her
finally; there is no need to go beyond 'like that'; a generality
can label such a life.

"You were too little there," suddenly she is very loud, almost annoyed and her smooth forehead hunches together.
"There was no discipline in that little church there, nothing,
everybody did what he wanted, the boys always had their
hands in the girls' skirts, that is all they thought about. Vulcan was different."

"We moved here because of the church?" I have heard this,
he said it often enough, but now she affirms it. In her dark,
walled-in silence will there soon be nothing but these scraps
of his opinions drifting about as if they were her own? I will
come occasionally and hold her hand and say nothing, *yoh,
neigh, dout es einmol so, yoh.*

"Your Mam," says Olena later, and stops. She seems to be
hesitating over words, uncharacteristically. She looks out the
small window at the new poplar leaves almost as if she would
find a tone among their bright shimmer. "She a strong
woman, she always very strong, hard."

"She had to be, married to him."

"Maybe from the start, and he fit in."

"You didn't live with them."

"How long you live it," she says not looking at me, "when
you old enough to understand something?"

"Old enough to get out."

"And you run."

"Yes."

"Who you run from?"

"Him!"

"Was it so good, the run?"

"It was terrible for a while, especially not seeing her, but it
was better than him staring over my shoulder, too old to do
anything but watch and find fault, finally a son after all the
ones dead twenty years ago and never doing anything right,

never enough, how could I, he was such an old man when I was born he'd never done anything himself, just what he was told!"

"He was just peasant, like me."

"But he was never happy unless something miserable was happening!"

She stares at me in the lengthening Sunday twilight, her eyes greenly unblinking. He never named her, she was just *di Russische*—the Russian, woman implied: not really cold, just a label for a thing, a convenient means if he ever needed it and he would of course, worse was always coming. But she seemed to like him, never raised her voice at the next approaching doom he predicted, though he did not dare order her to do anything; that was only for women in the family. She is looking at me now as if she were trying to decide whether to tell me something.

But she changes her mind. "Old Hildebrandt," is what she says quietly. "He died so good. Just go out of his boots straight into heaven."

When I emerge from the History Department mailroom shuffling a handful of redundant memos and publishers' flyers, I collide violently with ambulatory academic tweed. Harold Lemming. Unfortunately he is too broad now to send sprawling and too handsome to widely suggest his rodent namesake, though he always will to me who first knew him at three.

"Oh ... Dyck—yes," he rubs his lowered chin where my shoulder met him. He now outweighs me, whom I brushed off Vulcan sidewalks when he didn't step first.

"Sorry, sorry Harold, I was busy thinking about—" and guilt immediately, like a blow; my nose vivid with him for an instant: does she have to smell that every morning, English winter-flat stale? It must be the tweed.

"Actually," Harold stands there as I start to move around him, "yes, actually if you could spare a minute you know, I'd like very much to talk to you sometime."

He peers at me, did he see something flicker in my eyes? It's my jerk, I'm too surprised to suppress it, I — no tweed could smell like that, that long, he hasn't been in damp Oxford for two years. Talk to me the day after I've ... what does the modern well-fed — cuckold, face it — look like under the circumstances? What a heavy word.

"Is something the mat—" but that's stupid, as if I expected something.

"Well," he says easily, "we can hardly, right here in the hall."

He gestures; anyone may come around the corner in an instant. No doubt this is the modern style: smiling easy. There's certainly no point in postponing this.

"I've got a minute right now, if you have," my only hope his face, though I have never seen it adult angry to recognize that; but it seems more secretive. Ferret-ish? I am hoping.

His desk faces away from the window and the entire office is stacked with books, which fits: crammed in small towers on the floor and on the desk and in free-standing shelves double along the book-lined walls. It's simply ostentatious (and poor research method), most of them are not his, he has the entire mediaeval section of the Rutherford Library piled there, he could lie on them and vegetate. But he closes the door and shifts a pillar aside on the settee he uses to keep his visitors uncomfortable. "Please, sit down please," and lowers his size into the swivel chair. I sit; there's nothing to lean against but at the moment I don't really need anything.

"Yes, well I've been considering this," Harold says without preamble, "trying to formulate how I might best bring this to your attention. I'm fully occupied with my own research of course, as you are with yours, I know."

He knows a lot. I can only sit there stiff and try to appear natural, and be surprised — no, shocked, be shocked — when he tells me. Perhaps I am frozen, my mind seems not to grip anything, I have never talked to him beyond a passing 'hello' in the hall and this is not happening, there can be no connection between this tweedy — he's so goddamn handsome! — he has actually held her in his arms for years, what the hell is this, why? I grab, quick.

"I saw you at the party, the other night," I say, "but I didn't get a chance to talk to ... you or...."

I fritter away as he looks unblinkingly at me. Perhaps I never did know him at three small and carnivorous.

"Party?"

"At Albert and Ardyth's ... a week ago Saturday."

"Oh," shaking his head as if to unsettle a banality, "of course, yes, you were talking to Joy, yes."

"We got in our usual annual argument, about God."

"Really?" It is clear he talks about God only as a professional.

"When we were kids, in Vulcan, it started with worms, you weren't in school yet, and we've worked up to God, it's hard to say where it can go on to, if we live long enough, once a year...."

I have really mouthed myself into nowhere backwards; he gestures, brushing the clutter of his sister and myself out of existence.

"Gillian said, my wife, she'd met you."

"She ... did?"

He reaches for a pen to turn between his long fingers.

"Look, Dyck," he is crisp Oxford, sisters wives Vulcan irrelevant as any mosquito, "I am not trying to impose myself, or pressure you, anything like that, but I do know your research is on North (pedants know only research, glory be!) American aboriginals of the nineteenth century and I personally never tell anyone one iota of what I'm researching and I'm sure you don't either, one never knows what unscrupulous scoundrel will snatch an idea one has and rush into print with it half-baked just to establish intellectual claim, it's happened enough to all of us, destroying one's credit and years of labour," he signals grandly with his pen to volumes looming about him, if he took three words from each he'd have a treatise the miserly pack rat, he's probably found one fact he thinks is hot, but why me? "In any case, my area of concentration is the mediaeval papacy, as you know very well – you helped me come here, thank you again – on the eve of the Reformation and I've found a very interesting matter so far almost totally neglected by historians, at least as

127

far as I can discover, and if I mention it to you I know you will keep it in strictest confidence, I'm sure I can trust you—"

So memory makes fools of us all; as if on a green May day like this awash over the river valley, one May in Vulcan when I had a nickel for a revel and bratty Harry trailed Joy and me everywhere while we licked it by turns, whenever I looked back he was peering around a corner, from behind a cottonwood, under the school teeter-totter like some bad haunt of indigestion until I finally threw the chewed stick at him and booted his four-year-old ass and sent him howling home to Joy's fine sisterly laughter.

"O of course complete confidence, trust between us as professionals, of course!" I bawl now. Nothing is ever that 'of course,' he's still in the age of faith despite all mediaeval popes.

"Yes, of course, I just mention it in passing, but it is really an area so far quite neglected in Canada and it could be of real interest to you, I believe." He pauses, he is about to make pronouncement. And does, "The church and its attitudes to the aborigines discovered in the western hemisphere. It of course ties into the whole mediaeval debate on 'heathen,' whether they are human or beasts, and I came across a very early reference in an obscure statement by a certain pope ... very early fifteenth century ... and then there is the papal bull of Alexander VI, an exciting text and I was wondering...."

He pauses, almost as if he regrets already having voiced so much. It's little enough, good heavens Pope Alexander VI and Julius II's necessarily naive statements have been discussed since 1493, though Julius's bad generalship and Alexander's machinations to arrange estates and crowns for all his bastard children have proven more interesting to scholars. He's stuttering around a subject perhaps three other people in the world now would get excited about, and two of them because of professional jealousy, but his smile suddenly transforms him: he's a true antiquarian scholar, he has no personal past but lives in the fifteenth century somewhere between Avignon and Pisa and Rome and he has found a hitherto unknown reference to heathen glory be to God for dappled things! So I throw him a modern curve, quote Margery Perham:

"'The lawless advance of the white frontiersman against the North American Indian was one of several main causes for the American Revolution.'"

Harold stiffens slightly, "I'm not quite sure I—"

"Well, you see the colonial office back home in London was always much more—could always be much more Christian in its theory about dealing with natives than the poor nasty buggers who had to live with them on the frontier. It created lots of—ah, theoretical Christian tensions, the local exploiters' desire for land and the colonial government's desire for justice, at very least the appearance of it."

"Oh I see, yes, but this was the Catholic...."

Joyfully I push on, I have to show him, "Lord Glenelg, the British Colonial Secretary, sums it all up very nicely in a letter to the governor at Capetown, 1835, and I quote, 'It is a melancholy and humiliating but indisputable truth that the contiguity of the natives of Christendom with uncivilized tribes has invariably produced wretchedness and decay, and not seldom the utter extermination of the weaker party. This uniform result must be attributed not to any necessary cause, but to the sinister influence of those evil passions which in such circumstances found but too much to provoke and too little to restrain them. Of all the chapters in the history of mankind, this is perhaps the most degrading ... Everywhere aboriginal inhabitants disappear under the withering influence of Europe ... we are bringing upon ourselves the reproaches of mankind and the inevitable weight of national guilt.' End of quote."

Harold has solidified, at me as at an apparition shimmering in ordinary morning light; assaulted in his very office.

"What's wrong?" I ask, o so easily.

"You ... know that ... off by heart, everything?"

"No, no," and I chuckle even more easily. "I have this crazy memory, clumps of words stay stuck in it, I can read them off at inappropriate moments. It's nothing."

"Well," he grunts, stiffness crackling out of him like ice,

and he knows as I know that my memory is a damn sight more than nothing, "you're saying it's been done, it's not worth...."

"No, really no," professionally at least he has a good nose. "I'm saying there is documentation, and it should be possible to do better than give one more proof of Christian duplicity, probably its hypocrisy."

"Of course," he is obviously relieved. "You don't remember such a study? Other than Lewis Hanke, of course, *The Spanish Struggle for Justice in the Conquest of America*, which is good but just a beginning."

"No, no I don't know of one comparative, over such a long period."

He laughs suddenly; with a trace of scorn? Vulcan scorn? "Having had an example of your memory, I don't need to flog bibliographies any more!"

"Don't count on it." I have to laugh too or I'd kick him again, office or no office. "I can't, I forget the most obvious stuff."

"Really?" and like any scholar he has already lost interest in what sits before him, his mind only momentarily distracted from its thin rut in the past. "I sometimes feel we historians are almost too ... cloistered, we work so carefully that we begin to see history, the events of the past as almost too ... well, *narrow* you know, almost as if we *owned* them, we are so captivated by the very particular, precise facts we are trying to document that we fail to notice the larger issues, the subtle beginnings of opinions which eventually *order* the world and determine us today quite unbeknownst to ourselves or—"

"Yes of course," I'm relaxed now, completely relaxed, "quite unbeknownst, we get so tangled in details of past we're barely alive today, why if life suddenly grabbed us by the belt buckle we'd shrug it off unbeknownst as gas pain and keep on puzzling why Pope Alexander's Latin amanuensis misspelled a simple...."

Harold is watching me oddly, and I get myself stopped at last. But in doing so I've gestured too grandly for the atrocious settee: the Simon Stylites stack of Latin texts beside me crashes spine-wrenching to the floor, "O heavens Harold, I'm sorry!" and for a moment we are together at last gathering them up, me also gathering my relief into control. The small physical flurry seems to have reassured him completely; he tells me without hemming the two of us might try an article together juxtaposing (that's the word he uses, perhaps he's reading literature after midnight, influenced by whom?) the first papal opinions on how to deal 'Christianly with newly discovered aboriginals' and the actual practices of priests in the nineteenth-century Canadian west: "Four hundred years," he declares, "what remains the same, what is there of enlightenment, if any, you know, did Christian thinking make any change, progress? Just an article now perhaps, very precise, dealing with a few specific details, texts, but there could very well be a major book in it for us you know, a book for us both."

Into this contorted convolution of a morning (at a Canadian university in May one expects only the quiet contemplative world of search for whatsoever things are true) sodden with apprehension, guilt, jealousy, one-upmanship, a kind of triumph and dislike — more like detestation — and lust ... the lust of lusty memory at least, into this morning for a moment moves the bright, unambiguous, thanks be impersonal vision of a scholarly idea: before the Renaissance Christians either converted or slaughtered heathens, but then they began to develop a corporate conscience; if one worked backward and forward from Pope Alexander perhaps, perhaps....

And Harold smiles, "Well, of course history is never quite so simple, is it? One can never predict what one will find."

It certainly is not simple; not even the bit of history one lives seated in one's rolling chair in one's prosaic office. One can never predict, never. The weekend sheaf of paper is still in my hand, the air conditioning hums to reassure me: all is as it was. But it is not. To spend weeks, perhaps months and years consulting, perhaps regular lunches together, that was not latent Oxford I smelled on him, o no. Becca is now bent over her desk mauling uneven fractions, Mam sits at the window feeling the morning light on her face and soon Olena will come singing in to strip her bed, *du, du liegst mir im Herzen, du ...* Liv is either on the phone or waiting for the instantaneous computer; I will not go near the Micro-materials Room today. I have to sort what notes and xeroxes I have from the Glenbow and work something up on the stone wheel before I forget whatever it was I didn't notice there, I didn't take pictures because I brought no camera and where would I have focused in any case. I might have caught a bare leg in a corner, hardly prehistoric. Like so much of Harold, scholar or not. He is no fool and she married him, is still Gillian my jo.

'To live genitally is a beginning, also an end.' Words scrawled on a Palliser pad. I certainly needn't see them to remember, though the smudged evidence of a hotel ballpoint scribbling what the eye has not seen and what the head may never understand contributes to the kind of objective irrefutibility demonstrated, for example, by apples falling to the ground again and again (never from one only being picked and sadly eaten) – evidence if I ever doubt that diaphanous morning conversation. How can I not doubt it? It is merely absurd. 'Inharmonious, out of tune, insufferable to the ear,' declare the Oxford (it's everywhere!) English Dictionary genteel absolutes. Out of tune with the celestial music of the spheres perhaps? In modern usage, plainly contradictory to common sense, 'out of harmony (harmony still?) with reason, or propriety (good heavens!)' An absurd matter is one related to the ridiculous, it is suitable for derisive laughter – or the preposterous, 'an amazing extreme of foolishness.' First use of absurd: '1557, 9 minus 12 is an Absurde nomber For it betokeneth lesse than nought by 3.' Which is not so contrary to common sense or reason in 1980 – less than nought by two or three. 'Tis grave philosophy's absurdest dream, That heaven's intentions are not what they seem,' William Cowper, 1781. The logical explanation of one age becomes the preposterous assertion of the next. Even if heaven should have some seeming plain intentions, there is nevertheless a grave impropriety in them being spoken in a Calgary CPR hotel across a sleeping body. It is insufferable; my profane ear longs for repeatable logic, clear balance, a graspable sensible unity and completeness even though my life and discipline can never achieve that, not completely. Though I have written the words down, I could really do without a voice searching me out, asking where, asking why. I'm looking for bone of my bone, flesh of my flesh like they did in that garden on 'the day that God created man, in the likeness of God made he him, male and female created he them and blessed them and called their name Adam in the day when they were created,' the long desire for that celestial harmony of one name Adam which we all had before ever we started hiding, o have mercy upon us.

Outside the day has misted to silver; in the valley below the spring river slips along at the roots of the poplars furred with cat-tails in eddies of, as it seems from here, glistening mud. 'And a river went out of Eden to water the garden, and from thence it was parted,' no single simplicity outside Eden. *Du hast di dit selfst engerieht,* you've stirred (in the sense of mud) this up for yourself, my father would say with his infallible nose for doom, so smart you think you can run away and hide and live like any heathen, marry whatever you can't keep your hands off of, a Swedish one, and then think you'll be happy, ha, just try to run away from being a bound-for-hell sinner who thinks he can think his way to heaven, if anyone could do it that Einstein would be God, or Oppenheimer with his bomb or von Braun with his rockets or there's a new one every few years so smart he'll burn up the world and everybody in it, just wait a minute and another one will pop up like that Doctor Bernard cutting out and sewing different hearts into people, what does that change, the one you sew in is still deceitful above all things and desperately wicked, don't you know it?

Now this is truly absurd, a life-long purpose in guilt. My father is dead eight years and thirty years ago I was already so certain he was wrong that despite my hockey-muscle body I got the dry heaves at evening devotions, so-called, and I ran as fast and as far as I could and somehow even in the sixties carpentered together a decent life and several careers helped by a beautiful wife and beautiful child and the loving memory of a loving mother: how have I managed myself guilty again? Ask indeed, why. I have never suffered terror for my life, or political exile, or a depression that made me work for fifty cents a day for ten years just to feed my family—why should I feel purposeless without guilt? I didn't a week ago. Which was before she sat in my lap, Maskepetoon suddenly sang in my head like morning birds. Why, when I know so much, do I sit here feeling guilty that I cannot feel guilty except for possible discovery? I am blind somewhere.

Discovery is a part of conscious knowing, and memory; perhaps another life has always existed for me also, otherwise how could I sink in this so quickly? Perhaps it was always there somewhere at night when I slept and my incorrigible memory dappled and swirling like a Van Gogh starry night had no function and now it has come, she has pushed it into daylight too and my dream and daylight people are blundering into each others' emptinesses.

O to be an aging maiden in New England a hundred years ago, when one could write with complete confidence, 'The Soul selects her own Society — / Then—shuts the Door.' But this is now, and opening.

Of making many books there is no end. Especially about Jesus, three long sections of library shelves floor to ceiling at a university where Religious Studies has less faculty than birdy badminton. *The Human Life of Jesus, The Virgin Birth, The Humiliation of Christ* by the hundreds, and sections related, *Sigmund Freud and the Jewish Mystical Tradition, Sex Laws and Customs in Judaism, On the Flesh of Jesus* by Tertullian, *On the Discipline and Advantages of Chastity* by Cyprian, now really, *On Holy Virginity* by St. Augustine, also *On Marriage and Concupiscence and Eunuchs for the Kingdom of Heav....*

"Those third century North Africans laid everything on a certain line, they really did."

Behind me suddenly, so that the light between the book-shelves outlines him; again. My heart gives that thud! of recognition and he is smiling I think, perhaps at my mouth dropped slackly open.

"A library is as necessary as a hotel," he says. "You need to practise daylight living."

Between books he is too much, and words gather very slowly like dust in my mouth.

"It's pretty hard to live, hanging by threads."

"You need more faith then, but you'd feel better." He laughs a little. "It's really humanity's most natural position."

I do suddenly feel much better; if my life has turned, this is the expected. He steps closer, his eyes dark and enormous in the drifty light, a smell like cloves about him.

"They were passionately sincere men, but they got tangled up with neo-platonism," he says quite naturally. "Tertullian was married and wanted children, all Christians must be fruitful of course, but sex except for fruitfulness was concupiscence, barely half a step on the right side of adultery. That lovely old man thanked God every time he considered the resurrection for then, finally, there would be no more 'voluptuous disgrace' between him and his wife."

"If that's how he thought, there wasn't any anyway."

"He thought so."

"Purity!" I mutter.

"*Virginal* purity is the point. Every Roman and Greek and Hittite and Egyptian priest or priestess had to have it. It made them special, and how I prayed Christians should be beyond that."

"Then why have they never made it?"

"Partly because they got mixed up with Plato. They always fixed that awesome gulf between spirit and matter, you advance spiritually when you mortify the flesh. The theologian Origen starved himself regularly, always slept on the floor and since the greatest mortification of flesh for him was to deny sex, he finally castrated himself."

"What?"

"He was teaching a class that included women—they hadn't thought of segregation yet—and he believed that

135

would 'unadulterate' his thinking."

"Did it?"

"Of course not. Passion is a state of mind more than body. In old age he was sorry he had done it, the desire remained without the possibility."

My grab-bag memory makes me laugh aloud. "Luther once bellowed at a roomful of monks, 'For me, I'd rather have two pair added than one pair cut off.'"

He is laughing as deeply as I, but with the kind of quiet sibilance of hard rain among leaves; the world's most powerful sinner, a six-balled Luther screwing his way to all-encompassing faith! My laughter tilts the rollered stool on which I sit and my head bangs against a metal shelf, clunk! muffled and boomed simultaneously by a thousand absorbent books and he leans forward, fingertips that sting like vinegar, and the blunt pain evaporates with his face still smiling beside mine and I can't help myself,

"At least Origen puts his balls where his mouth was."

But he stops laughing; he seems momentarily further away, as if moved by a sudden grief. I re-balance myself, feeling the ribbed rubber under my buttocks, the round rollers shift squeaking on the tile floor. In a moment I will know this as more absurd than my night necessity in the Palliser, but just now it is as standard as straightening my kinked leg. Can sexuality be that, the profoundest mortification of the flesh? He leans against the shelves, against the groping wisdom of man moiled from the ages, and his face hardens.

"It would probably have been better," he says with a flip of irony, "if I had been born a woman."

I stare at him. "God can have regrets?"

"Of course not, it doesn't matter to God, who is both male and female and neither at the same time. It's just the human situation, the necessary language that splits everything male/female, and a human has to be one or the other, but it would be just as cosmically right to talk about God the Mother and Jesus Christ the Daughter, you know that."

And after a moment of stunned silence I do, of course.

"Then why ... " I manage, gesturing. "It would have been even more startling, you as daughter."

"It was bad enough as son. The Jews believed I was fathered by the Devil, not the One and Only Jehovah, because only the Baal and the Ashtoreth had children."

"And so worshipped with sexual debauchery."

"Of course, that's what the church was fighting too, we're not debauched maniacs, we're moral."

"So why weren't you a woman?"

"Mostly the hardness of the human heart."

"What?"

"Just like Moses agreeing to divorce, humanity closes its mind on something, men want to get rid of their wives, men think they are superior, and they develop their patriarchal ways to control society, what does it matter what God wants? A parent may not want the child to dirty itself, and if it walks in the mud and returns home it may be made uncomfortable for a while but it certainly won't be killed for being muddy."

"This is a bit more than mud."

"Magnificent. You kill for love?"

"There's the noble Othello with his lovely Desdemona?"

"He can't love. He's trained himself to kill and that's what he does when the world doesn't suit him."

"But he's great and noble, he's—"

"He's loyal. What kind of tune can you play with one finger on one string? He's a pathetically limited human being."

"Tragically human?"

He shakes his head. "Path-et-ic," he says in syllables.

"What about rape, violent rape, what if someone did that to your loved one?"

"They're doing it all the time."

"Be human!"

"You want a list of what's worth killing for?"

"What about rape?"

"A Christian deals with violence by suffering it."

"What about adultery?"

"Listen, haven't you read Hosea the prophet whose wife publicly takes a lover? He doesn't kick her out as any Jewish husband would, and destroy her in the society, no, he writes a poem:

But now listen,
I will woo her again,
I will go with her into the wilderness and comfort her;
there will I restore her vineyards,
turning the Vale of Trouble into the Gate of Hope,
and there she will answer as in her youth,
when she came up out of Egypt.
On that day she will call me, My husband!
and shall no more call me My Baal,
and I will wipe from her lips the very names of the Baalim,
and never again shall their names be heard.
This is the very word of the Lord.''

"That story just acts out Israel and God seen as wife and husband. It's not talking about everyday morality."

"Don't you see? God is passion; he is hopelessly, endlessly in love!"

"God?"

"Yes! He's no philosopher's abstraction, he's angry, jealous, tender, forgiving, head over heels in love and he won't let you go, he'll wait for years, a real fool."

I am pinioned by his black eyes, nose long and Semitic like a dagger.

"Your own best actions," he says, "and you recognize them, are pale but genuine reflections of the passionate goodness of God."

"So, the injured spouse responds to adultery with always more love."

"Nothing heals like it, both ways."

"And what if you're the adulterer?"

"Well?" he considers me steadily. "If you really want healing, that is."

I have to say it, there is no way I cannot, "There seems to be more than one answer to that, eh?"

His sudden smile is like the warmth of a wood fire soaking you up on a winter's day.

"If you express your question that way, there's only one. But with God there are many, an infinity of answers if you like, and anything you can imagine is possible with Him and even a few things beyond that."

"Even with love?"

"How, love?"

"'God is love, and in him is no darkness at all.'"

"Exactly, if you say it, light as the image for love. No more than you can quite imagine the limits of light moving into the limitless universe can you imagine the boundaries of love. That's what heaven is for, to explore the—"

"But I'm not saying anything when love grabs me right now and—"

"I'm talking about passion, can you for one minute forget about your balls? I was trying to tell you that reading Plato got early Christians hung up, so to speak," and he guffaws, almost ribald, "I suppose they were trying to make what I said sound acceptably intelligent and got hold of what sounded closest, and unfortunately these thinkers were so influential and their idea fit so well with that other notion—the Jews leaning over backwards away from Baal—that anything really physically lovely must somehow be wrong—God is *other* all right, beyond humanity certainly but not incapable of anything mankind can do, I mean why should God deny himself any of humanity's greatest blessings?—that sexuality is now connected to all the worst possible sins, especially for people like you who reject the so-called old-fashioned morality of their parents."

"Sexuality *was* the worst possible sin for my father."

"In what way, worst?"

"It was ... dirty, the sniggering secrecy, I think, it twisted his mind."

"Do you think he ever enjoyed his sexual body?"

I have never been able to imagine it; he was so cold, seemed to brutally despise his body, hurling it into such unrelenting drudgery and yet it was a good one, tapered and hard like iron. Despising others' bodies too; that was even worse.

"Do you think your mother was sexually attractive?"

"Oh," and my mind flips, "of course she was beautiful, anyone can still see that, incredibly."

"Don't you think he ever saw it?"

"All he wanted was sons off her."

"You're being silly."

"She had at least twelve pregnancies! Two early sons dead as infants, three miscarriages, what—"

"That's the way it was for most women then, you know it, brutal but all too usual. Why do you think there are three, four year gaps between your births?"

I have no idea; I have to laugh suddenly: "That's not something I can holler at her now, the people on the sidewalk would hear me!"

"Why do you think?" he insists.

"It wasn't planning by *him*, that's for sure."

"Oh grow up," impatiently, "understand a little!"

"Well why did he always make my sisters feel so miserable about their bodies?"

"Maybe he didn't want them to tempt anyone."

"That's a very charitable interpretation for ... " and I stop, his look making words unnecessary. 'With charity for all,' said a good man.

"I refuse to see bodies as mere opportunities for temptation."

"Even at sixteen?"

"Yes! I liked the way my body felt after working hard, skating and shooting hard."

"Good. Did he ever see you masturbating?"

"I was smarter than that!"

He smiles a little. "If you hadn't been so smart you might have learned more."

"What, for heaven's sake!"

"Understanding. Surely one reason he was hard on sex was because he knew it was so important."

"That's a stupid way to teach importance."

"Of course! But then he wasn't as smart as you."

And he laughs to the sting of that; all things to me except meek and mild.

"Listen," he says, "I was trying to explain I could as easily have been female as male, and speaking of God as 'Father' is strictly the middle-eastern patriarchal image of warmth and caring, not at all your modern father of one tiny family but the extended family patriarch whose responsibility and concern is for the whole clan, all related to each other through him, they give him allegiance and he cares for them; and if he is great they share his greatness. He, that One is not far from anyone, but if you want to talk of him today you really have to talk of him as *both*, father *and* mother."

"God as parent?"

"Yes, a good inclusive word, parent. But there's another problem. Many peoples on earth believe in God the great mother bringing forth all that exists and of course that's really a much closer image than the male one: the mother birthing new, independent life into existence, that is the primal work of God and to see the world and all that is in it as existing in and coming forth from the womb of God is as graspable an image of creation as the seed falling into the ground, being buried and then growing into a new plant is a graspable image of resurrection. When Moses asks God in the desert who she/he is, God says 'I AM THE ONE WHO CAUSES TO BE WHAT I CAUSE TO BE,' and the mystery of GOD THE MOTHER is an excellent image of the act of causing things to be. Too excellent, in fact."

"Too excellent?"

"All words are image, speaking is the only way human beings can handle large reality. But the difference between the image and the reality has to be clear, and when man speaks of 'God as Mother' her acts usually become so closely identified with nature – the physical world everywhere – that he forgets the image-ness and begins to think the words as physical actuality. For a person to say: 'All is brought forth from the womb of God' is so close to what actually happens every minute in animal nature that he starts acting out copulation and birthing and begins to think he's God while he's doing it. That's another reason why the very act of copulation became such a problem for Christians—"

"How many reasons have you got now, six?"

He laughs, "Always nine, counter," but will not be distracted, "People are always copulating and with it pretending they're God, and then they begin to worship Nature where birth takes place all the time, and that's idolatry, worshipping the thing made rather than the maker of it. But God subsumes and is far beyond both Nature and Image. So it is better to contemplate the concept of GOD THE FATHER because no natural father ever brings forth any life by himself. You are then forced to contemplate the creation of the world not as the act of physical birth out of God's womb, but rather as the act of being *spoken into existence by Words coming out of God's mouth.* That is an image so strange, so profoundly human, that no one can ever mistake it for what happens in nature."

It seems the whole building, the shelves, the tiled concrete floor, the books themselves looming over me with their multiplied millions of words are simmering in the fire of this voice, I am being steeped in the water of these countless words into something I myself will have to drink, the quintessence of myself beyond any essence that I could have dreamt to swallow; if this could grow in me, soak and surround and burn me up perhaps I could live beyond the mirror that walls me in and every existence itself would metamorphose from the absurd into ... what? Mystery.

He says quietly, "Forget about love connected somehow and only with virginity, penis, vagina, or bodies penetrating each other, even two bodies reserved for each other alone. On that level love concerns acts of ownership and physical giving and sometimes they are too overwhelming to handle, especially as you live them in your body; they mangle you with their particular power. But at the very centre of physical union there burns something else, like thought burns at the heart of all human life."

I have to shake my head. "Fire ... the image of fire is always only fire."

He nods. "The true difficulty with problems is expressing them."

"I have this problem with 'love.'"

"Forget the quotation marks. Think of love as a great wheel whose spokes are hope and whose hub faith."

I chuckle in sudden recognition. "That sounds like *The Book of the Courtier.*"

"Or the highest hill overlooking a prairie river."

But into my sudden silence he quotes Castiglione, "'Love is a certain coveting to enjoy beauty.'"

"There's the image," I insist. " 'Beauty cometh of God and is like a circle, the goodness whereof is the centre. And therefore, as there can be no circle without a centre, no more can beauty be without goodness.' "

"Plato via Castiglione," he says, and adds a slight twist, "neither of whom had a patent on circles. But the elements hope and faith are very different."

"Yes," I admit, "but just now his circle seems more relevant to me than your wheel because it begins earlier, with love as 'coveting.' Where's your 'coveting'?"

"Must you have it? The steel rim on the wheel?" he suggests.

"No ... no, that's too hard, why not tangled in the spokes as decoration?"

"Coveting is neither steel nor flower. It's desire, and desire isn't round; it's always triangular."

"A whole, cold geometry of love!"

"Because you're helpless without image. The closer the word comes to visual image, the easier it is to grasp. Circle, triangle, why do you think I'm so simplistic? I could use 'sphere' and 'cone' and immediately...." he gestures, palms up.

"Okay, okay!"

"Two-dimensional is tough enough. Desire is triangular because it always pulls two different things towards itself."

"What two?"

"The beloved and the body of the beloved."

"They're the same."

"Why don't you know yourself? You endlessly make the distinction and you have an endless desire for the difference."

Which is only too true again, true true, 'The world is everything that happens to be true / The stars at night seem to suggest / The shapes of what might be.' When she kneels over me she is there in the triangle of large dark entrances of eyes and the total clasp or bare touch of body, outside and in and with her groaning, which moves me to search through her like a blind man intent on the barest fingertip of recognition in a livid jungle. It is neither she nor her body, it is both and neither, it is myself and it is not either, o wretched

143

man that I am, who will deliver me out of this....

"I know. The image of God the Father hasn't really helped you much. I know."

Thanks be there is perhaps an angel standing here beside me. Sandals, brown legs, narrow blue-striped culottes and white top, shoulders mellow as cream.

"I dreamt this last night," Gillian says. "You were between library stacks, hunched over a pile of books. I'm starting to dream you before you do it."

"'The stars at night suggest / The shapes of what might be,'" I quote to her, very inaccurately.

She looks down at me steadily, then touches my shoulder.

"Hey, are you all right?"

"It's wrecked half the world, God being a father!" I may be bellowing, books silent in the farthest reaches of Level One could well be quivering. "God is no father!"

Her strong hands lift me. "Come," she says gently, "you need some coffee."

There is much I need more, but 'twill do; 'twill have to.

The University Mall offers no season; under five blocks of plastic skylights, which leak sievishly in the slightest rain or melting snow, existence is perpetually bright, cocoonish and vaguely uneasy, as if a very large – in German one could think *Ungeheuer*, a monster either animal or mineral or both – were panting just behind the nearest shop wall or behind the garbage can or even that potted tree, which will break out in an instant and devour its way through concrete, plaster, sidewalk tables and chairs, stairways, people, plants, everything vegetable, animal or mineral and leave the mall an immense wormcasing under the shallow earth of Alberta sky. Sometimes I shudder.

But the Rocking Chair Lounge is reassuring; if you concentrate on any one chair if seems old, almost venerable. Through a spray of poplar and leaves the glass wall faces morning sun which glints off the roofs of two acres of cars, all perfectly normal and civilized.

"Was I really that loud?"

"We were the only ones there."

"Don't kid yourself."

The waft from her coffee drifts by in a small brown sensation.

"What else have you dreamt?"

She does not answer directly. "Have you dreamt too?"

"About us?"

"Yes."

"I don't think so, not yet."

"You don't know?"

"I don't remember, every dream I have."

"Not yet, but you will?"

"Probably ... probably. I don't have much choice, I think."

"You always dream about your women after you have them."

"What?"

"You have no choice, you do after, dream a memory."

These are not questions, they are statements in the already ludicrous sunlight of a Monday morning in May.

"What's the matter?" I ask carefully.

"Before that you yell a little in libraries?"

"Gillian."

"I told you, I dreamt you in the library stacks!"

"Which means that in your day/night country, you are living the night before the day. My father would approve, it's biblical."

"You're not funny."

"I know. In Genesis evening and morning are always called a day."

"'And evening and morning were the sixth day.'"

"Exactly."

"When 'God created man in his own image, male and female created he them.'"

"That's right." Even more carefully. Unfortunately I detest liquor, but the strongest coffee is inadequate to juggle this.

"If I'm going to dream us before we happen," she says, "I need more protection."

"What?"

"You have to carry your share of this."

"What, please *what* are you talking about?"

"Us! Don't you understand English?"

The light in this lounge seems too dazzling, too heavy, I can't lift my head to look at her. Her delicate brown legs, feet in minimal tan sandals like a poor disciple. I have a sudden longing, one long gut-ache of longing for the irresponsible transparent impersonality of the dead, Maskepetoon brittle and depthless as carved glass, untouchable, completely there in words only, never again possible. Apparently; and that also was before I knew her. One black-haired woman and the world breaks.

"You don't know what I'm talking about," she says.

"This is no place to talk about anything, especially this loud."

"The impersonality of a public lounge?"

"Where people, individuals, see them? suck ice cream – it isn't public enough, let's get—"

"No," she says. Her face rigid. "I'm not going near your office."

"The library, the Micro-materials Room?"

"That's your territory too."

"Okay, you pick."

"I pick here," she looks about at three scattered coffee drinkers. "They're reading."

"They seem to be."

"I don't care, give them a little drama, who cares," she is almost hissing. "But you have to carry your share."

"Listen, I don't get this, my share ... I'm the one you dreamt in the library, did you dream the Palliser too?"

The pupils of her eyes dilate, strangely enormous in the fierce light and she stares at me without blinking. Intuition burns me and her eyes close, only an instant, "I'm not going to dream all this alone," she insists. "You have to dream it too, perhaps the night before or several ...."

"I have to? Your dreams come into my life, take it over, and now I have to, too?"

"You didn't want me to come?"

"I ... don't know."

146

"It's too upsetting?"

"No ... no, of course I did, when you did it I wanted it more than anything, no ... yes I do want ... " I say it, I mean it? Of course of course.

"But you'd never have done anything about that want, on your own?"

"I didn't know I had it, what I wanted, at all."

"Oh," she is abruptly sharp again, "I'm there and fall into your lap and then you know what you've always wanted, just as the glands lead is that it?"

"No, I...."

"Viscera, nothing but the guts secreting, waving their gluttonous sensors!"

"Gillian!"

But she's right; to an extent that's what I've thought several times in a very small part of myself: the simple modern adventure – but that's just plain truckdriver stupid!

"Get off your middle-class evasive," she says grimly. "I don't give a goddam for polite if it isn't honest too."

"Hey," I touch her bare knee, "what is it, what happened?"

Her lovely face is chiselled, almost polished in the sun and the echo of my words slashes across my thought – Liv, I am saying this to Liv, three days or four and already I am talking like – but her lips open,

"I've never done anything like this bef ..." and she stops, laughter is blundering up inside her. I can see it hunching her face and in a burst of relief I'm with her, the concrete and the glass echo, "I sound like a terrible movie script!"

"As bad as, 'Is that all there is to it?'"

"Wide-eyed and open-mouthed!"

But her laughter breaks off as quickly as it started. "Don't distract me with levity. I refuse to dream this alone."

"You're not dreaming it."

"I am. And you have to know the responsibilities of your dreams too. When I woke this morning you were as vivid as the daylight, sitting between the metal shelves, bent just like you were, the books spilled all around you as if you ... I don't know exactly," her face abstracted into concentration now, "as if you have been looking ... not for something but...."

The light off a windshield far below cuts my eye like a knife. I offer slowly, "Someone?"

Her eyes pinch together slightly.

"Who is it?" almost a whisper.

I can't speak; there is only image. And she knows without my word because she cannot imagine it, no more than I, though she has already known in a dream before me what she cannot articulate; perhaps tomorrow night or tonight she will recognize what her night eyes have already told her without day memory. Sitting in this perfectly cold modern building we seem both to have moved into the mirror; as if I took off my glasses and now saw my hand as having no part in me, the me that feels it there nevertheless, it is perhaps writing what I intend it to write or feeling the leg or toe I intend it to feel; which is no more part of me feeling them than the hand, hugely distorted now no doubt and possibly attached to me, is me as I stare at it. Later of course I may recall this and not quite know what I was thinking about because the sensation will then no longer be there. Perhaps I already dreamed it, last week.

"And then what happened? This?"

"No. I woke up, I was in bed."

I see nothing, I can only insist, "And then, what?"

She is silent; as if she were preparing to be frightened. So I plow on, past everything, "Harold asked you about me?"

And she is somehow relieved, but also truly frightened. "How . . . did you know?"

"I didn't dream it. He talked to me this morning."

"Oh." That may be worse for her. After a moment she says, "He asked, whether I knew you."

"And you said?"

"I'd met you, yes, you worked in the Micro-reading Room."

"Why mention that?"

"He knows anyway."

"I guess so, yes."

"It's always good to tell people what you know they already know."

"What?"

And I distance her detail by physical detail, a woman so striking if she had ever appeared at an IBS conference she would have been besieged with an absolute polite relentlessness that would have had no politeness about it whatever. And me then so proud of my integrity, my honesty; while all my colleagues frenetically tried to outflank the few women in the bar I would laugh at them, go upstairs and read a book and fall asleep thinking of my lovely Liv. I had, basically, the virtue of the untempted virgin (no woman ever really worked on me, there were always more than enough men about for them and willing) and the pride of one too. 'I cannot praise a fugitive and cloistered virtue, unexercised and unbreathed, that never sallies out and sees her adversary ... ' cloistered by the love and beauty of my wife. A spartan cell indeed.

"It's always best to say things as close to the actual facts as you can."

And now for Rocking Chair Lounge Course 101: Aspects of the Convincing Lie. 'We bring no innocence into the world, we bring impurity: that which purifies us is trial, and trial is by what is contrary.' Of course, dear John, but of course one must also endure the trial and not suffer failure. Because of what? An emotion? A shudder in the loins? And the trial is never from without, it is from the impurity within. What impurity? Love?

Gillian is silently contemplating me.

"Where have you gone?" she asks when I meet her dark eyes.

"The seventeenth century," and I chuckle a little, more in hiccough than apology. "To the wise Puritans."

"'The cruelest lies are often told in silence'?"

"Is that staying as close to the truth as is convenient?"

"No, close to a nineteenth-century neo-puritan, Robert L. Stevenson."

"Ah, he who also declared, 'To make our idea of morality centre on forbidden acts is to defile the imagination'?"

"The same, who ended that statement with, 'and to introduce into our judgements of our fellow-men a secret element of gusto.'"

"Don't you like that, *gusto*?"

"I just love *gusto*," she was drawling 'love' like a Texan.

We are laughing so brayishly that one by one the three solitary coffee-drinkers behind us rise in their Monday scowls indeed, and leave. At which we laugh harder; I am facing the yellow rape field dabbed on the concrete wall and roaring like a tickled freshman.

Then she has stopped; is staring at me with her eyes wide.

"What did he ask?"

"Something about history, not us."

"You're sure?"

"About an idea he has...."

"A project for you to work on, together?"

"Just a suggestion, I don't know it ... did he ask you something, when he came home?"

"That's not the way we live together."

"You don't talk?"

"Are you cross-examining me?"

"Does his suggestion, the possible project ... does that mean something?"

We are the only people in the lounge, and we are silent; her look has not changed: as if she were staring at a sudden stranger.

"Who are you?" she asks finally.

"Me?"

"Yes. Who?"

I laugh a little, she is so urgent. "I am James Aaron Dyck, barely associate professor of—"

"That's just your name, your job, I want to know who are *you.*"

"Well, I'm a Canadian male, forty-two, married to Liv Sorenson Dyck, with one daughter Becca, aged ten, living in Edmon—"

"Lists, numbers, who gives a sweet goddamn about statistics, I want to know who—"

And I finally turn the tables on her,

"Why?"

"I ... I," her words gathering behind her eyes. I can see them in points of brilliance as they issue between her perfect

150

teeth, "I want to know someone truly, not as friend – fraternal – not as daughter or student or customer or for god's sake not wife or pickup or good lay, this has to be...."

"No friend?"

"Your body ... the body is the closest image of the human being, who you actually are. A human is ungraspable without her body, ungraspable by another human, your body is an image of you. You know?"

"What is this, some kind of reverse Platonism?"

"Don't mix me up! I'm trying to understand something and I can't without explaining it, your body, which I see and touch and experience with all my senses and apprehension is the very best image I can get of you – it's an image because if you died suddenly your body would still be here but it wouldn't be *you*, something that most of my senses cannot register would be gone and that would be *you* – and some of this 'you' that is really only graspable as image is public and some of it is very private, for yourself only and those with whom you choose to be intimate. That's why rape is so dreadful; it's the violent tearing, the assault on your very centre. Because when I hold your body between my hands, you give and I take you into myself, I am ... that is also as close as my mind can come to holding *you*."

"Then why bother with me ... to want to know me? There are a hundred other possi—"

"No, actually there aren't so many. Over half the people I meet are women."

"So, why not a woman?"

"I've thought about that, a long time, and it would be a lot simpler, a woman would understand what I'm trying to say without a second thought, but—"

"If women are so great at understanding then two—"

"I think women have to know each other differently; for me the most profound unions are between opposites. A lesbian union seems more like a physical image repeating itself."

"Surely two greats, women, should make an even greater."

But she simply refuses my attempted irony. "It's possible,

but not for me, no," she replies straight. "For me this knowledge seems possible only between one woman and one man. I have a very close friend who's a woman and we talk and talk, and we touch each other easily and I've often thought – but that final physical intimacy, that way of knowing is...."

"Why, have you tried?"

"Yes." She is looking beyond the noon leaves outside, remembering something with a trace of smile. "We don't want that."

"Well ... " I can offer nothing but irony and her refusal annihilates that.

"In all the same places, there is too much sameness." She laughs a little, and I have to face her sincerity. "Place can destroy idea, you know."

"The base of 'metaphysics' is still 'physics.'"

"Indubitably."

"Well," I pause again, lame, my neck crimped from leaning forward too long and what is left of my coffee long since stale in its large styrofoam, "of the remaining forty-nine per cent, in the words of immortal Kipling, 'Each to his choice, and I rejoice / the lot has fallen to me / in a fair ground ... ' why me?"

She is grinning, her face quite lifted to me; if I knew what love may be, I could easily love her forever.

"It might have been anyone of course," she offers blithely, "but it wasn't. It was you. I watched you, you were impressively thoughtful."

"You're kidding me."

"If one has all the choice one wants," still smiling, eyes flickering roguery, "it has to be someone with ... brains and he may as well be reasonably good looking."

"Well I declare."

"Not repulsive anyway," and she laughs aloud.

Her 'has to be,' her 'reasonably' are shrivelling me up; I swallow stale coffee and regret that too. "Yes, I understand, yes, the body being crucial, if one finds one particular body conveniently available and not totally repulsive one can hardly expect to be ecstatically moved, "tis not so deep as a well nor so wide as a church door, but 'tis enough, 'twill serve' no doubt.''

"Hey," she has been trying to interrupt me, "don't be vicious. Listen I'm trying to explain something—"

"Well, do."

"—something that's really hard to ... I'm figuring it out and you understand it as well as I, don't try to cut it up. Are you ashamed of something? With me? Did you think my coming to you was some long long-range teeny-bopper adoration?''

"I'm sorry," and I am. "I'm being silly, okay? It's a matter of knowing."

"The old expression is 'carnal knowledge,' knowledge through the flesh. I want to know someone, you, through your flesh."

It's the impersonality of "someone" that twists inside me. She didn't come to me in that room then because she was ... overwhelmed, well, what would have 'overwhelmed' her? A pitiful philosopher across the room at a party, a professor bending his head with dutiful persistence into a micro-reader, of such are passion attacks made? Ha! even Isolde, despite all dragons and gaping wounds and a week at sea needed a potion.

But she will not allow self-denigration either, which must be showing on my face. She speaks steadily on:

"And that incredible stone wheel you showed me, that, exactly that is what I mean by knowing someone: who is this man who searches out this forgotten, lost, ancient holy place, this worship at the bare elements of the universe? Who is this man? And you told me, you showed me, and when the spirit of that place gathered, wrapped us up into one with itself, what did you think we were doing, eh? *Fuck*ing?''

I have detested that word all my life; it has never sounded more repulsively ugly. Her face is so close I have to lift my glasses.

"No ... no ...," I can mutter at last, "loving."

"Yes, dearest god I was strung by every nerve I have from all the stars and planets."

153

"I was scared at first, really."

"Were you?" perhaps misunderstanding me. "Why?"

"On that hill, everything is so open, so somehow endlessly revealed."

"There was nothing but cows within twenty miles."

"Oh, no person...."

"Yes," she says slowly, remembering that personality of cosmos. "And the act then, it seems rather ... small, so, I don't know...."

"Small?"

"Well, not quite worthy ... somehow inappropriate to the place, to the incredible feelings it creates, there. The great Maker must have had a very ironic sense of humour. The first time he saw that, one set of buttocks or another thumping away between his new earth and massive sky...."

And her laughter bounces from the walls with mine.

"What would you have done there" she says then, "alone?"

"I go to lots of places alone. I look, think ... just looked, thought myself into it."

"Masturbated?"

"What kind of juvenile do you—" I burst out, and stop; her understanding so gentle but quick as a knife. "I don't ... a couple of summers ago, once I was driving through rain all day ... I'd never seen Cutknife Hill and I got to the Pound-maker Reserve so late it was really hopeless but the rain stopped and I walked in from the road, just horrible mosquitoes, up some long muddy trail that didn't come out on the battlefield, it came out on top of a bluff between poplars and there was the ravine below me and the sloped field with Poundmaker's grave like crossed lodge-poles with their hide coverings ripped off and the sun was so low the shadows looked as if the Queen's Own Rifles were all around it, kneeling down, firing guns and cannon at the Cree all along the ravine and the evening mist like smoke from their camp drifting up between the trees, I could just ... see it all...."

"Yes."

"I was there. But I don't know ... why I...."

It seems too ludicrous, I must be scarlet and she touches my arm on the metal table.

"When I wiped the mosquitoes off I was all bloody, arms, neck, face, just bloody like I'd been painted!"

"You did what you felt, right."

"It's so ... crazy...."

"Look, you didn't frantically use all that last available light for Kodachrome."

Maybe she wants to know me, but at the moment I'm getting most of the benefits.

"Well," I can look at her again, her shining hair, "you're doubtless right about the Creator's humour, and I suppose the action is ... appropriate to itself, no sillier than the pace of a death march or the drumming of a grouse, body rhythm, the body's ritual of great passion, and it's good ... we seemed so utterly naked, out there."

"Aren't you usually naked then?"

"Yes, but behind a closed door, not on such a high ... open to the cosmic eye of four winds," and I grin, remembering suddenly, "no Jew could worship on top of a hill. Those high places were where the heathen built altars."

"But David built his temple on Mount Zion."

"You're right. You know everything."

"'Why hop ye so, ye high hills?'"

"And that's why no Mennonite is allowed to make love standing up."

"Why?"

"It inevitably turns into dancing."

And she laughs aloud, rocking back in her chair at last. The sun has moved, only the far side of the parking lot glares at me now. And then Gillian does another lovely thing: she reaches for my left hand and takes my forefinger in her warm mouth. Completely. After a moment she lets me have it again, smiling.

"You close the door," she says, "because of intimacy."

"Wir sind abgesondert, set aside?"

She nods. "And on that stone hill all the sky and all the earth are watching, the ultimate intimacy. You captured me there, did you know?"

"Captured?"

"Yes. Did you know that?"

"No."

"I was silly, I thought I could just learn to know you. That's all I wanted. I thought."

"Capture." I groan. "In knowing, inevitable capture."

She looks at me steadily, her eyes wide and black. I ask her finally, "How many people around here do you think are captured?"

She tells me without blinking.

On the prairie the only graspable image for time is the movement of a body in space; consequently, the only image for a person's outlook on humanity is direction. Therefore the life of Maskepetoon I am now discovering reveals itself as a body continuously moving into an ever tighter and tighter circle of contortion. If one ignores Indian racial differences (all popular culture does), then it seems he begins life facing in the direction now simplistically known as 'typical Indian warrior': he accepts the tribal values, trains himself in fighting, considers the tribal enemies his personal foes, tests his young manhood against them and over years kills as many as he can so that he becomes the ultimate subject of their warsongs for them in turn to test themselves against; in other words, his consciousness seems untextured by any complexity, either extended thought, doubt, or even hesitation. But as his days lengthen, experience and irrefutable vision turn him toward peace and away from the Indian veneration of war and blood revenge, so that when in middle age he encounters the Christianity of the Methodist Rundle (whose unwavering teaching about love in the Church at first glance makes him quite unsuited as a missionary to Indians, and whether 'love' means the same to Maskepetoon as to Rundle does not really matter since there appears to be a large common ground in their respective understandings of it), Rundle's teaching seems to largely corroborate what Maskepetoon himself has already come to understand about life. However, by the time of his death at somewhere age seventy (so few Indian men who began as warriors survived to such an age that this in itself appears almost a cosmic intention, a demonstration that only such a life could carry with it the affirmation of three score years and ten), Maskepetoon has been turned even further, twisted shall we say three hundred and sixty degrees so that his body is again facing in the traditional direction, but there is something very different about him also. He is still as it were looking back, over his shoulder. Looking at that point of Christian world view directly opposite to his originally accepted Indian one, that world view toward which he was himself once completely, bodily turned. His body now faces Indian, his head faces Christian. At his death he still confronts his traditional Cree enemies, the Blackfeet, as any warrior of his people must every spring when the new grass is long enough to sustain travelling horses and the sloughs are full on the prairie so that when the buffalo make their daily journey to drink along the paths they have worn to their waterholes like the spokes of a medicine wheel, the long lines of their brown bodies will move slowly, gradually down into the deepening paths as if they were slanting under the horizon and when they lower their great heads set below their massive shoulders down to drink they will be gone altogether, taken away under the earth. He confronts these enemies every spring and in the middle of his life he destroys his father's killer far more devastatingly as a Christian than ever he could as an Indian: 'My son,' the old man says to him in the circle of his listening tribe, 'you have killed me,' and that Blackfoot sees only his Indian destruction, not comprehending at that moment (perhaps he never did) that when Maskepetoon has destroyed him with forgiveness and offered him love for murder, that forgiveness has destroyed the original killing and that love has created life again: Maskepetoon has brought about the Blackfoot's only possible life, that is, his resurrection.

The end of Maskepetoon's life is not like that, however. At his death he faces his enemies with words only, and with the fact of his word-defended body forgives them and asks their forgiveness in turn. But in both the Blackfoot and Cree camps his forgiveness ultimately destroys, and has destroyed, nothing; his proffered love resurrects only hatred. That is neither Indian nor Christian. It is, sadly, both; and therefore I must see his life as a movement of contortion. Or at best perhaps a spiral. But whether the long rhythmic spiral of his life moves in an upward or downward direction is now, it seems to me, certainly indeterminable.

Nevertheless, the ancestors would have known. *Our ancestors knew that nothing ever happens that someone was not listening for; everything has already been heard. They taught us we must rise before dawn and listen very carefully for the voice of the wind; it sounds like two people singing the same song together. As they sing they come nearer and nearer and they have picked up a leaf, a stone, a bone and they are passing these three back and forth so that each always holds one and the third is moving between them, as in their song, which is the fourth thing that they pass. We listen and we hear in their endless dreamlike song of those who have been and will be carried ashore by the tides, who are white as a peeled log with iron axes and knives stuck in their belts and who will make dreadful sounds which no one has ever heard before.*

So we know of Whiteman long before we ever see him with his inevitable rifle in his hand, in the same way that long before we first saw a horse we had already heard of them from the dawn, how they were larger than four dogs and so strong they could carry a grown man on their backs and still gain ground on a running buffalo. That is why our name for "horse" is "skydog."

No one doubts what he hears in the dawn songs of the wind; the world is too amazing for anyone to doubt any possibility. It is astonishing to us that Whiteman can carry the gruesome smallpox about with him in a small bottle that looks empty, and which he threatens to open any time he pleases, but we do not doubt that he can do this any more than we doubt that he has another bottle which contains the killer of the smallpox. After all, the sickness is his own and he should be able to do with it what he pleases (though sometimes, when he only has one bottle and not the other, it turns on him and kills him too); all this is merely astonishing, at most strange. But to fix words on a white piece of wood or leather, not merely signs but words which always say exactly the same thing and which can make you say the same thing when you have touched them with a pen, that goes beyond strange. When we first saw words we could lift and put down with our hands, we thought such words would destroy both listening and memory altogether. However, after many long thoughts around a centre fire, we understood that this was not so. Rather, the knowledge of how to fix words in wood or leather or paper gave them their ultimate power: now one could handle them, make them and send them in silence, see them as well as hear and remember. That moved words beyond the power of sign or declaration into mystery, and if we had thought about it further, as some of the wisest among us surely did, and if we had listened even more intently at dawn, we would soon have understood that it was not Whiteman's gun or his disease that would end our living as we did, no no, it would be his words that would destroy us. As it was.

"But mystery is that which is hidden to some and revealed to others," our great chief Maskepetoon told us around his centre fire. "Once we were deaf but now we hear; once we were blind but now we see. The mystery of words and the world is revealed in the Book for those who truly want to know."

He was the first of our people to make words, and also the first to read them, and he understood mystery in the same way that it was given to him to read. When he first tried to make the three- and four-edged curves and lines and tails of words, whatever he made was smudged, he said, though the shapes were very sharp to us who could not understand them. He said they were all smeared, draggy like the tracks of an old person in river mud. Then Rundle gave him two pieces of Christian glass with a wire to hold them in front of his eyes and suddenly he laughed aloud, roared in his huge voice so that women and men and children from all around the camp came running.

"I can see," he cried, "I see!"

And he saw not only the sharp limits and edges of words but also the gnarled old scar of his broken left arm, which *had always been so close to his eyes yet he had not been able to see it distinctly since his vision of heaven. That glass on his nose, which clouded the world for us when we put it on, made everything he could touch as exact as his memory and fingertips told him it was; wearing that he could say words slowly, saying them in parts in the same way that they were made on the paper:*

"In the be-gin-ing God made the heav-ens and the earth...."

After that his favourite words in the Book were about Creation, the way things were made and held together by the Great Wind, the Spirit that made all things and gave them to people, and the young missionary John McDougall later told the story again and again of when he first met Maskepetoon he was seated with the log wall of the mission house at Fort Victoria against his back, the Book in his hands and the glasses on his nose. The North Saskatchewan River endlessly repeating itself between the striped banks of clay and shale and coal in grey-green reflections as he read aloud, slowly,

"... our sufferings of this time are not worthy to be compared with the glory that will be revealed to us then. For all creatures, the whole created universe waits with eager longing for God's sons to be revealed ... because then the universe itself will be freed from the chains of mortality and enter the glorious liberty of the Sons of God. For we know that until now the whole creation groans in all its parts as if in the pains of childbirth, and we also groan while we wait for God to make us his children and set our bodies free.'"

Maskepetoon looked up at young John, who had spoken our language since he was a child, and who therefore also understood the laughter of our old chief as it bounced off the cliffs across the wide river and came back to them, its image repeating itself like the river in their ears.

"I will be set free," Maskepetoon said then, "free from the groaning of my heart in the day, the cry of my heart at night. And I will walk across the water of the river and up the cliff and over the buffalo prairie to the Blackfeet and give them my two empty hands and we will sit down together and make words of peace forever."

Perhaps somewhere beyond flowing water and rock and time there was waiting that completed paradise; Maskepetoon brought us as close to it as we ever were that fall when he and his grandson faced the Blackfoot warriors at the Blindman River. He had moved that far south because the buffalo had not come north and in those short days before the snow hunger was already visiting our camps. But of course our enemies needed the great herds as much as we and they followed them north toward us until there did not seem to be so much as a grass blade to separate our two People. And the camps of their fierce friends, the Bloods and the Peigans, were at the Red Deer River crossings not even a day behind them. In the Falling Leaves Moon some of us had already eaten our dogs and were going to start on our horses.

Then Maskepetoon said he would ride to the Blackfeet and six of us, only six, said we would go with him. Our horses had barely broken through the slivered ice of the river when their scouts noticed us and disappeared south up the spruce of the valley draws. Maskepetoon rode after them and we followed, saying nothing while we stared at the skyline ahead. We were half across the wide valley when heads bristled up there, at least thirty of them and with a whoop they charged us on their summer-fed horses. We swung around and rode back hard for the river, there was nothing to fight for against numbers on such a day when the snow whispers it is coming, but when we dashed through the water and turned to look at the pursuit, we saw that the Blackfeet had not followed us. And we also saw that we had two riderless horses running with us; Maskepetoon and his grandson were standing where we had turned, facing the wide line of charging warriors alone and on foot.

And then, as we looked at each other and were about to gallop back to die with them, they sat down on the ground, both of them, and in an instant they were surrounded, Blackfoot horses running around them in three and four circles so that we could see nothing but our furious enemies and hear their screams and our own hearts pounding with fear.

So it was Chief Child, Joseph's son who was only sixteen years old then and stayed with him, he told us the story:

161

"My grandfather stood looking at those horses, there was nothing to see but heads and knees driving, their riders so low on their necks, and I stood beside him. Then he said to me, 'It is time to read,' and put his hand inside his blanket and took out the Book and the glasses, and he sat down. So I sat down too. He set the glasses in place and began to read from the opened Book, his voice as strong as if he were seated in his own lodge in the circle of our People:

"'... in the same way the Spirit comes to help us when we are weak; we do not even know how we should pray, but through our inarticulate groans the Spirit himself pleads for us.'

"And that is how the Blackfeet rode their circle around us, my grandfather not looking at them but reading on while the hooves of their horses threw grass and dust over us until the riders finally stopped their screams and just sat there on their shivering horses, staring. They had not shot a single arrow or bullet; I suppose not even Blackfeet kill a man sitting on frozen ground and speaking words into the air breathing winter over him, and suddenly the oldest of them shouted,

'It is The Young Chief!'

giving him that old name they had first given him when he was young and killed them better than any man of our People, and my grandfather looked up and said in their tongue,

'Yes Red Sky Bird, I am that one,'

and he stood up and the Blackfoot slid from his nervous horse and they took each other in their arms. Then Red Sky Bird said,

'What is that you hold in your hand?'

and my grandfather said,

'My friend, I do not need to ask what it is you hold in your hand.'

"The Blackfoot looked down and seemed surprised that he still held his Hudson Bay rifle in his hand, its long barrel rubbed so blue you could see it lay with him under his blanket every night. And then he understood that my grandfather had embraced him even while he was holding it, and he dropped it to the ground and said very gently,

'Forgive me. What have you?'

"And my grandfather smiled. 'These are the words of the Great Spirit,' and he showed him the marks on the Book and translated them into Blackfoot. Then Red Sky Bird and some of his men put the glasses on their noses and looked but the words were more smudged than ever and they still could understand nothing without Maskepetoon as interpreter so finally Red Sky Bird said,

'It must be the will of the Great Spirit that we meet as brothers today. You are the only one who can tell us his words.'

"And his warriors agreed, so they sat down with us and our men came back from the river and all the horses grazed the fall grass of the Blindman valley together while we smoked the Blackfoot pipe. Even I who was not yet a warrior, but had stood by the side of my grandfather."

That is how Chief Child told his story. And that very evening eight Blackfoot men came on foot into the large camp of our People, and Chief Child rode out with sixteen young men to escort them in. Hundreds of us would have been happy to kill them, for who did not have blood vengeance crying in his heart, but we honoured Maskepetoon's word and Chief Child's young courage and the Blackfeet walked through our camp as if they were being led through a great bluff of silent trees. Straight to the centre of the camp where our chief waited to greet them at the door of his great lodge. And that night the drums called us to Peace Dance.

Our war leader at that time, Starving Young Bull, stood up first to the beat of the drums. He was following the guidance of The One He Dreamed Of, he said, and he began to move in the rhythm of the drummers. Long and marvelously he danced, finding a song that reached up from the ground and through his voice and under the raised edges of the lodge past the People watching all about to the sharp cold stars of the winter sky. He danced around Maskepetoon's centre fire and The One He Dreamed Of gave him words, gave him courage and he lifted his blanket from his shoulder and gave it to Red Sky Bird singing, "I will live in peace," and he stripped off his beaded shot pouch and powder horn and gave them to a second Blackfoot singing, "I hunt only buffalo." How we

163

cheered him as he sat down in the circle, exhausted and naked.

Then one by one our greatest warriors danced agreement with Starving Young Bull, and when they had given their most precious possessions as gifts to all the Blackfeet, at last Red Sky Bird, sitting beside Maskepetoon on the side of his heart, rose to his feet. He stood in gifts to his knees and he held the blue rifle in his hand as softly he began to sing. Our drummers passed the drums to the Blackfeet and they beat out the rhythms of our enemies, but different too for the words we knew were strong like the man standing motionless in his great song, singing of comfort and peace and trust, words that a mother or a father could have sung to a snuggling child though his hands reaching out were like a black tree with the rifle grown blue into its branches. Then he bent at last to our chief Maskepetoon and laid the long rifle at his feet.

Maskepetoon sat motionless gazing into the fire; it seemed now as if he had seen and heard nothing. The Blackfeet drums grew quieter, quieter, and then Maskepetoon's broken arm reached out, picked up the rifle and laid it in front of Chief Child sitting on his other side.

But Chief Child said nothing either, nor did he move. He sat beside his grandfather as if he were one with him like the roots of a tree and slowly the drums died away and silence came upon us all, silence as when one person is alone on the prairie and all things under the sky make their sounds but they mean nothing: it is their endless silence you must be able to hear. So we waited for that other silence. And it too came, walking like mountains opening their mouths or soft bones when they move into the order of birth. And in this silence at last we heard a song, whether from the fire or the ground or the poles and skins of the lodge or the rifle or Chief Child's hand we could not say; perhaps it was Maskepetoon's Book itself talking to each of us in words none of us had ever until then been ready to hear:

The wind at dawn
Gives me the words

To teach stones to speak.

The knives of the wind
Open my eyes to see
The hills cry yes, yes.

That was the best peace we made with the Blackfeet, and it lasted longer than any we had in all those years of our ancestors when we rode anywhere on the prairie that our horses would carry us and we had friends to meet. In a few years we would have to agree with Whiteman that we had to live on the little Land-Set-Aside, and the Blackfeet would have to agree to that too because the buffalo were suddenly all gone and there was nothing to eat except what Whites agreed to give us and they would agree to nothing unless we touched the pen to their words they made on their paper. We did not have the power then, neither the strength in our arms nor the words to hold what the Spirit had given us we thought forever; our heads then seemed to have been shaken loose somehow, it could have been by disease or whisky and bad eating; or perhaps we had never truly understood what our greatest leaders tried in many ways to tell us, so we talked only small, but this peace lasted three years, and it was the last peace we ever made with the Blackfeet. This is how it was.

It was summer three years later, in the time of the Hatching Moon and we were south much further than ever, on the Bow River trying to find buffalo. Two hundred Blackfoot lodges were on the Little Bow. We stayed away from each other, hunting in different directions, but one night three of our women went to the Blackfoot camp to play and in the morning four of our men went after them. They all came back alive, but now the peace was broken.

So our old chief Maskepetoon asked us to help him onto his horse and with Chief Child and two others he rode to the Blackfeet. When they came over the hill above the bend in the Little Bow where the huge camp was, Blackfoot warriors came riding from four directions, but Maskepetoon rode on holding his Book high. And Red Sky Bird was coming to meet him, smiling and holding his hands up, empty, when suddenly from the back of the pushing horses a shot was fired. Maskepetoon pitched forward, he fell from his horse. Red Sky Bird screamed so loud his voice was heard high above all the warriors,

"What have you done?" he cried. "What have you done, stop, stop!" and he stretched his empty hands to the sun, praying for them to stop but the warriors had smelled blood, they beat their horses and rode circles around our men and cut them down screaming, there was no power could stop them and when their frenzy was at its highest they threw ropes around Maskepetoon's legs and dragged his body down the hill and round and round through the camp for the women to see, screaming their triumph as the dragging dust churned up behind them.

A young man was living in that camp. His name was Rattlesnake Boy, his father was Blackfoot but his mother Cree, and he ran to see what was happening. When he saw the torn, insulted body of Maskepetoon being hacked to pieces for the dogs, he went back to his lodge to cry. That night he slipped away, stole a horse and rode to our camp. So we learned what had happened to our great chief and ahh, how we wailed.

But before we could finish wailing there was something we had to do and next morning at dawn every warrior in our camp was at the bend in the Little Bow. There was nothing there however; the Blackfeet knew we would send a war party and had broken camp and fled. We tracked them south all the way to the Medicine Line and they crossed that and later met American traders there who gave them smallpox and that winter they came north again to escape that and then in spring we finally found the few Blackfeet that were left, weak with disease and hunger. And we killed them, we killed every one of them we could find screaming, "The Young Chief! The Young Chief!" Our peace chief Maskepetoon, The Broken Arm whom they killed when he held only the Book of his Words in his left hand, the one nearest his heart.

The air of my office tower moves like some sonorous messenger past my ear; telling me nothing. Especially not silence. The hand nearest my heart holds a book but not to any discernible purpose. Across the river, there where the Mountain and River Cree once traded, the line between land and sky is erupted by concrete and glass and glaring aluminum; only the long black bridge repeats the horizon. Perhaps my own life must be considered a continual slow turning, certainly not a spiral but more a level intermittent twisting away from things, which of course must result in an inevitable level facing of something else. I turn from whatever has become too much for me and still I am faced with the view down along my nose which is — irony is the fundamental attitude of slaves; of those who react to their world but who are not strong enough to determine or create for themselves. They live the mollusk's life of waiting and reaction, the only self-determination a supposedly superior sneer — who said that? Perhaps I thought it myself. But I could not bear my life if I thought it a sneer; I simply try to avoid the uncomfortable, and the soft Canadian life of myriad opportunity makes it so easily possible for me to make that half turn, simply away, avoid. I am no longer helpless like the young, needing flight. I am not leaving. Anything. Anyone. I will not; like Maskepetoon I want to have both rather than either, I want to encompass the entire duality spreading itself before me. I am a profess-or even when no one seems to be watching, especially then. I profess, my notes precise, nothing biasedly remembered sprawls across my desk: each word copied to the exact turn of its given comma, 'In Maskepetoon's dramatic turn to Christianity there was certainly no trace of those political motives which are so distinctly visible in other great converts of history, such as Clovis and Constantine for example. He was no absolute ruler as those men were, and it is difficult to see what else he could expect to gain [on turning to Christianity] than misconception, scorn and hatred.' That easy historian has it right; it was impossible for an Indian in the Canadian Northwest to be a 'rice Christian' when trade was the complete monopoly of the Hudson Bay Company which in two centuries had developed every commercial ad-

167

vantage from the convenient fears of pagans. And to be an avowed Christian at this university would scarcely earn anyone scorn or hatred – no modern professor would waste such emotions, supposing her or him capable of them, on anyone's religious beliefs. As for having a beautiful – mistress – I haven't thought that word before (avoided it?) but there's no question that is what they would call her, 'You can give her any nice name you want, Dyck, friend, soul-mate, muse, inspiration, spiritual partner, pal, it doesn't matter, she's a classy luscious lay, your meno-pausal (haha!) medicine, the tiger (growwwl!) to hold the terrors of your impotent forties at bay and you're double-crossing your beautiful wife,' – a certain arousal of male jealousy or feminist scorn but hardly professional persecution or ostracism, and a jealousy (scorn?) streaked with liberal envy, not hatred that professional achievement would stir – professional jealousy is the only true passion a professor can generate for a colleague, and that of course must be hidden under professional congratulations: the more deserved, the more fervently hidden with inner seething. Otherwise anything goes here, there can be no opposition to anything I care to do because nobody cares a whit what I do. Except my wife, my daughter, certainly my mother, and now perhaps ....

Ahhh I am looking for a shadow, straining for parallel. Even in mirrors I wouldn't see it. If there was something, anything in my world I could lay my body and all I am, whatever that is, on the line for, if somewhere I could put my balls where my mouth is, that would be glorious. When a policeman stands at your door night and day for years, as they sometimes do in Czechoslovakia, or you know your telephone is tapped as in Argentina because you often hear breathing there and the pounding on your door comes just before dawn, then the world becomes comprehensible, as precise as copied notes on a desk. A telephone call assumes the dimensions of heroism, a five-minute visit is a declarative political act defying an entire national system. There would be nothing brave or political in my turning, returning to Christianity – for that is what it would be; a re-turning – though I might then become precise enough to eventually be

168

a body lying before a congregation on the steps of a pulpit, a much better place than with head and shoulders slumped inside a micro-reader in a charcoal room, the small shadows of someone else's devastatingly insignificant words caught on my stiffening skin, in my mouth fallen open. I have done some small things with my life, notes re-gathered at Glenbow (my profess-or life is one unending, impeccable verification) shift and expand and shrink across my cluttered desk, details spaded into fresh air like inestimable treasure, the sudden tragic drama of a ride to my enemies as far beyond me as clean, total hatred. What enemies? I have none. I will drip and measure out my life into some intravenous tubing, hovered over by solicitous machines that will insist my mechanical juices circulate even when there is no heart muscle left, no brain cell alive to offer a signal, go! Nothing will change that, no re-turning to what I once furiously (at sixteen I was somehow capable of sustained years-long fury) cast off, 'as a dog returneth to his vomit,' the wise (noble?) Solomon said, 'so a fool returneth to his folly.'

Am I being tempted by Christianity? In what possible way? By the image of a minister who dominated two hundred families with a formulaic simplicity of ultimate salvation, finally all groans and prayers gone into that other silence, inert and flat like sod? A body destroyed by ropes in the dust?

Because what I do not believe is not enough for me. The certain temptation of Gillian drives me to the possible temptation of the personal Jesus. The temptation not of formula but of a singular certainty. 'God does not reveal himself *in* the world,' Wittgenstein asks. 'It is not how things are in the world that is mystical, but *that* it exists at all.' And Teilhard answers, 'What exactly are the essence and direction of passionate love in a universe whose stuff is personality?'

"I'm certainly not an expert in this matter," Harold Lemming must of course be boringly heavy on scholarly evasions, "but what I've read seems to imply that in the upper classes of mediaeval Christendom love was more a source of fealty, a longed-for contrast to the brutish marriages of the time that were contracted almost always for motives of gain. The theology of it was that every marriage was arranged in heaven, but among the upper classes marriage actually became a convenient way to enlarge your estate or secure your borders by contracting yourself or your son, if you had one, to the heiress daughter of some neighbouring estate, and it didn't matter if your son or you were thirty or fifty years old and your betrothed a child of ten or twelve; it was the marriage contract that mattered and so the 'heavenly arrangement' theology really underwrote the inviolability of the estate. For the woman involved, once grown, why she finds love wherever she can."

"Husbands, wives are not loved?"

"No. They're necessary to life but obstructions to love."

"But then they're always unhappy."

"No, they're happy in their unhappiness. Love cannot be happy."

"That's perverse."

"I don't know," Harold says with a mild stirring of his powerful shoulders. "We don't think people perverse today because they go around saying only love can make you happy."

I must be looking at him blankly, because he continues, "Courtly love is really the love of love, and in that sense it becomes the desire for death because the most intense love is achieved by the most intense obstruction. The secure constancy expected in Christian marriage makes such love imposs—"

The telephone clamours and I reach for it immediately.

"Excuse me ... yes?"

"James."

It is Gillian; with her husband staring meditatively at his pant cuffs six feet away.

"Yes," is all I can say again, breathing.

"What are you doing?"

"Yes." I say again and she hesitates.

"You're ... there's someone with you?"

"Yes, that's right, and I really cannot—"

I am waiting for Harold to signal and leave, but he doesn't; won't. After all, I asked him to come here.

"Good!" and she laughs deeply, "then I can tell you anything I want and you can't answer back, something shocking and you'll blush purple and you can't say a thing, oh this is marvelous, is it someone really important, a president?"

"Yes." All I can do is face the wall as if listening.

"I know, it's somebody stiff and important," she goes on, "and so you'll blush incredibly if I tell you I want to—"

I am ransacking my mind and I cut across her as levelly as I can.

"Of course, thank you for calling back. I ... I intend ... I am putting up a new fence, around my place, along the alley, and I need an auger for the posts, holes—"

"Come over here," her voice suddenly sensual as licorice, "my future's indefinite right now, come here and augur me."

Curse me for grabbing such an image.

"A posthole auger, for the posts," I mutter feebly, turning to grab a pencil from under Harold's abstracted face.

"Auger me any way you want. Come here, be my sooth-sayer, my long diviner."

"What is your address, please."

She laughs like a crash of cymbals; I squash the earphone against my ear, surely Harold must hear, and scribble a name, any name Hortense O'Shame and then her numbers, voice fluid as a woman turning in silk. It would have been a gracious address in the Edmonton of the nineteen-twenties, but now a high-rise of poured concrete, a view over the long teeth of the city and the unchangeable sweep of the banks and the river like an enormous brilliantly green snake flung down between them.

"Can you?" she asks suddenly sober. "Right now, please?"

"Thank you, I will," and I hang up. But not daring to turn to Harold seated there, oblivious, more certainly bulging with data on the mediaeval Christian systematization of land and adultery, his own address blatant on my pad! I smear an elbow across it.

"It was heresy, of course," he says finally to my back.

I turn. Pedants are so reliable. "Heresy?"

"Courtly love. The church performs marriages in the name of God; and Christ is the only true bridegroom of the church, so there can be only one true bride or groom for every believer."

"The one the church blesses?"

"Yes. Hence courtly love is of the devil."

I can but stare at this big tweedy academic. The devil. She has lain in his arms and held him within herself and cried out, she loves him, those very hands.

"After all," he bores on with devastating logic, "if Jesus personalizes the creator and goodness into someone he calls God the Father, then surely he must also personalize evil into someone, that is Satan the Destroyer. Mustn't he? After all, there are both in the world, good and evil."

Whose soft lovely wife opened her young body, arms and legs, to me in ecstasy. God and the horned Devil!

"There's a train going over the High Level Bridge."

"Hmmm."

"It has one–two–three blue Alberta Heritage cars, one wheat-sprout Government of Canada car ... and no Saskatchewan car at all. Discrimination."

"Who cares."

"And one big engine pushing seven cars. Wasting taxpayers' money."

"CPR is private."

"And still gets half its income from the public purse."

"I don't care."

"What do you care about?"

"Not counting boxcars."

"It's such a fine view."

"Fine to get tired of."

"Even from the floor?"

"Even. The shortest distance between two points, straight and black."

"You don't like straight black lines."

"Nothing natural is straight."

172

"A body, any body falling?"

"Down."

She says and I raise myself up on one elbow. She lies on her stomach, a five-pointed slender star, face hidden against a thin cushion. At this instant I am overwhelmed to see such a body simply lying there, being. I have to savour her, I have to run my tongue from one heel along the ineffable back wishbone of her legs to the other, then from her centre up to her neck; and settle myself into her every indentation.

"Hello my friend," I say through flung hair against her right ear.

She mutters something into the cushion.

"What?"

"We're not friends."

"Then what are we?"

"We'll never be friends, we're adulterers."

"Hey." Even into the cushion it sounds ugly. "We're adults all right but—"

"No no, Latin *adulteratus,* to defile, to corrupt by adding impure, base materials."

"Isn't that Latin *adulterium?*"

"You looked it up too."

"Not now, years ago."

"Why were you interested then?"

"Well, 'adult' and 'adult-ery,' they're so close, I wondered why they had such different meanings."

"Why do they?"

"I still don't know."

"You know."

"I don't, really."

"If you don't lying on top of me, you're not very smart."

"I'm smart enough."

"I know. You know they're not different."

"What?"

"They're the same thing."

"Is that why we can't be friends, we're adults?"

She mutters something while trying to burrow out of sight in that tiny cushion. I touch my tongue in her ear.

"I can't hear, I'm a base material?"

173

Abruptly she rolls herself and me over, I am on my back on the floor and she is stretched out upon me. She lectures the stippled ceiling:

"We cannot be friends because we are lovers."

"Mutually exclusive?"

"You do this with your friends."

"Not till now."

"And you never will. Could you walk into a high-rise party now and see me across the room and just come over with a drink in you hand, 'Hi, how're things, courses going okay?' Are you crazy?"

"'All our life is like a dream, but in our better hours we awaken just enough to know that we are dreaming. Most of the time, however, we are fast asleep.'"

"Who said that?"

"Didn't you hear?"

"Come on!"

"Wittgenstein."

"Well, I've woken up, just enough."

"With me you can't dream?"

"Not of friendship you silly ass."

"Come back to sleep."

"Wake up!"

She does not move; I am shrinking in the warm fold of her buttocks soft inside my hips. Her insistence a slick of ice between us.

"Why do you do this?"

"We're both doing it."

"Don't play games."

"It takes two."

"You're twenty years older, you should know better."

"When a beautiful woman appears from nowhere, sits down on my lap and kisses me?"

"Tell her to go home."

"You wouldn't have listened."

"Do you have any idea how long I ... just turn me around and send me home."

"With a pat on your nice ass, go girlee bye bye."

"Nobody pats me, not ever!"

174

"So what would it have helped?"

"Then why didn't you invite me and Harold to your house for dinner?"

"To ... eat, with Liv and Becca ... Harold?"

"He has excellent table manners."

"Dinner, at home?"

"Don't you know anything about short-circuiting these things?"

"But you suggested Calgary and—"

"You're older, you should be smarter about this."

"And you're feeling guilty all of a sudden."

"No." With a hunch of muscles she rolls off me a quarter turn; she may be staring along the carpet and out the glass balcony doors straight down the tracks of the black bridge to the city piled on the other bank. She says slowly, "Love is not a matter of guilt."

"Do you love me?"

Her back-body remains motionless. And I am suddenly cold; I want her warm, I want to see her eyes but I'm not sure I could face them. This is no Rocking Chair Lounge graduate course; no easy word of capture here, or friend. Certainly not friend.

"I could still take you home," I say at last. "For dinner."

"It's too late."

"Why?"

"What do you think we were telling each other this morning."

In retrospect, who knows what he has told anyone else? Words being what they are, irretrievable. There is certainly no simple two-hundred mile flight home on the airbus from here. Nor have I ever before lain naked on anyone's floor, and something black twists in me, he pays the rent, it's his floor too.

"If you just want to get laid differently you could just walk across the campus, find yourself some muscled frisbee chewer."

"I guess ... I should have."

"No questions, no problems, in, out, finished."

"No. In, finished, out."

"That's what I find so thrilling about you, your sense of humour."

But her body is shaking; she is crying almost aloud, as her tone told me. She turns, curled, and we hold each other tight.

"Why does saying 'I love you' make so much difference?"

"Why does it make us sad?"

"Yes."

"It shouldn't, we should be happy...."

"I know women who would kill, I mean it, just to feel once what we've felt together, again and again."

"Is it so rare?"

"Don't men ever talk about that?"

"Not to me."

"Women talk about it all the time, women who have never, never in their lives come with a man. They're just sick of wanting that."

"Orgasm isn't everything."

"I know. But it is so good when you make me come and come. I'd be crazy to give you up."

"Even if you feel awful?"

"At that moment I feel ... totally and completely myself and completely with you, in a way I'm wiped clean of everything and in another way I've never lived so absolutely in all my mind and body. Like I was electrified...."

"Singing?"

"Yes, singing but not just one voice, a whole orchestra, being yourself and a whole orchestra, together, you understand?"

"Could we be friends if it wasn't for sex?"

She is curled like a ball against my stomach, the skin over her knobbled spine grained faintly red by the rug pattern.

"It's not the sex, is it?"

"No," she says then. "That's never it."

"I am not depriving anyone of anything with this sexual act."

Her black eyes flick up at me instantly; she will not, we have agreed wordlessly that there will be no words between us on what she is thinking—but why not. Why can't I tell her that when I came home I wanted Liv with an incredible intensity of difference, of doubleness and something rediscovered? If I am depriving no one of anything, why don't, can't I tell her that sexuality is suddenly a much larger terrain in a world I long ago thought I had completely explored, forever, stupidly thought so? Because she thinks this too with her husband?

"You haven't told her about meeting me, have you."

"No."

"That's it, the lies."

"It's just to protect...."

"Of course, dear god we sound like a tv soap."

"Living a French novel."

"No need for melodrama, we just disappear."

"Yes! Now cash, let's see maybe four thousand in the joint account, six in the trust company ... say five, six thousand."

"I only have about two hundred...."

"Well, wait till the end of the month."

"Great, six hundred more."

"Fly to ... where, an island?"

"As far as possible."

"The absolutely farthest place in the world from Edmonton is Kerguelen Island, sixteen thousand miles away straight through the molten centre of the earth. Owned by France too."

"Kerguelen? Yes, France, who lives there?"

"A few penguins, I think, and whales. The Japanese arrive every other year to hunt rorquals."

"Not even a weather station?"

"I don't think so."

"Where is this?"

"On a big curve south, three and a half thousand miles from Capetown on the sea to Perth."

"Sounds cold."

"It's absolutely miserable."

"How'd we get there?"

"I don't know, catch a whaler?"

"We have to go fast and it has to be hot."

"Yeah, I don't want you wearing clothes in the house, ever."

"I'd love that, and we'd save so much money."

"How about Fiji?"

"Hmmm ... their hair is frizzy."

"Seychelles?"

"The Indian Ocean ... there are really only two places, Singapore or Rio."

"Okay, wherever the plane goes first. If it's Rio, we'll become voodooists."

"Or buddhists in Singapore."

"You'll want a bicycle to get around."

"Perfect. You can research the history of the Brazilian sand dollar on a beach grant and I'll play jazz piano for a supper club. We will turn quite brown."

"And love each other browner every night."

"It's all the necessary lying," she says as if bending to a stone. "I do love my husand."

"I love my wife and daughter."

"And your mother."

"O god, yes."

"We could run away to the medicine wheel."

"'Love is a wheel,'" I quote to her. "'Its spokes are hope and its hub faith.'"

"'Hope' as in 'anticipation'?"

"Part of that, maybe more faith as 'the substance of things hoped for, the evidence of things not seen.'"

"You mean like 'blind'?"

"There are some powerful realities one can't see."

"Such as?" she asks flat on the floor of the place where they live.

"Trust."

"We've known each other exactly one week!"

"And all I have with you is ... hope."

"Why?"

"I have no holds on you."

"Like family, like a common mortgage?"

"Sure, or promises too. Nothing like that."

"Me coming into the Micro room wasn't that?"

"Of course it was, but you may walk out too in a minute."

"I have even less from you, I at least came there."

"I came here."

"I asked you, you know I'm a pretty good lay."

"Is that what you think I think?"

"How can I tell?"

"Is that what you felt at the medicine wheel?"

"No ... I could tell there."

"Can't you tell here?"

"Yes. But I can't tell tomorrow."

"Neither can I, neither can anyone. Even a shared mortgage doesn't amount to much."

"I could get the police after you."

"And they'd force me into your bed at gunpoint?"

We have said it all, all the little pieces of it we can gather up at this moment since there is certainly a great deal more of it to be lived. We are at stasis. The ordered necklaces of our lives seem to have burst, the beads—pearls I hope pearls— have scattered all over the floor, scattered together and it's shocking to discover how unsortable mine suddenly are from a young woman's whose existence was no more to me than an 'x' on an unremembered form a week ago.

Her body uncoils, her arm reaches past the couch upon which we first lay: at the piano leg a lined writing pad, words inked and scribbled out.

"I wrote this," she says, "when I came back, that's why I phoned you."

She said nothing at all when she unhooked the chain on her door; simply engulfed me. And I listen to her read now, after she is ready:

There's a name for this.
Consorting with the enemy;
betrayal.

But oh, my lovely enemy,
here between my empty palms
the echoes of your bone and blood
stay ringing.

Pleasuring with the enemy is
an outrage punishable

by endless measure upon measure upon
measure.

Not longer partisan
but traitors each to our own side,
how can we ever justify ourselves?
My enemy, my own,
we're adamantly traitors.
Pleasure taken
can never-be revoked
and where's necessity
to lend us virtue or sufficient
reason.

Only ecstasy.
And that's a simple loyalty:
> *a cry,*
> *a mouth,*
> *a faint and longing bruise,*
> *the long curve of a muscled back*
in silver light that slides between venetian blinds,
the silver light that seals out
all our savage loyalties
and our forgotten causes.

Consorting with the enemy; we
can only close our eyes,
wrestle in another slippery fight
as honorable foes.

For oh, my lovely enemy
if you and I were friends,
we'd blast all causes
blind all light
make pleasure sprout in grass
and wake the farthest stonefields with our cries.
Better we stay enemies,
my enemy; my own.

"It has to be possible."

"Do you really think so?" she asks against my lips.

"Otherwise why have we been given each other, to want?"

The brilliant light of the long May afternoon darkens slightly over us. And I sense a distant shiver, almost as if the girders of the building were flexing steel muscles. She says softly,

"Lay your ear against the floor. Do you hear that?"

And I do, then.

"A train," she says. "A long one on the black bridge."

THE BLACK BRIDGE

There is a certain moment before dawn in an Edmonton summer, they say, when a mist fills the river valley like water fills the hollow of a winding lake. The enormous, slightly sagging line of the High Level Bridge, which spans that space where the banks lean in closest over the river, is hidden then and for a moment the sounds of birds waking under the trees and gables of city houses are silenced, and out of the white mist one can hear the bridge, singing. It sings with the voices of all those who have fallen from its high, cold steel, fallen down into treetops, into water, onto inexorable ice.

No one has ever seen a long train spill like seeds from the bridge, nor a streetcar, automobile, wagon or truck, and perhaps they never have because individual vehicles can move only through the spacey tunnel of girders below its top and the train down a single track centred above them, though open to the sky. But many have seen people falling, the riveters transfixed by their three companions' gentle twisting spiral from the tip of steel reaching for the north bank of the river, the Christmas or Easter morning motorist crunching his fender into a pillar as he flings his car door open, screaming at the naked girl who swings first one leg over the rail, and then the other, and then is gone.

They say the half mile of bridge is held together by two million one hundred and thirty thousand steel rivets, one for each dollar it cost to build in 1913; they also say that six hundred and seventy-two people have fallen from it. No proof is offered for either statistic, and perhaps there is none; except the anthem heard only at the moment before dawn when white mist dry as snow levels the valley and the bridge vanishes and the log church that broods over both, and may materialize once in any person's lifetime where the steel enters the north bank, the unseen church is about to offer its hewn columns and cupolas and unused porticos like a blind face to the coming sun. Perhaps then it is also true that at that moment the bridge itself is unnecessary; that a human being could cross the wide valley on the mist, on the final amazement of that incredible, terrifying song.

SEPTEMBER
ONE

In winter, he remembered, the grey roofs above Blackmud Creek blended into the delicate hoar of bushes like architects' trees frosted on blueprints, but in early September the houses now appeared to him like slabs of slate jagged between green mottled by summer heat, the trees against the cliffs sheered off above the creek now variously touched with yellow and orange. Orange, as if small fires had been lit everywhere in this gaping, twisting crevasse between careful suburbs and soon the entire sprawl of it would be aflame to the very banks of the North Saskatchewan River; when all things truly, and all creatures would confess their ashes.

"Did I ever tell you," he said to Liv, trying to be usual, "this was once part of the original Papa-chase reserve? They let themselves be robbed of it in 1888 for about five hundred dollars a square mile."

"Just watch where you're driving," she was peering down the road scratched across the valley's blackish flank. "There are a lot more potholes here than buffalo."

So he hit one, deliberately; the Volvo staggered, shuddered like a shaggy beast and Liv almost thudded up against its watermarked ceiling.

"James!"

He sang without tune, "'Though the road leading down be rough and steep, I go to the de-epths to fi-ind my sheep, I go to the ... '"

"Don't be grotesque!"

"Ira B. Sankey. Scared more people into heaven with song than all of Moody's sermons."

Liv shook herself, silently, a small haze of autumn dust rising about her from the tufted surfaces of the car. If she had not been glaring so hard at him, as he told her soon after, she would have had time to scream before they rear-ended the limousine halted just around a sharp bend. As it was, he saw it and she screamed a bit late.

James sat rammed motionlessly forward in a long moment. This road was nothing but a scar, it jerked almost at right angles around a sliding coal-streaked bank: because of it he could not see why the Lincoln had stopped and the instant before they hit he had seen Liv's angry face through the dust of his silly song and he had felt like a lovely effortless swimmer wafting downward into that final green spasm of evening light, an effluence of both dreaming water and fire. His heart still shuddered between that image and this sudden, as it seemed, annihilation; seatbelt burned across gut and shoulder.

And the car shivering with Liv's cry; her mouth still open. He touched her shoulder and gradually she looked at him. Silent. He felt for the door handle then, to get out and perform the usual car-accident necessities, but her hand groped for his at the belt-buckle, her face pale in fierce, frightened beauty.

"We shouldn't be going down here," he said softly.

Level sunlight was a spear through her eyes.

"I know it, never," he said again. "It's no good."

"It's so hard to get reservations, everyone says it's …" she was saying exactly what she had said when she first brought the two reservations home and dropped them on the kitchen table, printed bits like detonators simply waiting a connection, but now she stopped abruptly. He was halfway out the door and he leaned his face toward hers.

"Sweetheart, are you all right?"

"This thing," she gestured at the belt crossed between her breasts and he touched one moving under silk. "It really works."

185

"Thank God," he brushed her lips with his fingertips and got out. Autumn like blue smoke prickled in his nose, with a flare of gasoline and in the same sensation he swore at himself and this stupid limo driver and all stupid Edmontonians clammering to get down here, if somehow he had hit this hearse's enormous gas tank – but by a miraculous industrial coincidence their bumpers had met dead-centre, their Volvo's bumpers had recoiled inward, as they should, and nothing at all had really – just then the huge black vehicle lurched away from him, forward, down the steep incline it might have been hesitating to tilt into moments before, its round cushioned windows too dark to distinguish any shape or even number of heads inside. Leaving him to stand as if he did not exist on a splotch of tacky tar.

"Why didn't they get out?" Liv asked. "Did you see who it was?"

A car horn blatted behind them; he buckled himself tight, settled, carefully shifted into gear.

"There was nobody in it," he said. "It's empty."

"What?"

"It's just a black message, sent to us not to go down here."

It seemed to him momentarily that the road had been scraped out for hoofed animals; he and Becca and Liv and Tolstoi had hiked in the valley for years and never seen it. How had they ever hauled coal out on this, 1927 to 1972? Here for a space the gravel leveled, circling along a raw cliff though the limousine was not visible ahead, and he realized Liv had said nothing. He glanced at her, a silver Porsche 911 hanging on his left rear bumper as if trying to nudge him to a decision.

"Sent by whom?" she said.

"Maybe by 'what.'"

"You'll have to go to the very bottom anyway, to turn around."

"Don't you want to go now?" he asked, concentrating on the road that bent down again.

"I don't like accidents," she said.

"Accidents are better than intentions," and he laughed.

186

"Nothing happened. Our bumpers met and really it's okay, nothing happened."

"Are you sure?"

"Sure."

As confidently as he could steering at a crawl, gearing down. He would not admit again, even in his thoughts, why his heart had leaped when she got reservations for this evening of all possible evenings. The road dipped abruptly and in ten seconds ended under giant poplars in a small puddle of cars.

"I don't believe this," he said. "The most expensive, secretive club in western Canada and it has a gravelled clearing to park in. It's more ludicrous than the road."

"If you're exclusive enough it doesn't matter," Liv said. "There's space there, to turn around."

"You had to pay for those reservations?"

"Och, you Mennonite!"

"Then there's no way!" He laughed and she laughed a little too as he eased the Volvo forward between two vehicles, both of them suddenly lifted from their astonishing depression at driving down into the Blackmud Valley where they often struggled through parkland brush and Becca would insist it was the Cold Lake homestead with Tolstoi's shovel nose following he never knew what, lifted back to the anticipation they had felt while dressing and for him the happy apprehension of seeing Gillian here somewhere after three weeks' vacation in Rome when they got inside the door, he knew he would because she had told him in summer that Harold had reservations at The Mine for September first and they had talked five minutes on the phone this morning, while Harold unpacked in the bedroom, and he would hardly have to pretend surprise at their meeting he would be so happy, the introductions necessary and perhaps he could sit beside her and ask her about the eternal city and touch the length of her thigh with his—for a few minutes, what about that? What did people do here, just eat and drink? He had no idea, perhaps all evening. And he could see nothing but trees over the glaring roofs of the vehicles, nothing; not so much as the top of a building or a door flickering in the heat. It was devastating heat; as if they had contorted their way into a barranca.

"There's that car," Liv stood looking across the lot. "That black one."

He bent to lock his door. "I'm not looking at it. It doesn't exist."

Through the car windows he sensed her stiffen. The Porsche chortled to a stop at his heels and he straightened to see Liv staring at the long black roof and a very tall man sticking out over it. Six six at least, enormous. The trees and the cliffs and the blazing car surfaces buckling about that head and shoulders seeming to melt into a shapelessness as flat and unsubstantial as an instinctive lie. Or the prayer for eventual release.

"It's Cedric Whitling-Holmes," Liv was saying, or saying again. "He's got himself another car."

"Oh."

"The cabinet minister."

There was no possible avoidance it seemed. She was already moving ahead between fires, her hair itself a monochromatic flame.

"Ah, Mrs. Dyck," voice booming, "fancy seeing you here. How utterly delightful!"

The English immigrant incongruity in a provincial cabinet distinguished by dull, dutiful lawyers; a massive imperial accent that had purchased his party many a good opinion where none would have seemed natural otherwise. Already resources minister, second only to the Leader himself, O he sounds so cultured, so utterly ... cultured! Cultivated with never a plow.

"Your new car is quite lovely," Liv said, even she sliding into fruit-edged talk.

"Quite. Long enough for my legs." He laughed, "Some idiot or other just tried to knock me heel over scuppers off that terrible road, oh, have you met my wife? Rikki, this is Liv Dyck, the marvelous travel agent who used to tell you all my flight plans on the phone."

"Before your husband inherited his government jet."

"Charmed, I'm sure."

London, East End. Charmingly bucked teeth, a ruddy face of probably mindless laughter, and breasts fit for those enormous paws: a perfect conservative wife except she was too young by a quarter of a century at least, how could he stump the province with such a popsy tailing him? Why, he left her supine in the limo or accentedly sucking round chocolates the length of a hotel bed.

" … my husband, James Dyck," Liv's lips awry at him pondering those naked shoulders in the shimmery light leeching red through poplars.

"How-do-you-do!" Whitling-Holmes engulfed James' hand, though not annihilating it as he might have.

"Hello." There was no point in mentioning they had once met at a computer demonstration in South Bend, Indiana in an earlier business incarnation for them both; not while that huge left hand was still massaging that neck-post for whip-lash. Rikki's superbly folded musculature was obviously more resilient, she could take any unexpected jolting and no doubt had, from any direction, but what she said then was as blind-siding as a rear-ender.

"What a gorgeous man," directly at him. Crunching close over gravel and leading with her thighs as some women do on high heels, her bare arms reaching so his hand was closed between hers and he knew her for one of those effusive liars though her palms were warm as thighs closing and when his smothered hand balled into a fist her eyes widened enormously as if with a bit more evidence she could actually be convinced of what she had said.

And behind her Liv was laughing; she slipped from wry to laughter while he extricated his fist with a moist sigh. "Not bad, not bad," she exclaimed as though they two were bartering on a village street, her accent as deliberately bald as short-grass prairie, "if he grew five more inches he'd be as gorgeous as Whit."

"How about a trade?" Rikki grinned, fishwife incarnate.

"Straight across?" Liv countered and a twitch of incomprehension, almost a crease heaven forbid, smudged Rikki's gorgeous brow. "I'll throw in a badly used Volvo for nothing."

James discovered Whitling-Holmes on the edge of a leer, his iron-curly hair fairly bristled; all he needed was a fired pitchfork.

"You want to inspect my teeth, before you shake hands?" James asked Rikki, leaning forward, molars bared.

"Teeth aren't really my interest, my dear," and she patted the top of his head.

Whitling-Holmes' guffaw splatted about the poplar clearing and scattered a few brilliant leaves, no doubt. And his voice announcing:

"You all seem in particularly fine fettle for The Mine. We'll have a lovely evening, come along then, Liv."

She accepted his arm as if by right and they zagged away between tight cars; there remained nothing for James but to offer the same to Rikki, who was still shaking in various places from her giggle.

"I've heard the most terrible things about this place," she shivered in anticipation, moist weight in the bend of his elbow. "Whit thought perhaps he should come incognito."

"How could he, indelible as he is?"

"Easily. Look at that."

She had seen more than he; for a moment he thought she was indicating the manufactured redhead passing between cars beside them and rentable no doubt in that mint condition from any modelling agency, but it was the woman's companion, a tall draped figure, hooded, its face hidden by a mask that must have been designed for a hockey goalie. Pointed like a beak of a gigantic predatory bird, designed in livid red and blue slashes to deflect pucks at ninety-seven miles an hour, unshatterable plastic and the mouth a small protruding zero shaped only for sucking.

"What gender is that?" James asked, amazed.

"Only search would tell," Rikki chuckled. "Anyway, what does it matter?"

"Well I once thought there were essential differences, requiring you know either codpiece or brassiere ... a differentiation almost ..." her high heels in the gravel balanced her as surely as the trees running in light gently overhead, flushed scarlet, "vital, but I guess that's irretrievably nineteenth century where I spend most of my waking hours. Though the brassiere did not exist until 1912."

"It didn't? Whatever did they wear?"

What, what, when would she get to how? "They didn't become popular until the thirties." He did not bother to think why she was so easy to natter to though Liv would have instantly offered a suggestion, "A very large opera diva, soprano, Madame Grisl Haeklenwurst if my memory serves, found herself uncomfortable singing, probably she couldn't wear a high tight girdle breathing so deeply and rather than leave her unmajestically pendant a gallant Frenchman, it would have to be a Frenchman, invented a ... well two ..." he gestured with hands cupped and she was laughing in rhythm with his upward gesture, she might momentarily have been a Chaplin heroine though far too rubensesque. "It gave such enormous relief to her diaphragm, reaching high Cs."

Gillian would have broken up over that one, but verbal niceties were no more Rikki's forté than teeth. It appeared Liv and that giant had followed the indeterminate pair around a cutbank; he saw now it wasn't rock at all, rather a processed plastic barrier glued together from the photograph of a Blackmud Creek cliff.

"1913," he tried again, "the year of the High Level Bridge a Frenchman named Aristotle Robespierre rescued mankind from the shapeless chemise and the strangling girdle. Only pantyhose was a larger step for mankind."

"You seem to know everything." Rikki was a little breathless, from what he could not say. The camouflaged corner had hidden a bolt-studded door of planks under an arch of rocks. Plastic too? They've even got their motifs crossed, stupid Albertans, mine and castle. Would a Japanese garden be rippling inside just because they could afford it?

"Maybe I seem to, for a little while," he smiled down the length of Rikki's nose into her tremendous décolletage so artfully contrived it seemed unpowdered. "When we've known each other a few more minutes you'll understand

191

what kind of historian I really am."

"What kind is that?"

"Inventive. 'History,' declared Professor Michael Oakeshott, footnoting Professor Collingwood, 'is the historian's experience.'"

"What does that mean?"

"Whatever you want."

"In school they always told us history was what had happened."

"Hopelessly nineteenth century. Happened to whom?"

"Oh ... kings, people like that."

"There are no more kings. We now shoot republicans at the moon."

Fortunately at that instant a grated slot unnoticeable in the planks slid aside or he would have been forced to discover more of her cliché/empty mind. And revealed his own? ... he should manage for the evening ... if only it wasn't too dark in there to accidentally recognize someone ... the other two couples had disappeared as if into some apprehension but he had no time to consider that for the eyes and mouth at the hole said, "Reservations," and he was pulling them from his breast pocket, unfakeable coal-tar mauve, and the mouth said immediately, "Okay, down."

And it must have been down they went for sky and the incandescent leaves vanished above them and he realized there was no superscription on the planks over the door because there was no door, that no ceremonial ring of fire would welcome them here only blackness, thrust up so swiftly around them there was no sensation whatever of down; on his arm Rikki could not even gasp before the darkness clampled shut above them with a clang and they were breathing suddenly together, enormously aware of their panting as if to compensate for their useless eyes and they were feeling, clutching for each other in this abruptly terrifying deprivation.

"James!"

She was too large. A soft tree, he had no image of face, no idea whether his eyes were open or shut until his bare eyeballs nubbed skin, her voice then with his name seeming

192

double as if he held both Gillian and Liv transliterated into each other, voice and face and body exploding more than familiar but simply too much of them together as if he had been blown entirely to the ends of his fingers, though that was what had materialized in different beds and floors and office chairs and all summer, in this darkness it was screamingly possible, both together beyond sight and any dream and guilt and unbelievability swallowed into a globe so black it was unseeable anyway up, down, right, left, front, back, all orientation gone in this equidistant unfathomable richness between his arms and hands and legs along his body, his face pressed into this one metamorphosis of inevitable woman he was seeing with his tongue and just too rich to contain merely one, still growing larger, he could control nothing while he wanted everything.

"I'm sure the light will be on in a sec."

Like a revelation he saw Rikki's face: immediately in the cool accent of her voice with his long tongue dry. A face so stunning in profile, so lengthily horsish head-on. Though the English might still instruct the deepest provinces how things must be done, in a world of revolutionary colonels they were now at best unrufflable butlers, their unexcelled taste like a worn hand-carved wooden mask when all the universe displayed machined plastic. It was the road, the blazing valley descent, the unexpected lurch into one sense deprivation: like being slammed sideways into dream without the warning of sleep. Rikki, good grief what a child's name, Rikki.

"I'm sorry," he managed, backing away, feeling his hands fall from her shoulders past her breasts, but she found them immediately and brought them up, her breath still against his face as if wanting his inside her.

"You were screaming a little," she said gently, not at all flustered. "Gilliv, something like that, Gilliv? ..."

He caught his gasp in a twitch of horror, trying to laugh it aside. "It was that quick drop, nonsense, my nonsense left hanging in the air. They should warn you, they must lose a few with weak hearts."

"We're still going down."

193

And so they were; when he concentrated he was aware of a sensation more delicate than her hair against his face. A strange woman hooked to his arm and his head so full of smart-ass that with one jerk every sense had betrayed him, before this woman he had stupidly assumed stupid. He was so furious with himself he wanted to spit fire but of course that was beyond him too and it would have illuminated too much here; there was nothing to be done but give praise for darkness and swallow bile.

"They do call it The Mine, you know," she said against his beard.

He realized he had been expecting a cave. He did not want to taste her in darkness, his mind's eye was not good enough, he needed light and he needed to be away from her, this feeling of enormous fusion was asinine: if he was spinning like this at the mere entrance, what would he do inside when Liv and Gillian, dear god, were perhaps actually together before him – perhaps he should avoid that, perhaps for the good of his soul (if he still had one after all this summer, and he did, he more certainly did) he had better avoid that – he swallowed again, bitterness and fire.

"Well," he reached for anything, having no idea what he had been about to begin, "it seems pretty clear, doesn't it, I mean, why they insist on having couples only? What they do, here."

He sounded so sententious even to himself that he wasn't surprised when she loosened from him; only vaguely relieved.

"They're probably watching us, they probably watch everyone coming down."

"What? In this hellishly dark...."

"What can't they do with cameras these days?"

She was of course absolutely right, but the implications of that could no more than tweak him before actual light dawned, Rikki was an outline and then bluish lips and eye-hollows and forehead and immediately where he was staring space opened to sound: of applause. Someone, apparently many people could see them and appreciated it, them and also the masked, hooded shape whirling just beyond them which he now saw fumbling clumsily into the existence of light, like a bulging column of swarming sparrows and there was the little redhead materializing as it seemed out of folds and imperturbable plastic, her body still, twisted as if cast into molten steel: either she had known of this descent and was a brilliant contortionist or she was catatonic with terror. Rikki had shifted around out of his clasp and was applauding too as the postured pair swung toward them, themselves motionless on what could have been moving platforms. The mask, the beautiful woman sprouting up, straightening to face him.

"Don't tell me a wig and a pushup bra fool you, Jim."

It was Gillian's voice; he registered only make-up clichés, and then abruptly he saw her: that was her snakish body! His mind tolled literally blank, blank, were those the bones he had felt so lovely, and they paused for an instant past Rikki's shoulder as if both couples on twirling turntables had hesitated on a programmed point. Out of the grotesque sucking mask he heard the sound that Harold Lemming had imagined for a silly lifetime was an ironic laugh.

"We were in the car right behind you," Harold's voice muffled by hockey mask and snigger. How inappropriate, James thought, the first time I meet them together, and could only ask,

"You drive a Porsche?"

"If one must live in Edmonton, one needs all the help one can get," and they were gone, twitched like icepans spinning away on an ocean eddy.

It was the first time he had ever seen them together, and he felt a spasm of joy that he had not recognized them. Gillian was here, yes, but unrecognizable where all his life and country senses saw and Harold appeared as silly as he had ever been, only import pretensions to disguise him, and there was Liv standing motionless while coming towards him, her hand still hooked with that unrufflable grace on the arm of Whitling-Holmes, o, how he had missed her, his rock in a weary land and he wanted her like the sudden warm touch of a tongue. As the applause trickled out beyond the lights surrounding them their movement coincided and he stepped across to Liv, leaving Rikki to do what she chose.

"It's a delight to see you again," he bowed, trying to laugh and she looked directly into his eyes, pupils enormous and asking, and then she came to him from Whitling-Holmes as easily as ever she had left any bear-skinned doorman. "You disappeared so quick," he murmured. "I didn't know, where did you go."

"You miss me?"

"Hey!" he held her facing him, filling his two hands, "I came here with you, don't run off with the first big big-shot you see!"

"Well, you ran off with the first beautiful woman."

It was all perfectly banal and hilariously funny of course and they were all four laughing together like the cool, unrufflable people they of course were in any company even if the edges of their words cut closer to their feelings than their laughter could admit. The low light brightened about them into distance where people sat around tables, glasses and candles and gleaming foreheads winking, gesturing welcome, and by some extravagance of floor machinery all six new arrivals were turned in one direction, side by side, and attendants stood there with arms poised ready to hand down the women.

"Watch your step please," one attendant said. "Tables for two or four or six please?"

"What do you say Dyck?" it was obvious Whitling-Holmes so convivially had already decided. "If your friends here," he gestured at the mask while staring at Gillian, "would they care to join us?"

"Well ... fine ... " James said, "if you—"

"Do you know them?" Liv asked, not incredulous at all.

"Why sure, they're the Lemmings, from my department. Harold and Gillian Lemm—"

"Oh!" Liv laughed, "I'd have never recognized you."

"That's the whole point," Harold whistled through his mask.

"Really, Dr. Dyck," Gillian began at the same time.

"Oh sorry, sorry," and he guffawed loudly to interrupt her tone, "at least, the transfigured Dr. Harold Lemming, and his

196

gorgeous wife Gillian Overton, nowadays it's hard to make connections, it's just—"

"Would you step down please," one waiting attendant said, arm still up. He wore a beaver cap and fringed buckskin closed high at his neck.

Whitling-Holmes glanced down at him as if an adjacent post had spoken. But Rikki moved immediately, and then they all stepped to the rock of The Mine floor.

"There must be others coming down, Whit," she said.

"Table for six," Whit declared. "The more the merrier."

Liv left James' arm for the waiter's and they trailed a certain order into what seemed a rock cavern crowded on all sides by people clustered about tables; bluish video light shimmered on their faces, cancelling candles and a low radiance diffused from below, somewhere, to create a kind of distance like heat on open prairie but not golden, silverishly gold somehow. And then he realized they were simply walking a narrow aisle crowded between narrow tables for two and the depth surrounding them was two parallel mirrors infinitely repeating each other's images. Finally, he thought, here is my country inside glass ... reduced to the size of two walls.

"Gorgeous my ass!" it was Gillian twisted around to him hissing, her lips slashed straight across her hollowed white face. "I'll gorgeously connect you!"

James blurted out, instinctively covering such excesses here with his own, "We started upstairs in the parking lot, talking gorgeous, it just stuck in my ... craw."

Whit loomed beyond her, turning, over her, "What, what was that?"

She was too angry to bother changing her tone. "It's a stupid word!"

The huge politician almost hipped a woman onto her table, but recovered and stood still looking back; he managed almost to manoeuvre himself beside Gillian despite intrusive flanks, the back ends of chairs.

"What word?"

"'Gorgeous.' It's so ... down-putting, contemporarily puerile!"

Whit snorted, finely amused. "Wait till you've been down here a bit longer, Ms. Overton, and mere words will pale."

"Who are you?" Gillian demanded.

"I'm sorry," James blundered in, "when we get to the table I'll...."

But Whitling-Holmes would make his own introduction; all James had to do was follow the unnatural gleam of her hair, the superb shift of her body he now knew certainly like a devastation under cloth, there never would have been a doubt had he seen that first, 'when as in silks my Julia's free, o how that glittering taketh me.'

Their table apparently was to be one of a cluster at the enlargement where several mineshafts intersected; here the endless multiplying mirrors showed gaps. James discovered himself backed against the edge of one with the brittle glister of the coal seam behind it. Liv was seating herself opposite him, chair handled easily by the sucking mask; Whit already had a chair for Gillian in his paws so there was nothing to do but to assist Rikki, who must be on his right. She was already seated, not having waited for regalities.

Abruptly he ached to talk with Gillian; he had not seen her in three weeks and for that moment she was the only person there to talk to or hold or love and she within an inch of his left sat like a silken stone and already he had shoved distance like anathema between them with his stupid chauvinistic 'gorgeous' and there was Liv looking at everything except him, she would get over the surprise of six, maybe she had really wanted only two, as in a way he had wanted also, two, though with both of them at a table with him, he had to face that, there was no avoiding it. Two? Or three? Five dear god. There was a kind of rush in the air he was breathing. He felt it; as if he were being hyperventilated from behind the mirror, his awareness snagging on bits of now that made no substantive present. The coal crumbled when his finger touched it – soft prairie seam, too shallow to bother cutting, here – and he sagged in the leather chair where the enormous white of tablecloth draped over his lap – and immediately Gillian's knee touched his. There was surely the length of her thigh, touching silk, his heart leaping. He dared then to

198

glance quickly at her, but she was talking to Whit, no words it seemed, just the inimitable voice above him flat on the floor without moving her leg away and he staring up into sunlight a blazing canopy over them.

"Do you think your fine friend Jesus ever did this with a woman?"

"I don't know ... this?"

"Take it easy, take it easy, don't hurry, just ... yes, do you think so?"

"It's hard to tell."

"If he was a great man he—"

"None greater."

"Okay, he was, could he be a great man do you think without ever doing this?"

"I don't know, any more."

She sits motionless on him, he reaching up inside her and her arms braced against his ribs pushing her pendant breasts together. The windows of her living room burn around the black piano.

"Would it help you to know, right now, if I moved?"

"Not very much. It's more or less ... blasphemy."

"More than less. As blasphemous as a John Donne sonnet, too full of sting and sensuality to be properly spiritual too."

"Don't don't move please, please ... 'Yet dearly I love you and would be loved fain/ But am betrothed unto your enemy' ... that's not such a good line, for me."

"For either of us, my friend."

"I was trying to get to the last lines, you know."

"Yes. 'Take me ... for I,/ Except you enthrall me, never shall be free,/ Nor ever chaste except ... '" she stares down at him, eyes widening. "What?"

"'Except you ravish me,'" he completes.

"You can't ravish me."

"Why not?"

"I'd stop you."

"How?"

"Like this, and, like this."

So for a few moments they say nothing in that roaring sunlight lifting them across the floor.

"There's another sonnet that's even better," she says slowly. "It starts, 'Show me, dear Christ, thy spouse so bright and clear.'"

"I don't know."

She is relentless. "'Betray, kind husband, thy spouse to our sights ... / Who is most true and pleasing to thee then/ When she is embraced and open to most men.'"

"God! The husband as pimp, the wife as public whore, hideous!"

"But she's 'most true and pleasing' to her 'kind husband' then."

"Have done lecturing!"

"It's biblical, my friend, the church is the bride of Christ. What do you think brides and grooms do when they get where they both want to go?"

He can think a moment. "What do you think," he counters, "what do shepherds literally do with sheep?"

Her face creases in laughter. "This?"

"The standard ones! Jesus is also called the good shepherd."

"And shepherds feed their sheep, and shear them, and...."

"And slaughter them and flay them and roast them and eat them for supper!"

"Even the good, 'standard,' shepherds?" she is completely lascivious.

"Of course. They don't raise pets."

"I know," she says, and bending double all along him until her lips find his shoulder; held thus, she cannot quite reach his lips. "I'm torturing the image, I know, I know."

He sings her tighter, "And now I know and now I know and now –"

"What do you know?"

"You that's who."

"Donne does it, deliberately." Her crown fills the hollow of his right eye.

"Why?"

"He's building a careful structure out of oxymorons."

"Why, tell me."

"If you can say it, you can do it."

"Huh?"

"I don't mean you *ought* to or have to, do it I mean, but if the words can be put together and it can be thought, then probably it will be. David the good shepherd certainly ate some of his sheep so maybe Jesus the bridegroom literally made love with his bride. All bridegrooms should; it's not really nice otherwise."

"David wrote the poem, the Lord was the good shepherd."

"All the more to the point."

He squints his left eye to focus what it can see of her: the spray of black hair, ear skin tawny as sun on water.

"You're too literary, I got lost in the language somewhere."

"I'll explain again," she says. "After I eat you." And she begins.

"There are only two main courses on this menu," Whitling-Holmes said, amazed. He was holding a sheet of birchbark down into the blue light.

"Like Air Canada?" Liv laughed, raising hers.

Whit guffawed. "No! Beef or buffalo!"

Harold Lemming had unmasked himself, face glowing reddish like a sick ghost. "Every item on the menu is Albertan, every single thing except the pernod and the pepper."

Rikki read aloud, perhaps stunned, "Heart of Bullrush salad?"

"Still beating no doubt," Whit told her.

Harold's lips twisted slightly. "No one has to come here," he said. "There's a waiting list four months long." Perhaps three weeks in Rome had turned him nationalist, perhaps he would leave ancient popes for present politics, god bless us all.

"I heard the magpie tongue hors d'oeuvres are remarkable," Liv said carefully between them. "I didn't know they were edible."

"Rarer than caviar," Harold said, "and twenty times as expensive."

An entire evening devastated by data, and James felt a sodden lurch: despite all Oblate and papal records, despite half a summer of St. Albert and Rome, a project here was impossible, no, Gillian's fingers moving across the piano while city lights emerged one by one over the frosted valley.

"Just the tongues?" said Gillian now in a kind of horror.

"If you split them," James murmured to her, "they'll never squawk again, just sing as sweetly as great poets all in choir."

"It's a paté," a voice declaimed behind them: an enormous man in leather fringes with a cloth draped on his arm. "Every night," he continued, "one main course special is chosen for one table." He bowed slightly to the three women like a tasseled tree bending, or perhaps a centre pole with cloth offerings, "We would like to offer this distinguished table the special for tonight."

"That sounds ... " Whit began, "what is it?"

"*Bison in utero* with cactus dressing. Very special." He bowed again with discretion, "I'll be back," and disappeared.

They looked at one another. Rikki said, puzzled, "I've not heard of that."

Whit asked James, past Gillian, "Did he say what I think I heard?"

"Undoubtedly," Liv said. "James, where are you?"

"They ate it whenever they could get it," Harold chortled, clearly ecstatic. "The most delicate meat on the prairie, more succulent than tongue or beaver tail or prairie grouse, oh, it sounds fabulous!"

"Buffalo *in utero*?"

"James," Liv said again.

Harold insisted, "Even a century ago it was extremely rare, you only get it by sheer luck. They didn't even have any at the Paul Kane Christmas banquet in Fort Edmonton in 1849, it was so rare then, imagine what it is now."

"I don't prefer my meat rare," Rikki laughed, and her flawless skin seemed to dance in the quivering light. "It's too savage."

James saw her naked as a faded mushroom fore and aft risen after rain. "They'll have dipped it in buffalo gall," he said morosely, why was she sitting here, this fulsome Anglican, "the way true savages ate."

"Not buffalo foetus," Harold had committed himself to the nineteenth century; if he now heard of medicine wheels

202

the fate of all western Indian historiography was sealed. "Indians only ate raw liver that way, to kill one sharpness with the other and—"

"And the poison of one with the other, yes, yes," James said impatiently, bloody literalist. He realized then Liv had not been after the buffalo; but she had given up.

And he felt Gillian's hand on his knee, slide along the inside of his thigh and he dared not glance at her bending all his sensation about her like a cradled egg, her hand at last familiar as taste he wanted to mouth and swallow, swallow, but the foreign froth of her hair at the red corner of his vision and the tilt of her breast hoisted it seemed so violently out of contour: Liv, he concentrated on Liv. The blue light silhouetted her against deeper black, austere goddess saddened into frown. What exactly was it? He made obeisance to her.

"Bison in utero," he orated. "Shaped in that eternal silence which speaks when soft bones move into the wistful order of birth, amen and amen."

Upon which invocation Whitling-Holmes' sudden diplomatic heartiness was not as obtuse as it might otherwise have been.

"Well then," he declared, "we'll certainly have the special, thank you very much, with the cactus dressing, and begin with magpie paté, and wine, what possible wine...."

The fringed waiter said at his shoulder, "Dandelion, 1974. An excellent year, sir."

Which more than resolved the eating problems, though it eliminated a great deal of possible conversation. And as it materialized, the meal was startlingly delicious, a kind of wild searching out of areas of the palate none of them would remember discovering before, the paté on tiny crackers astringent and faintly nutmeg, the buffalo calf appearing stuffed entire and curled like a piglet within itself, a slightly drier but as delicately sweet as butter turkey basted in its own wine (dandelion too, or saskatoon?), falling into diaphanous slices under the knife Whit's long fingers wielded skirrily: was it really the food? Gradually texture soaked into James, as if he were seeping into the mine's cool musk of earth and coal and water trickling somewhere behind him, it was certainly not the wider surround of implacable eaters, though perhaps the incredible triumvirate of the women? Who said not a word, directly opposite to him his wife so devastatingly regal, her hair a light-frozen tiara; on the side of his heart his lover in a wig flaming like any Rome or Alberta tart but her profile against Whit's tuxedo white sliced paper, and on his right the woman he had embraced in darkness when she momentarily seemed both of them translated, all he could want and more than the tactile world had ever given at once or the world of mirrors or the world dreamt as undreamt because it was explorable only in unremembered unconsciousness, offering appearance only, no order, not even that vague general order which must be believed to achieve a fortuitous conjunction of small, personal orders, 'the body never formed to mind or voice/ Like a body wholly body, fluttering/ Its empty sleeves ... oh blessed rage for order—' where would it be possible, when. He sipped dandelion wine, a clear distilled cloud fraying him into invisible rock pockets, into the angles of cracked rhomboid crystals where coal still blazed with blackness, into the spaces of pick points, shovel cuts and dynamite tendrils, he was spread fine as smoke so that wisps of him breathed in the abandoned recesses of the farthest mines of Edmonton, of Alberta, of the black horror crawlways of the world, Harold blithered on, "... sixty-three miles and a blizzard howling at the tipple when we got there by noon, but down in the mine it was so hot, really *hot*. That was the first thing we kids all noticed, hot."

"Wasn't it the smell too," Whit interrupted, "a kind of dusty, fiery smell?"

But Harold rushed on, determined for his story before inevitable imperialism would overrun him, "It smelled like horses, they were there, two little mares, they'd been *born* seven hundred feet underground and never seen sunlight. Their eyes were pale, almost a, a creamy white. I remember that," Harold's fork suspended on a bit of buffalo, his long face almost ascetic. "Quite ... creamy."

"'Truly the light is sweet'," James contributed, "'and a

pleasant thing it is for the eyes to behold the sun.'"

"James," Liv said again. He decided he must now fulfil her worst male expectations; and Gillian's withdrawing hand drove him.

"Ecclesiastes chapter 11, verse 7," he insisted, "and the eighth is like unto it: 'But if a man live many years and *rejoice* (he did not try to resist the emphasis) in them all, yet let them *remember* the days of darkness for they *shall be many.*' Thus the wise Preacher (left finger aloft) instructeth us, to remember our future!"

Harold continued as if only an idiot had bumbled,

"The miner led us down a *wide* tunnel, the main shaft half a mile under the river, with branches going off in different directions. The seam at first was almost eight feet thick and they had just dug—"

"So a grown man could walk upright," Whit said.

"Oh *yes*, at first, and wide with steel rails for coal cars pulled by the horses. It was easy at first, and lights strung from the cross timbers holding up the rock but when we got under the river the seam dropped to maybe three four feet, that was really where they were mining then."

"Three feet?" Liv asked, stared at the granite wall beside her.

"They've blasted rock here," Whit explained. "For this club. It's quite useless for coal miners to do that, it's a waste, waste."

Deep useless digging the useless secrets of earth, Tolstoi's tan brush flags furiously, red earth sprays back between his legs, and suddenly a bit of metal clinks as Becca bends to pull him out, "Leave the poor gopher alone, you dum-dum!" hauling with all her might and his head squirms out with a growl and flare of teeth, vanishes again. Becca laughs, brings something between grubby fingers.

"What's this?"

The dog knows nothing of gophers, the girl of rifles thank god.

"It's the shell of a bullet, a rifle shell."

She shifts it between her fingertips as if it intends immediately to explode; grimaces, "Something to kill people...."

"It could have been hunting," Liv comes over. "Antelope on this empty prairie."

She sniffs the shell; by the evening sheen of Hand Hills Lake the heat presses them flat like piled logs. Becca surrenders the shell, gladly.

"Not hunting," he says, "look, '45-75 W C F,' that's old North West Mounted Police issue, could be as early as 1878."

"A police bullet?"

"Probably a Winchester, it's rimmed, necked, centre-fired, see, that's where the firing pin hit."

Becca says, "How does it ... hurt you?"

"The gunpowder's in it here and a lead bullet about an inch long sticks out of here so when you pull the trigger the pin hits it, the powder explodes and the bullet shoots out of the barrel, 1,300 feet per second."

Tolstoi tunnels on desperately; the woman and the girl look at him holding the shell grained with earth between his thumb and forefinger.

"A bullet," he lectures, "kills by penetration but even more by shock. The shock of a hit depends on the mass of the bullet, and its speed. The RCMP now use 7.62 mm NATO rifles and their muzzle speed is more than twice what this was."

He is awake, the camper roof very low overhead and after two weeks he should be used to weight over him, sky perhaps or earth pressing him out thin, and now he knows there is someone folded into the corner at the foot of the bed. He is not asleep, someone very small, crumpled down. As if in fear.

"Becca?" he asks.

"Da ... ddy," it is her voice, yes, and movement. Terror. He sits up, avoiding the roof, and reaches for her past his feet.

"Hey."

"T-there's a police," she whispers.

"What?"

"Outside," she gestures slight as a shiver. "The door, with a gun."

Night insects sing at every camper window and ducks answer on the lake. He listens, his hand broadening on her small waist, hip.

"There's no one."

"He came," she whispers, "I heard him step, he's there, by the door."

"Who?"

"The man with the gun."

"Then why isn't Tolstoi barking?"

"He choked him, he's dead."

"But if he has a gun...."

"It's for us, not Tolstoi."

The Hand Hills blazing out to the northwest in a long sunset, the corrals and chutes of the rodeo grounds fading from whitewash to prehistoric post, then outline like a giant causeway leading down into the burnished platform of the lake. Liv burrows away from him, deeper into her pillow, muttering sleep.

"Come on," and he clambers down, scooping her with him onto his neck, she twists her legs about his naked waist and he is glad of that as the night air finds his body, the ground cold and Tolstoi grunts as he uncurls by the rear wheel, his moist nose touches his ankle. "See, there's Tolstoi," he says, and she nuzzles closer, not looking. He carries her in a circle around the truck, the west and east north sky bronzed as if sunset and sunrise were joining in celebrating together beyond the mound of the hanging earth. Tolstoi's chain clinks.

"See," he says again. "There's nobody."

"Why do you know so much about what doesn't matter?" Liv says to him. The plank chutes are grained with animal hair; above the centre chute he can barely read '1907 Hand Hills Stampede, May 24, 1980.'

"The oldest in the province," he muses. "Warm-up for Calgary. Some of it matters. I know things, that's how I make my living."

"No one makes a living knowing the muzzle velocity of every known Mounted Police rifle."

"I also know the name of the superintendent in charge of police in 1878 when Laird tried to give Big Bear some money at Sounding Lake ninety miles northeast of here. Something else you care to know?"

207

"Ninety miles as the crow flies?"

"The crow or the nasty thought."

"I don't want to 'make a living,'" she says.

"Then what?"

"Live."

"I thought we were."

"We seem to have ... slowed down, this summer."

"Isn't this trip good?"

"Of course, it's lovely, but lately you've been so...."

"What?"

"As if you'd used up all your patience, not with me, somewhere else."

In the arena Becca has announced herself the only woman contestant in the bareback bronc riding class, but it develops that the mount she has drawn, Tolstoi, is more whirling or seated dervish than bucking horse. Finally despite her spurring he lies down gently in the soft dust; she stands over him, a small abusive silhouette.

"You don't have to work night and day," Liv says.

"What if sometimes I'm not working?"

Her slim arms clasp his, surround him, her breasts tight.

"Sometimes," he says, and stops. " ... I wish I could just go, walk away out of myself and not ... just somebody, not me. Everything is so drifty, loose ... nothing is quite as good as it should be ... or significant ... ahhh," he rubs his face against hers, if he could only drink her and drown thirst forever.

"Why?"

"If I knew don't you think I'd do something?"

"Maybe not."

"I'm forty-two and what have I done?"

"Why should you be special?"

"I'm all I am!"

Becca is hurling herself about the huge arena, arms wide, trying to catch Tolstoi. But the dog is in his manic running, cornering and barking just beyond her reach, mouth slavered, tiny leaping figures. Seventy-three years, the last of the day's light, the whitewashed planks and posts watching through dust and snow, watching daughter or lover or husband or son and meaning whatever that is may be somewhere like a whiff or wolf willow momentary in spring. Beside him on the corral Liv answers a question he probably asked, sometime.

"You've loved me."

"Is that enough?"

"I've loved you."

"Is it enough, several lovings?"

Liv says after a moment into the purple darkness of the hills' shoulder, "How can there be *enough*?"

Somewhere a smell had been drifting far back across his awareness, a smell of words out-Englishing Harold's Oxford, it could only be Whit of course " ... critical seam thickness ... crawl every day to the working face of the coal ... a mile or two if the seam is only ... " Whit had donned his rightful mantle and Harold was left to glumly spear a final Heart of Bullrush; the white faces and necks and shoulders of the women set like mausoleum pillars holding apart the darkness "...props of course, but the roof always ... the rock always...."

"They can't stand to shovel?" Gillian, Gillian was beside him and said that.

"Almost never."

"How...?"

"On your knees," Whit said and James began, but caught himself in time, and cleared his throat. "On a three-foot seam you're bent double all day long. There's a belt running behind you and you shovel onto it all day, like this," Whit suddenly translated onto his knees beside his chair, his table-fork a minute shovel in his giant hands, head bent forward and sideways throwing invisible forks full of coal over his left shoulder, bending, heaving, twisting in the manic rhythm of a machine. "The conveyor rattles like, an endless machine gun, and the deeper the shaft, the hotter, and black, the air so full of dust, the lamp in your hat shines maybe three, four feet into the dust, and you're breathing it too, and shovelling steady, your gang is paid by the ton, you can't let down your gang, it's all in the arms and shoulders, and muscles in your belly, shovelling."

They stared across the cluttered table at him working, his head twisted aside to keep it level, an enormous man kneeling in black tuxedo and gleaming shirt clawing the coal out of the air that had built the city above them with a silver table fork. James thought, whatever has been will be again, though different. Whit was suddenly tearing at his collar.

"In the deepest, hottest mines," he muttered, "they wear nothing, only clogs on their feet and knee pads." His black tie was crumpled in his fist; he knelt there, opening and closing his fist as if the next time it opened some miracle would appear. "The line of miners ... " he pushed to his feet but stood bent in half, then pointed down the tunnel between bluish tables, "as far as you can see the most magnificent muscled bodies working, crusted with coal dust, their eyes crusted, steel black muscles...."

They saw him on his knees shovelling, black and naked.

Harold said finally, "It was afternoon break when they took us kids down there. No one was ... doing anything."

"It's almost peaceful then, isn't it," Whit said dreamily, straightening, sitting down at last. "Sheltered."

"They were stretched out on their elbows drinking cold tea, their eyes white below the yellow spot of light in their hats, like three-eyes one kid said, it was spooky ... three-eyes."

Whit mused, "They already had a unionized lunch break."

"They just stared at us," Harold said, "lying on one arm in a space no higher than this table and propped up here and there by columns of coal like toadstools, you had to crawl there and three thousand feet of rock above you. I'll never forget that."

"That's right," Whit said, "the whole earth above you squashing you inside a flat, thin slice of hell."

He was looking at the invisible ceiling; as if spring clouds were about to carry him softly away sipping his creamy wine.

"Did you work in the mines?" Liv asked.

"Our whole civilization rests on energy and we'll be back to coal soon, we already are, perhaps not to children and women pulling the cars in hell-holes, but—," Whit gestured, "we'll be back, pretty soon."

Gillian opened her mouth to speak, but didn't; James watched her mound golden corn on her plate, a surrounding circle.

"No," Whit said to Liv. "When I was twelve I was already five-ten and my father said I was useless and my mother said thank god and sent me to school. On my grandfather's pension. He was buried in a rockfall and his mates uncovered his head and he was alive and talking to them but then they had to run for it because the roof was coming down again, and they got him uncovered a second time—he had his head crushed between his legs so he had some breathing room—"

"Whit," Rikki said.

" ... and that time they got him out altogether before it came down a third time, for good, but it got two of his mates that were helping dig him out. The others dragged him for miles on his coat, crawling, his body smashed like a piece of paper and he refused the weekly pension the company offered and they were stalling, hoping he'd die and then they'd be free of him altogether, but the Board ruled for him finally, a lump payment and he could die in peace. That's how I went to school," Whit was still flattening his crushed tie.

"You shouldn't tell that story," Rikki said, chewing steadily. "It's just frightening down here."

"It's essential," Gillian said abruptly. She had decided where to place the golden rubbing stone, her face set in that particular stasis James had sometimes seen above him, momentarily, bending down and she should be there like steel but wasn't, as if her thought were searching past impossibilities she wanted to push beyond.

"It's this mine, I admit," Whit smiled across at Harold. "Don't let me spoil your story."

"You lived it," Harold said with sudden generosity. "I was a thirty-minute visitor in a pretty good mine, but I won't forget it."

Maybe today the roof caves in, or the cage cable snaps; James could have laughed at himself falling from one foam-cushioned occupation to another with no external necessity. He would feel better if there were. But Gillian had finished her stones; they aimed past him at no rosy-phallused dawn.

211

"Why shouldn't women work in the mines?" she said level as stone.

Whit asked, after a short silence, "Why would they want to?"

"Why would the men?"

"Well, it has to be done, someone has to."

"So why exclude women?"

His face hung bluish and blank.

"It's power," Liv said.

"Of course," Whit said as to a child, "that's it, you have to be very strong to work down...."

But Gillian was talking across the cluttered table with Liv: "It's like stupid bloody Lawrence, in *Sons and Lovers* the big strong miner marries the pretty little woman and promises he'll labour for her in the mine every day as long as she...." she threw her pale arm up, flicking manly coal away into air.

So Liv completed it for the men, " ... as long as she stays pretty and gives him sons and cuts his potatoes right for supper."

Whit uttered in his heaviest ministerial tone, "I'm afraid you ladies don't understand the brute strength that's needed to shovel coal all day."

Liv said gently, "All men are just naturally so *brutally* strong?"

"They have to get that way, or they don't last."

"Well," she declared, as if he had explained everything. The women all bent to their last bits of meat, chewed assiduously. James had unhooked his left shoe but Gillian's scarlet nylon – the tips of his toes read that colour again through brown wool – gave off nothing, not even a ruffle of friction. He felt cold; so separate. Whit steered them to public, restaurant safety:

"Oil and gas are so easy, compared to coal, but they won't last."

"Aren't they strip-mining in Germany," Harold was helpful, "up to a thousand feet deep?"

"You can't strip mountains or the sea, and that's where the big coal is."

James mumbled through wine, "God should have put the

big heat and the big squeeze on a lot more animals and plants, a lot earlier."

Harold could be irritable with James at least. "What are you talking about?"

"Oil, oil, it's so easy to suck out eh Mr. Minister?"

"Are you using any less of it," Whit said, "for all your ironic tone?"

Harold said, "I want light when I trip the switch."

"And if it's not there," Whit laughed, "you'll yell at me."

There was slight laughter for them only where Whitling-Holmes permitted it; the women were of course unherdable and the men his sheep, not even James with his erratics could be expected to shake himself quite loose, but an abrupt darkness did swallow them just then. So densely it seemed they still saw each others' faces trying to crinkle into some kind of mutual politeness avoiding the unease of a disagreement not one of them at that moment could have explained why or even what, but of course there was really only the memory of the round table scattered with dishes and the square blue eye of the video light glowing out between them and fading as gasps, small whispers and cries grew along the recesses of the tunnels. And an androgynous voice spoke at each ear:

"We ask silence of you now, only silence. Please. This is your second darkness, and unlike the first it is without movement. And brief. We ask you to use it to reaffirm the touch of the friend with whom you came, or the friends. If there are only two of you, no decisions have to be made, of course, to prepare yourselves for the third, the Long Darkness. In the Long Darkness which is coming you will experience the inexpressible and the so-far unimaginable for which you have always longed, though perhaps you could never quite decide what it should be. You may decide now. It will be ready for you when you have finished dessert. You will have one further minute of silence now to make whatever decisions you need about the Long Darkness, where you will spend it, and with whom. Silence, please."

A speaker built into the back of each chair; when James leaned back, not quite believing this, the voice was as intimate and sexless as a moist whisper. His head swam, almost

213

frantically: this entire evening, the flaming valley, the bump and the descent, the incredible menu and memories and the Minister of Energy's story, the two women suddenly strange as ... women, there was no other analogy: he was being steeped / yeasted / marinated in the wine of his own unclotting and unhealable juices. He did not, in that moment, know what to do with his feet or hands, The Mine hovering still as a consecration in ether. Perhaps other diners were actually making ultimate decisions – what a silly – well, perhaps it wasn't obviously silly, he needed hands suddenly and he felt for Gillian, her thigh at least, and her fingertips now brushed the edge of his hand as if almost willing to be familiar again and he slid after them, where had her fingers not touched him and her body stretched where sunlight glanced off the black piano like a scar, and then he felt her dress stir. Immediately he was certain, absolutely certain, that Whit's paw was on her other leg. And a hand – Rikki's it must be – was on his own right thigh, searching, dear god only Harold was unaccounted for and if he stretched his shoed foot for Liv's, as suddenly he longed to very badly, would he encounter four other feet searching too? There was a hole opening somewhere, a black hole in all their universes about to swallow them.

"The light will come on now," the voice murmured discreetly. "Ten seconds."

Which left them nothing but count. Hands scrabbled against cutlery, glasses clattered; when the light grew to distinguishability they were all there with forks and a few knives in hand as if they had not yet finished the main course, glances skipping aside and certainly nothing decided like teenagers. 'About the woodlands I will go / To see the cherry hung with snow.' O metaphysical Geronimo, no.

"Well!" Whit's hard, muscled face was slightly flushed. Perhaps he had not received the immediate assent he had of course expected; had he had time for a second or simultaneous manoeuvre? Was it imaginable he might have been rejected, or even hesitated at, twice? Liv's head set at that particular tilt of abstracted stubborness.

"Quite a scenario," Harold exclaimed, his glance slipping

aside from each woman in turn without actually pausing long enough for any decisive encounter. "As if they really want to give us our money's worth."

"The women," Liv said distinctly, reaching for her wine, "will decide what has to be decided when the time comes. In the meantime, we should finish this extraordinary meal."

"What is to be decided?" Whit asked.

"Everything about the Long Darkness."

"They said nothing about what would happen then."

Rikki recited, "'You will experience the inexpressible and the so-far unimaginable for which you have always longed.'"

"Terrible script-writer," Harold said, but of course no one laughed with him.

"'For which you have always longed,'" Liv repeated. "The happiness will depend on our decision."

"That is, the women's?" Whit grinned, not believing it.

"Yes."

"And what will *they* contribute, once *you* have decided?"

"'They' who, the men?"

"No, no, that sexless voice, The Mine."

"It didn't say, did it? And neither do the women, but I'm sure both will be highly unexpected."

"At least!" Harold laughed uproariously. Perhaps he was still negotiating with someone – though it certainly wasn't Liv.

"So, we men are to be helpless." There was perhaps banter in Whit's voice, or simple irony.

"It will do you good," and Liv smiled. "Look at James, he's been quite helpless for a long time. Does he look peaked?"

James tried to out-stare her craziness, to look innocently about while avoiding Gillian more or less; and decided he must be decisive.

"Liv has the best possible idea," he said. "Men think they have to decide everything, so give us a break and do what you want with us."

"Who needs a break?" Whit said.

His tone was too serious for the candied sugar-beet slices, certainly for the *crêpes saskatoon flambées* the fringy waiter was about to incinerate at his shoulder. But Gillian spoke up suddenly.

"I agree, don't you, Mrs. Whitling-Holmes? We should decide."

"I think it's a gorgeous idea," Rikki's lovely shoulders quivered with mirth, her deep breasts no less.

"We have listened long enough to the men talking," Liv said.

"They've been quite good this evening, considering," Gillian said gently.

"Of course, they're tremendous storytellers, they've had millenia of practice and they've charmed us since Adam. It's time they listened to ours."

Rikki laughed aloud as the brandy flames leaped up, "Eve told Adam a better story than he her."

"Stories," Harold interjected, though somehow pleased. "You're talking about the Long Darkness, whatever that is, and...."

"Whatever it will be," Whit amended.

"Probably freezing cold," James said.

"You mean Arctic?"

"That's profoundly Canadian."

"Good god!"

"We're talking about talking and listening," Liv cut in, "and you'll listen for once."

"How will we decide?" Gillian asked her, and James' heart jerked to be with her alone out of this fencing, teetering, squeezy balance, but Liv answered immediately.

"You know," level and clear-eyed.

And Gillian seemed satisfied; James could not comprehend. Something had passed him silently, swiftly by, and he had only one resource to catch up.

"'In his own image he created them,'" he recited, "'Adam and Eve he created them and blessed them and said, Be fru—'"

"We hardly need Genesis," Liv interrupted. "Neither the fruitfuls nor the first verse."

"That was verse 27."

"You know every damn verse?" Harold with his lip curled.

216

Behind Liv the orange flames settled in the silver pan, and abruptly James let his hatred flare.

"Don't tell me Miss Charity Graham didn't sing in Sunday School with you, 'Thy word is like a garden, Lord, with flowers rich and fair,' every Sunday bright and clear?"

"You certainly never sang it with her," Harold muttered.

"Of course not, I was one of them immigrants in the ship-lap church in the wheat field and Fraulein Lizzie Warkentin crowing, '*Al die Voeglein sind nun da*,' with all us little Mennonite bohunks."

Whit sang in an astonishingly lyric tenor, "' … May pluck a lovely cluster there, Thy Word is like a deep deep mine with jewels—'"

"Oh please," Rikki exclaimed, "spare us!"

"The men are already singing before dessert," Gillian's heel on James' instep was an instant needle, excruciating. "There'll be nothing expected of us, soon, but to run."

James realized then that all three women would decide on Whit; to devastate such a man was too great a temptation for them to resist. And he and Harold would be left to heap coals on each others' heads as it were; ugggh.

"You can't run here," Whit leered exaggeratedly at her. "You're under-ground, cornered."

"You've got us cornered?"

He should be so lucky. It was that usual female/male innuendo which Gillian could manipulate as easily as anyone, but he knew her—he had to convince himself suddenly—so much better when she thrusts her body against his and holds it there, tight, and then pushes her hand between them, "What's this?" she says, "Old man?" laughing against his teeth and he: "I'm tearing your clothes off?" and she: "Just one track—and it's not *mind* either," and he trying to reach up and behind her: "How about you, what's that eh?" and she: "You can't feel anything, there's nothing," and he: "You're as bad as me but *secret*ive!" and she: "The natural superiority of women, never give ourselves away," male and female, why doubleness? Why not three or one, more choice or none, the swift, instant destruction of all present morality. If the Creator is one and three, never two, why this silly human duality that forces everything either/or? Since it was all spoken in the first place.

"Maybe he made children first," Becca says.

"They're still one or the other."

"They don't think about it so much."

"Do you?"

"More than I used to," she admits. "I never did before I was a double number."

Her tenth birthday had been painful. In daylight now she seems more or less resigned, but evenings she still resents it.

"There's a Blackfoot story," he says, "where Napi starts mankind by making a woman and a child."

"Is it a boy-child?"

"The story doesn't say."

"That's nice it doesn't," Becca hunches a bit further into her pillow. "Just women and children."

"Oh yeah? Why?"

"There wouldn't be any schools with principals."

He laughs out loud. "Did you like the way Genesis tells about making?"

"It's funny. God makes it all by talking."

"Yes," he says slowly, unable to think where she may be going and not wanting to deflect her. "Yes."

"The world is just God's talk."

He says even more slowly. "'Day unto day uttereth speech,'" trying to hear his lovely innocent daughter beyond awe and possible alarm.

"But I don't know, who is he talking to?"

To talk to someone else is a given? "Who is there?" he asks blindly.

"There's just God."

"And...."

"Nothing else."

"Isn't there?"

"And what he's making."

"Yes, so that's two possibilities at least."

"But what he's making is talk, so he's either talking to himself or to his talk?"

And Becca lies curled trying to unravel that behind her

eyes. Then suddenly she smiles. "What I really like," setting deeper with a truly beatific wiggle, "is 'way different!"

"Getting cuddled in Gramma's quilt?" reaching for her.

"Oh that, I mean Adam. When God brings him all the animals and then he makes names."

"'And Adam gave names to all the fowl and every beast of the field; but for Adam there was not found an help meet....'"

"Yeah, when he does that," pointing, "you're pig, you're alligator, platypus...."

No help meet for him. If he could name, he would know. *Hast du di vielieft?* his mother says to him, naming it in Low German. Not, have you fallen in love, but have you yourself in-loved? "As Hazel Motes would preach," Gillian whispers, spread naked under the rough blanket of her wide bed, "'there ain't no sin because there never was no fall.'" What could a man named Motes say to understand so much? *Enloved*, 'En: a prefix meaning primarily "in" or "into" ... with the old concrete force of bringing the object into a specified condition, as "shrine," "enshrine."' Enlove? If he could only gather the words to speak.

His mother and Becca and Olena shell peas. The air green, irrigation trickles between four green rows past their feet against the sun-gorged wall of the garage, his mother sits so tiny leaning into heat, the black edge of water soaking in the soil a delicate steam of summer with Becca's fingers from the bucket placing peas in her hand which she splits and spills quick as touch, wide-legged Olena lifting the edges of plants like rows of broody hens for their long curved green eggs attached, not a word, he sights along the runnels of mud-coloured water through the constellation of garden and long-eyed women and the green golden mound in one lap that points the sun's one eye in the sky.

"The *crêpe saskatoon flambée* is marvelous," Rikki said, chewing lusciously. "Isn't it, Whit?"

"Quite."

"I must ask the chef for the recipe."

James snorted aloud: Liv and Gillian's expressions were echoes of each other's horror; which as quickly changed to relief.

"It is very good, thank you, Rikki," Liv said rather strangely, and Gillian nodded, barely polite. The corn on her plate was gone, golden stones could you fall all May and summer and then three weeks apart and still be falling together? A fall was once for all, exclusive, probably requiring single-minded recovery. Enloving should be different.

" ... but when you pass fifty," Whit was saying quietly to Gillian, "the past is more and more forgettable, it's the shrinking future that starts to concern you."

Gillian said, as quietly, "If you hadn't been born, the question would not have arisen."

"Which question?"

"The one we're trying to ask with our lives," James said and she grimaced sideways at him malely horning in again. "Sorry," and he tried his sheepish smile for her acceptance but swiftly she ignored him.

"I was about to say," she said, "the question we're all answering, whether or not we know it."

"An unconscious question?" Whit asked, floundering. "Politicians are not much given to contemplation. They have no time."

James wanted to say, Contemplation is not given to anyone, it must be taken; but Gillian saw his mouth open and looked silence before she turned to the cabinet minister and said, very clearly,

"Then they should not pretend they are fit to run the world."

Her face was growing dim beside him, and he looked across the table. Liv. Always Liv, she must have been contemplating him for some time, the pupils enormous in her dark eyes as the darkness grew. 'Is she kind as she is fair?/ For beauty lives with kindness./ Love doth to her eyes repair/ To help him of his blindness,/ And, being helped, inhabits there.' Behind her gleamed the irridescence of coal, darkness visible mocking him with its contradictory doubleness, the eternal light and heat of the sun trapped in cold solid blackness, somewhere black light: here was duality to the point of oxymoron. Both! both! was screaming in his head; doubleness must not cancel itself!

"The lights are now dimming," the androgynous voice reassured them. "In two minutes you will receive instructions for the Long Darkness."

"Counting, counting," Liv laughed happily, "as if they're sending us into space."

Rikki echoed her: "They're running the time on our little tv screen," she said, "look."

And so they were; all its four faces clicked over second by second.

"Two minute penalty," Harold clapped the grotesque hockey mask to his face, "two minutes for holding!"

In the fading light James could no longer resist. "Harold," he said, "did you ever put on skates?"

"Did you," Harold asked too pleasantly, "after you ran away?"

"Well, well," Whit the charmer switched on all burners, "have you ladies decided?"

"Of course," Liv said.

"You have? I didn't hear you ... consult ... "

"We didn't have to, women always know exactly what they want."

"Okay for the moment, but what if one of you changes her mind, suddenly?"

"Let her."

"Consistency is a bare male virtue," Gillian said. "Do you still want the recipe?" she asked Rikki.

"Do you?" Rikki asked her.

"I never cook."

"Neither do I," Liv said to them both.

The men considered each other in amazement.

"Well, I suppose I should," Rikki said in her broadest Cockney, rather dampened. "Though I've tried most of it already."

"That's why I was wondering," Gillian said.

"So have I," Liv reassured Rikki quickly. "But it's the new combination that counts."

Whit said, "I'm not sure I know what's going on."

"I'm damn sure I don't," Harold muttered.

"Of course not, how could you?" Liv said and smiled

round the table quite regal, perfect. James had managed to keep his mouth shut so he could smile expressionlessly at Whitling-Holmes and Lemming, his mind on this point blanker than theirs. And all of them seeing the fringed waiter emerge at Liv's shoulder as the last light faded with the runing clock. Gillian was not touching him.

At first he was aware only of warmth and silence. No smell, no sight. The warmth was understandable, but if this was to be every Albertan's dream then surely he should have been swimming in a jacuzzi of libidinous oil and eating and drinking it, every cell awash, wallowing and screwing and screaming in it for every happiness with a few thousand chosen others, smeared over, rubbed and scrubbed raw with it while they all twirled their solid gold taps farther open to get more and more and what was there to life but endlessly and eternally *more*. But now that hardly seemed necessary. As it had never been, when he considered it seriously; the necessary decadence of enormous wealth was merely ridiculous, and with that one glance he simply forgot about oil and its stiff cousin coal, the one with all the character, and would not remember them again.

Into the solitary silence holding him came light. Silvery, as on a winter morning when the first sunlight glisters through the crystals of frozen air. He was walking in white, his steps led into snow but snow warm as summer moss, snow that lounged on spruce towering about him into a distance of multiplied tender spires, snow so thick it transformed every tree and shrub into a mere green fringe stacked like a child's picture of a winter forest. And through this abundance there shone a clear austerity of light, sourceless, uncluttered because there were only two entities, or three, and they were all growing here. There were no things, and in luminous silence that was very restful.

At first he did notice sounds: snow shifting against needles, bending branches, the mice in their tunnels fleeing the thump of his feet as he walked, the whisper of falling. Birds tiny and busy, somewhere. Even his own breathing, the sibilance of his chest and legs contained by clothes, perhaps even his face moving through silver air: he heard that, the place not soundless but silent, and as his awareness grew he sensed the opening silence that would continue after he was dead as it had been from the beginning before he was born. And then he smelled the numinous damp of spruce needles in snow, breathing on moss, to the outer edges of his body and he felt the distension of the silence that inhabited space before the world was and which will be there still after it has vanished in eternal light.

He knew then that silence was the foil that gives words their brilliance, the container that contains their power and he felt very close to weeping for all the words he had scattered, those great words his mind gathered and piled within him like rocks to fence in the enormous, o endless field of his longing and ignorance.

And all the words that still must speak to make worlds possible.

Gillian took his hand in her warm hand, walked with him between the bending spruce; immediately he felt physical desire flicker along his nerves, centring. He felt ... petty then. Not because she was there, loveliness shared made it only lovelier, but for what struck him suddenly as his almost programmed banality: no matter what or where, given her presence the same synapses snapping, and he was so furious that for a moment he experienced only his own triviality. But Gillian's arm folded over his, she swung smiling to him in all her full bodiliness with her face wiped clean under black hair, and her quick happiness toppled him beyond sensuality: she was there and they loved each other walking or lying in the bowl under spruce or standing between them, whenever, however, in the snow that sprinkled them with glister out of the very particles of the air through which they moved without effort and he understood then, sharp as morning light, that they were no flowers dumped beside each other at the random whim of some omnipotent gardener; they were particular, they moved of themselves, their very shadows on the snow spoke as uniquely as each frozen crystal reversing

223

itself into dry heat; they were complete and nevertheless a tiny cell of all that continued to be. In fact, their feet were so vividly warm that Gillian bent in one lithe motion and unstrapped her unnecessary heels. His hand rested on her back, curved like a sensuous letter and she looked around, laughing, then straightened and he reached under her skirt the way he always liked to reach (his head in the pungent darkness there sang in its chains like the sea) and slid her stockings down one round leg and then the other. They left the stockings there, somewhere between her shoes and his.

When they emerged from the laden trees they saw they were on the last high rim of foothills before they break down to the plains. The mountain peaks were at their back and they could look east over parkland spruce and poplar and white plowed fields and tiny sloughs fringed by dry, green bullrushes to where the prairie lay adrift somewhere at the meeting of sky and land. A covey of quail whirled up behind them and darted down the air's incline of the land as if snatched away. They knew then that they had asked excessively and had received only because they had so asked: nothing but passionate insistence could have given this. They were on the Medicine Lodge Hills, the silver coin of Gull Lake flung below them seventy miles away and that meandering stream was the Blindman River, a heart beating here was drummer for every world and so holding hands still they walked down, easily and ran in the snow-like lawn, paths opening for them between deadfall and brush down slopes and Gillian ahead over ravines where birds nested and he through tangle brilliant as frost, down to the flats. When they reached the lake, breathless and running because they could impossibly walk between trees cascading snow on them and always running faster to catch the next warm shower of it on head or neck or uplifted face, James wore only his shorts and Gillian nothing at all. And there was Liv, leaning back on her elbows with her face tilted up as if breathing light, her creamy body stretched out of the snow into the whistling lake. She heard their laughter coming towards her along the white beach and turned her head to watch them. But it was Gillian who spoke first when they arrived.

"This is the Long Darkness," she said, shaking her head like a splendid horse, sweated, and her hair seemed to flicker with gold perhaps, or red. "May I never see the sun again."

If there was light at all, and the world shone clear as day, it dawned from the aurora flaming over the lake like immense torn curtains, and reflected upwards so that the water shone numinously deep purple within itself. Perhaps that was also the source of the warmth they felt in the undreamable snow which was sifting over them and sprinkling the burning water of the lake like shredded coconut over the limpid bay of a coral island, the snow like sand shining against their skin.

"Why are you still wearing those?" Liv asked James.

He realized he was too embarrassed by his erection to undress completely; brandish a gleaming pointer pointing only to itself. He envied the women their mounds brilliant with curled hair so hidden and delicate. Their breasts they carried as casually as their arms, and he could not have said which was more beautiful. His eye and his emotion found them both awesome, choice was stupidity; only some grainy memory threatening on this beach of sweet snow.

Gillian placed her hands on his hips and slid his shorts down; he had to step out of them for her. Then she knelt at the water's edge and began to build a snow castle; tamping snow into the waist of the shorts and using the legs to give a shape to large embattled keeps. James hesitated a moment, but more than ever aware of his distended shaft gesticulating like some peeled pole for a royal flag, so he quickly knelt down and Liv's toe was there to contemplate. The water flickered over it, it might have been extended to him in the sea three miles deep where he would certainly drown long before he could touch it.

"I will have to start quoting history," he said, finding it merely impossible to laugh and looking up the twin columns of his wife and the rounded singleness of her belly and between her breasts to her face glistening upward to light. "In self-defence."

"What is your defence?" Liv asked. The snow sifted over her like unending filigree.

"This is Gull Lake, the lake Maskepetoon, The Broken

Arm, saw silver among the trees when he had his young man's vision on the Medicine Lodge Hills. Later," he added, trying at least to count the hairs idly adrift on that superb toe, "he had a silver medal hung around his neck by the president of the United States, whose profile was on it. Also the words, 'In God We Trust Cash.'"

"Which president?"

"Jackson, general and Indian Killer Andrew."

"No one needs presidents to verify they are."

"It helps to go down in history."

"Sweetheart, all that is hidden will be revealed."

But before he had that quite unleafed, Gillian said across her castle, "The English language is bi-polar. All critical words are either nouns or verbs. However, nature itself is not necessarily so polarized, and neither are many languages. Nootka for example is monistic and sees all objects as events happening for longer or shorter times: a house is something 'that houses,' a flame 'a burning occurring.' 'Man' or 'woman' are simply longer events than others: a female child is a comparatively brief 'womaning,' a girl a rather longer one."

"And I'm a longer one still," said Liv up into the snow light. He did not seem to exist in their conversation.

"Yes, a little longer," Gillian was building a wall with great care. And continued presently, "On the other hand, Hopi is a timeless language whose verbs, and therefore thoughts, can make no distinction between past, present or future. All time for it is psychological, always of a personal duration that varies for each observer, and never has a number greater than one. Hopi speakers cannot say, 'I was with him four days,' rather 'I left him on the fourth day.'"

She had completed the snow castle with walls and two tall keeps of stripped shorts and was now developing the surrounding earthworks and moats, digging into the snow almost to the hot ground. The lake shimmered, clicking along its edge at the silver curls breaking.

"Or the forty-ninth day," Liv said and sat up. She watched Gillian. "If ever at all."

"Greek cannot say 'forever,'" James could not remain silent. "Only 'from the ages to the ages.'"

Liv said impatiently, "Which then may actually mean forever as far as they're concerned."

But James did not want to accept that. He insisted, "Just like German has no word and so no concept for 'goodbye,' only *aufwiedersehen*,' literally 'till I see you again.'"

Liv dropped back to her elbows, closing her eyes to the sky. The cut from which Becca had been taken was a thin silver line from navel to mound; the track of the worm upon her, or snake.

"James," Liv said steadily into the air, "must you butt into everything, offering, offering?"

Gillian said to her, "There is no universal natural logic fundamental to language which explains the world to everyone in exactly the same way. Every language is its own personal logic. Our language makes us think in one personal way, and we cannot see another."

"All four of us," Liv said gently, "have the same language."

"Not until today," Gillian said.

"We do?" James could not quite believe it. "Four?"

Liv reached behind her and offered Gillian her discarded bra; James could only stare from one to the other. The girl's hair now flamed so witchy red in the light that she seemed to be shaking fire from her head as she lifted it smiling faintly at Liv; he would not have been surprised to see the snow burning between them. Well, he thought, if hair can turn stone white in one morning of horror anticipating Babi Yar or Belsen, it can surely turn brilliant red in the Long Darkness between the Medicine Lodge Hills and Gull Lake; and how inexpressibly sad it was that the world knew so much about one and nothing at all about the other. He suddenly could not hold back his tears watching them together.

Gillian kissed Liv's hand and hooked the bra from her fingers. She hesitated, the snow castle sprawling wide almost to Liv's folded legs, the moat so deep lake water lay below the castle's main entrance. Then she patted the bra full of snow and took three long strides around to the side away from the lake and set it, straps tucked under, a double anchor of a new

227

line of defense beyond the moat. Liv leaned over and began idly to shore up more snow.

James said to Gillian, "That's a strong, lovely breastwork."

Liv laughed enormously, then Gillian, and finally James through his tears, realizing what he had said. He found himself mainly detumescent and the two women laughing so happily together that he put one arm around each and hugged them together working in the snow, their bodies so thick full of being he could not encompass them by half and wrecking part of an extended wall they were building, but happy and separate and unashamed. He felt hilariously wonderful tears still sliding down his cheeks for no particular reason that he could remember now or that anyone remarked upon, so none of them heard Harold until he yelled at them. By then he was already in the shallows near them and striding through as if coming out of violet fire.

"What's going on?" he yelled. "Hey, what's going on?"

He had lost his goalie mask somewhere and obviously stripped to swim: he wore only briefs and undervest. On the snowy beach, still laughing quietly, they watched him power himself towards them, livid water spraying from his muscles, a veritable glistening Achilles rising from the burning foam. James was suddenly astounded that Gillian should leave such a man – but now he realized that was a ridiculous thought: she had left no one, perhaps simply added. And what was Liv adding this very minute, who had cracked such cruel jokes when they had known nothing of this body built under damp tweed. Or the person. Gillian felt known in his arms, but Liv's larger body suddenly seemed strange, Harold splashing them with warmth as he muscled up and Liv laughing at him very much as she would have had she loved him.

"I thought you were settled with the Whitling-Holmes," she said.

"You mean stuck. Can you imagine that, the Long Darkness with a Conservative cabinet minister and his wife! I'd climb the highest mountain, swim the widest – "

"Oh Harry," Gillian said, "Rikki could be fun."

"Not in a threesome with that politician of hers."

"You mean a politician doesn't –"

"He won't blow his nose without getting it cleared by either a lawyer or a make-up expert."

"That's a grotesque pun," Gillian grimaced, and they all laughed together.

Harry shook himself, energy spraying from him, "That was a fabulous swim, and this is a fabulous place. So what's going on? I wonder who owns this?" He was striding about the narrow beach, staring. "Maybe we could buy it and develop it, build an exclusive resort and Liv you could send your winter-weary Edmontonians here, how about it, short trip, make us all fortunes."

Harold Lemming – now Harry – prancing about like the developer, did every Eden generate a snake?

"Harry," Liv said quietly, "wake up."

But Harry was granulating warm snow like sand between his fingers, as if weighing it for price.

"Wonder who owns this," he said again.

"Two hours," Gillian said, "across from a businessman and you—" she stopped. "Nobody," she said. "Nobody ever owns anything."

That's right, quote Crowfoot, James thought; you can have all you can carry, but the land remains a gift; all is gift.

"You've swum the lake," Liv said, "now take off your clothes."

"I think you should all put yours back on," Harry said slowly. "If anyone saw you, they'd get very funny ideas."

"Like what?"

"Well ... and I might too, my wife prancing around naked with my old school enemy Jakie Dyck here."

"You were too young," James said carefully to him, "to be an enemy."

Gillian said deliberately, "This is not a story about jealousy."

"What is it then?"

"About love."

James had to shout to them all, "Can you have one without the other?"

Gillian's eyes dilated, they seemed to swallow him. "You, sir," she said, "are the one who's always rebelling against the bi-polar world."

"There don't have to be victims or victors," Liv said.

"No consumer no consumed, no owner no owned."

Harry stood with his underclothes plastered to his body, face blank. Somewhere in the snowy trees leaves were talking, and flowers almost.

"Will you please wake up," Liv said intensely.

"You have a beautiful body," Gillian said; he might have been a stranger to her. "Don't hide it."

"And anyway," Liv was laughing gently as the snow floated out of the sky, warm and light against their bare skin, "those wet shorts don't hide anything."

Harold stared down at himself, quickly astonished.

"It's lying," he declared, "I don't feel like that, that's for sure."

"I believe him," James said. "The betrayal of the body is not easily overestimated."

And at that Liv finally exploded, "Will you both for once in your lives *forget* about your silly cocks."

"I might," Harold said, suddenly black. "If I knew what had been going on all summer."

"What?" Liv said without surprise.

"Between those two."

"Don't you know?"

"Do you?"

"They'll tell us," Liv said calmly.

The world wheeled over. Their sharp bright eyes shifted to Gillian and James; who could not look at each other and so could not sense what the other was thinking. But before James could gather some words, any words to follow into speech, Gillian said softly,

"Have you missed anything, Harry?"

"I don't know, I intend to find out."

"Has this summer been so bad?" she asked steadily; as if she were being overheard.

"The summer was fine, I—"

"Then what is it?"

230

and again again, through passion into spaceless ecstasy. He could barely endure Gillian's hand on his, or Liv's; Harold stood there looking between them as if he had seen that too. Was it possible for them all to endure this and live; all of them knowing the unimaginable for which they had all always longed?

To love totally, without debauchery. Nothing heals like it, as the man said.

They stood there in that small circle which it is possible for one woman and one man and one man and one woman to make, but whether they all knew to awaken and then could truly sleep or whether they slept in the snow castle and awoke to love and sleep and woke again to see the great beasts of the Long Darkness gather themselves together from the trees and the crystal air and the hills and come down to the lake to drink, it is hard to say. For though it is certain that the buffalo came for some of them, came with their little calves licked creamy and led by the great albino cow who could smell water like stars down to the shining hub of their radiant paths, and heard the cowbirds singing as they rode those humped, woolly backs, chirrupping over the plains grizzlies lolling about like shaggy, shifty-shouldered mountains scooping up snow like manna while the buffalo calves gamboled between them and the birch and diamond willows bent low to the lake till their white, greening branches drank with the animals and the garter snakes, quick as quicksilver across paws and hooves, swam over the sweet snow and onto the water, their tracks interwoven strings of fire until the great canoes came to them all sleeping there and watching too, till the canoes came in silence sweet as wind chimes and the breathing of pan flutes over the burning water for them, it is hard to say. Perhaps it is enough to know that in the land on the other side of waking, where we may sleep with all our five and wilful senses open, they dreamt they were free at last from the necessity of both want and freedom and were only good, and found themselves unimaginably happy in that; at last.

SEPTEMBER
TWO

When the mortician eased the coffin completely off the back of the hearse and the full weight of it hung on the children's arms, James saw them stagger and thought, o no it is too much for them, Young Aaron was right. He sprang forward, reaching, as did Young Aaron and two of the older brothers-in-law, but the mortician made no move and in fact there was no need to do so. David and Becca, very sturdy at the head, held it firm and the seven smaller children behind them on the long coffin bars straightened quickly—perhaps they had not expected quite that weight despite what the mortician told them—so the coffin sank a bit but then bobbed up as easily as if it had touched water. The mortician reached down, took Elfie's tiny hand in his, and led her forward with the pot of crocuses.

"Where in the world could you find crocuses in September?" James had asked.

"And blooming, purple and absolutely lovely," Liv said.

"They tipped over twice in the car," Gillian smiled, "but didn't spill."

It was Liv's idea that Elfie Hasserl, barely two and the only great-great-grandchild so far, should carry the regal flowers before the coffin in the procession at the cemetery. Elfie's grandfather, Aaron Bargen, called 'Young Aaron' to distinguish him from his father though he was only three years younger than James, his uncle, declared in his most sombre ministerial tone,

"This is no wedding, this is a funeral,"

236

but no one in the family had ever yet defied Liv on a matter of taste on the rare occasion when she offered it and Elfie's mother, Katerina, said immediately that that was a terrific idea, she'd look cuter than a button doing it. There was no point appealing to the good sense of her husband, Tim, since Katya definitely wore the pants in that family (and the suspenders too, her great-aunt Ruth giggled) though Susan's middle daughter Janice, who had left all her four pre-schoolers at home in Vancouver because she wanted them to remember their Gramma just like she was, objected to any of the children being there at all, much less mixed up in it like that.

"You want them to remember her helpless and blind and deaf?" James said. "What kind of a Christian are you?"

"Jakie," Ruth said gently, "don't, not now."

The only son after all those born dead during the revolution and civil war and starvation and anarchy in Russia, then finally a living family like a sentence of six girls, Lena, Ruth, Maria, and Susan born on that night train from Moscow, Eva and Katja in Canada who died in Sunnynook and Cold Lake and at last, when Mam was forty-two, Jacob: the only son, who changed his name to Canadian James, the fury and despair of his father and hopeless hope of his endlessly forgiving mother. Even Young Aaron, who had seminary training and could preach like an angel (mostly avenging, James snorted), could never out-argue him.

"All I meant," said James very quietly, though unable to force the familial technicality of 'I'm sorry' out of himself, "Christians of all people know death is as much a part of life as birth or marriage or ... eating. Why hide your children from such a —"

It was then he realized that the children should carry the coffin. No one had spoken about pallbearers; they had merely expected that, as usual, it would be the grown grandsons; there were eleven of them now, five more than at Grampa's funeral eight years before, and room for only six so some equitable decision would have to be made: perhaps no more than two from any one branch of the family, since James had no son, and let each decide for themselves but the mortician had to know that evening, he was getting the programs printed.

"What do you mean, the children?" Young Aaron asked, astounded.

"Twelve and under, pre-puberty. Let them carry her."

"There are only three boys, and Johnny Eigsti is barely six, that's impossible."

"There's lots of girls between eight and twelve."

"Girls?"

"Yeah, you know," James drawled, and only Liv's elbow, hard, prevented him from adding, 'they're human too,' though he couldn't quite keep it out of his tone. Just being in the same room for ten minutes —"There must be seven or eight of them," he said, fast, "let them all do it. One last, small service for the Gramma none of them could ever talk to, whose hands they all loved."

"It's ridiculous, it's too heavy and it's too far, the grave is dug so far back ... it's just never been done."

"I'll talk to the mortician," James said, and when he did that the man looked at him as if he had swallowed a revelation.

"For their grandmother and great-grandmother?"

"Yes," James said, but suddenly felt queasy before the man's relentless, ancient eyes: what had ever been hidden from them in a lifetime of preparing the dead so one could bear to look at them one last time, those who died senile, the young destroyed in brawls and drunkenness, the life-weary, the murdered, those smashed in cars or wasted to death in despair, the annihilated children, the ones who mutilated themselves for loneliness, o have mercy upon us. "I ... I just thought, but...." and he was ready to give it up, admit big-headed stupidity again. Only his mother was not here to label it correctly.

"Some die happy," the mortician said strangely, as if answering his thought. 'That would be beautiful, the children." His venerable face was shining as if a hand had passed over it. "No one has ever done that, in thirty-three years."

And he had parked the hearse by the iron gate; he obviously expected the nine children to carry the oak coffin not only across the grass to the open grave but also that they lead the procession down the cemetery lane itself. And they were doing that, between the tall, spaced poplars through September light that lifted the leaves in crimson foam the coffin seemed to float, a gleaming brown cloud hovering near the earth between the heads and hands of children. For a moment through the stout bodies of his sisters and their husbands before him in the line it seemed to James the coffin was drifting, the children swimming around it in bright, golden water, perhaps buoyed on leaf chatter or the whistle of ducks passing high in the mares-tailed sky holding it there for their contemplation and possible happiness snug and brown. Liv held his one arm, Olena praying steadily in Russian the other, and all the grandchildren and great-grandchildren and the old friends from Cold Lake and Vulcan (walking here so regularly, next week they might be the ones carried) and the long following of the community where somewhere Gillian walked far away from him on Harold's arm though her purple crocuses guided them in a straight line between acres of stones, the tall black mortician with Elfie's tiny hand still in his leading them, knowing where they were going. At the cemetery there will be no pictures, he had told them. Some things in this world are so beautiful we should remember and let them go.

The children had stood around the opened coffin, silent, looking. The mortician seemed to have done nothing more than comb Gramma's grey hair and lay her down comfortably in satin, certainly there was not a touch of cosmetic on her grainy skin hollowed into her skull; her false teeth were not even there to give shape to her lower face, though she had not worn them for years because her jaw had shrunken so badly and she had adamantly refused the assault of being fitted for new ones. *"Dowt lohnt sich aul nich,"* that isn't worth it anymore, her hand brushing him away when he roared himself into her comprehension as she mauled a bit of bread soft between her gums. *"Loat dawt maw toch,"* just leave it alone. Even the scattered coarse hairs growing on her upper lip, two high on her cheeks, almost everyone in the family was indignant, she looked just awful, what was the matter with the man? Eight years ago he had made Grampa look so handsome, lifelike and dignified as a doctor (which I never saw in life, James thought) and they should just dock his bill now, he'd just done nothing for her, one of the granddaughters saying that of course that was only natural since no man had ever done anything for a woman since the Year One, exactly nothing. But the children, there before the adults arrived, were merely awed, saddened by her ugliness.

Becca said, crying, "She was so beautiful."

"Yeah," David Bargen, Young Aaron's tall son said, crying too. "Sitting by the window all the time."

But the youngest children had no tears. They pushed to get closer and looked intensely, a kind of awed, puzzled wonder shifting their limbs, then one reached out and touched Gramma's cheek; then another her folded hands, and then even the smallest had to do that, every one of them, and tiny Elfie gestured until Katerina lifted her up and let her touch Gramma's hands too. A small voice said,

"She sure looks dead,"

a recognition that drove down the back of James' neck and through him to the very soles of his feet, 'Old age should burn and rave at close of day, rage, rage,' and they all seemed to agree, even Becca and David who had stopped crying. Then they all looked at him, the adult who had brought them there and who had asked them whether they wanted to carry her to her grave.

He said, as best he could, "When the soul leaves the body, that's what's left. But she is really beautiful, in heaven right now."

Another little voice said, "Then why are you crying?"

So he had to let them see the tears running down his face, since he had asked them to do this.

"Because she was my mom, and because I won't see her again ... maybe, for a long time."

The older family began to come in then for the viewing, including Tim to pick up Katerina and Elfie, so he piled all the small pallbearers into Aaron and Lena's stationwagon and took them out to the Daddy Lacombe on the highway. Driving down Main Street he saw Gillian standing alone on

240

that corner of the sidewalk and his heart lurched, he stopped without thinking and she crowded in too – Harry was in the bar with a dozen ancient school buddies and not a woman among them, all just staring at her, so while the children ate Daddy Lacomburgers and onion rings and drank wheat beer, James held Gillian's hand and looked across the highway at the immovable green and orange and red grain elevators and felt a little easier. Thank god he couldn't see the hockey arena from there.

"Wouldn't it be nice to have a family as big as this?"

"Nine?" She laughed aloud. "I'm only twenty-four!"

"Oh, they'd be a bit younger, but if you'd started at sixteen and were really regular, every year more or less with a few twins and triplets thrown in for efficiency, you could have done it."

She wrinkled her perfect nose at him. "I'd be fined for littering," she said as they both laughed quietly.

Becca, sitting beside them, smiled. "It would be easier for two moms, daddy."

And he said, "Personally, I know it would be impossible," and all three laughed, louder and not for the same reasons.

The procession was beginning to sing under the trees. Until then he had not recognized any tune for it began somewhere among the old people far behind him and the cemetery was a green patch of stones and trees on a ridge surrounded by wheatfields and the only sound when they arrived and shut off all the car motors was a faint murmur like relentless bees swarming. Combines, wavering in heat. August had been unseasonably wet, the harvest was late and everywhere now red and silver machines gnawed dust along the endless swaths around and around the giant fields. But low as it was, droning, he recognized the tune from the old people as if the bones of his body groaned the words he remembered when his mother had gripped his small hand following Eva to the hole chopped out of snow and frozen earth into such a terrifying little size:

Es geht nach Haus, zum Vaterhaus,
Wer weiss, vielleicht schon Morgen . . .

241

a melody they had sung so often and loved, his mother said it had slept in his flesh within her a decade before he was born, loved so much in the winter days in Moscow when no one had a home any more and no one knew whether they ever would have another on earth, having fled the only one they had known; and the one certain heavenly home such a happiness then, they had thanked God for those he called there,

We're going home, to father's home,
Who knows, perhaps tomorrow.
And then, o heart, all pain depart,
Away all woe and sorrow.
We're going home

the song rising between the brilliant poplars like fire into wispy sky as the mortician turned right. He was carrying tiny Elfie in his arms now, and she still clutched the crocuses in hers, leading past raw mounds into the open. The low coffin followed.

We're going home, who knows, perhaps

Doggerel more harrowing in memory than eloquence, Eva had been home and her face still open, the women laying her out had not been able to close her lips or quite one eye. He could see, looking over the edge of the coffin as he had to, the under-curve of her eyeball which should have been all white but actually was almost as yellow as her teeth, they had turned so yellow while she lay in the granary on the planks frozen hard, and they could not get them to stay closed decently. She was going home, he knew that and was so happy because all her pain was over and all her woe, but when he saw the hole that was the entrance to heaven in the ground like rock under the squealing snow he thought she would have been better off hard and frozen at home in the granary where at least he could go and his sisters and his mother and kneel there to pray when the grey cat came through the mousing hole and sat on the slight mound of her knee, listening, Eva who held his small body so warm and snuggly between her arms and legs against her soft chest and belly, he had loved her, Eva Eva, eleven years old when she died, the first of all the loves of his life, he was weeping for her in this death march following his mother's body out under the unshaded sky blinding as snow, the deep long groan rolling like surf deeper and deeper to her long home,

Es geht nach Haus, nach Haus, wer weiss

Liv turned to him suddenly in the soft bed where they always slept in her house, and where he had wanted so badly to sleep now, Lena and Aaron directly below in her bedroom and the rest of the families scattered between Olena and friends and the motels on the highway for those with smaller children, Becca on the couch in the living room—you can sleep here, sure, like you always do, it's all right—Liv clutching him as if she would claw off his skin behind the paper-thin walls and he rolled over to face her inside her desperation and held her tight with arms and legs but she shook her head, no no o no, tears slippery between their faces and her naked body spread open against him and he entered her quick and completely like falling straight through hot sky and they clamped inside each other, he could not tell if she was crying or he or both and motionless, bared teeth to teeth

"Sweetheart, why? Don't ... why?"
between them and only her head shuddering, her whole body delicately no. Where was that life motionless as a knitting needle, the fire in how many stoves she had worn out cooking and forever cooking the same food for the same endless hungers that chewed down comforts like salt, comfort they now must themselves forage for in this soft bed; they suddenly had to have it so passionately far beyond passion in a convulsive necessity which their mutual bodies prayed might be there, somewhere, she must have left it to them somewhere in the house, in a whiff of promise perhaps or an abyss they could hurl themselves into with dreadful joy, a fall that would transfigure the abhorrent edges of their bodies into an elixir or nothing but bloods intermingling until all their cells lost identity in a singular oneness that knew neither longing nor desire nor want, above all not repletion.

"It wasn't such a terrible life," he hissed against her face.

243

"How could it have been worse, what was there to it?"

"It wasn't so terrible."

"Mine is worse."

"What?"

"Helping people choose Hawaii today, Puerto Rico tomorrow, and then Hawaii again, there's the big volcano erupted, something new, you can see boiling lava, o you have to see it o dear god!"

"It makes them happy, they have something to remember, or anticipate —"

"It just makes them more miserable! Either you have too much work or too little, it's so useless, you always want more, to be where you're not, to be in somebody else's body, more money, more —"

"Liv, stop it!" He was so hard inside her the back of her head beaked over him scraped the headboard, but she had his face between her hands and was pushing it back against the tangle of sheets as if she would break it off and hoist it for eternal display on a pole.

"She believed in what she did, useless as it was! I don't even do that."

"Useless? Sitting blind and deaf by a window knitting?"

"I'll be lucky to be blind and deaf. You won't be there."

"Sweetheart."

"The men never are. They live out all their little purposes and die quick, heart attack or something nice and quick and leave the women wondering another twenty years."

"She knitted vests and stockings for third world children and —"

"And how many millions of them are there in the world?"

"Don't be silly, what does it matter, she did what she could, what's the ma—"

"I help people go take pictures of them," she was crying in his face. "They always look so picturesque on slides, they're never starving, Kodachrome is always so horribly blue, you know!"

"Will you listen to me? She lived in this house and cared for my father and —"

"Whom you hated."

244

"Yes," he said slowly, and he began to carry her rhythm with his body, "yes, I did, I did, did," as he moved his other hand to grasp the other full globe of her buttock and spread her wide so willingly that her legs came up folded around him like wings, when had she last so lifted him, "but I don't, now, she prayed that out of me, you know, she prayed it out, that's what she was doing, here for all of us, praying."

And they left their bodies so far behind them they were beyond touch.

"You want to be, good for something," he whispered.

"No. Just good."

"You are, really you are...."

"Are you?"

"I ... I want to be, too."

"But are you?"

"I ... hope."

He felt her so hot and full and slippery that hardness roused in him again, but distant, it seemed no more than a tiny ocean breathing against some isolated beach. And he was suddenly alone, dreadfully there in her arms, as if he stood on naked shingle on the far side of the world.

"Sweetheart, sweetheart...."

And her voice against his skin as if waking, "This is me, you know it is."

"Mom. Mom."

For some time he thought he was breathing that, a gentle persistence of longing, of course he was terrified, awake, there in the enormous black world of responsibility and naked, so overwhelmingly stripped while she was far away and sleeping with her face closed against something else, but it could not be he, he would have been saying "Mam, mam," Low German against the darkness, it was Becca in her long cotton night dress. Beside the bed still. Creaking a little.

"What's the matter?" Not wanting to move, or let go of all he held; he did not think what she might not have understood standing there.

"I ... it's so ... cold ... downstairs," she murmured unsteadily. He could see her shape shiver in the hot autumn room.

"Come here," Liv said, lifting her shoulders off him, "just crawl over here, come on."

"What?" he said sharply. "What?"

But Liv reached across him to Becca's hand and his lovely lithe daughter slid her nightgown over him, the frill tickling his nose around her feet warm and separately sweet, smell and touch burst awake in his nostrils, and Liv turned completely wet away from him easily, gave him snug all of her back and settled tightly into him again like a soft living spoon all curves and several spaces, he found himself in replete wonder pulling her tight with one arm below and around her soft stomach and the upper one beyond her drawing in Becca too, who clutched it, her breath escaping, snuggling in and he found Liv again as easily as she had left him and tightened into her, his body grown, reaching.

"Ho!" Becca chuckled deep in her throat. "You're so hot, Mom."

Liv laughed against her hair, he could hold these two women in his arms, and a third he knew, as full as a circle, one perfect ball. "Two people are always warm, my sweet girl."

"Then three are even warmer," Becca murmured dreamily. "We should sleep like this all the time, why not?"

Upstairs in the small room where the rafters closed the roof and she could not go for years, always apologizing for not having made the bed; that was her work of course, how could a man make a bed properly in a room he had fled as a youth? He remembered then this soft moldable bed was not his painful narrow one but the one where she had slept with his father for years before they bought the new one with the rigid mattress for his back, in which Lena and Aaron were now (unless they had fallen asleep immediately, no doubt huddled together in amazement at the sounds overhead), had she felt passion; had he? There are things the body can no longer hope, the mind no longer feel; when the head is severed and gone the body cannot see, or smell or hear, or taste; there is only the whispering touch. To recreate all possible sensations of the world from the texture of a leaf and a single pebble; but in this his mother's bed with Liv pulled tight around him by

246

Becca between his hands, he finally felt the heaviest weight creation has to carry: no body can ever touch enough, deeply.

"Three is too crowded, they make beds for two," Liv whispered in Becca's ear. "Can you lie very still, all night?"

"I don't really like her living room, now," Becca explained.

"Why?" he asked. If she said it immediately it might help her.

"I was just thinking about Gramma, sitting by the window...."

"She couldn't see anything," he said, not to the point. "Not even the shadow of the water tower."

"How come she's so ... so ... she looks so bad, now."

"'Death be not proud,'" he said over them into the darkness. "'Though some have called thee / Mighty and dreadful, for thou art not so; / For those whom thou think'st thou dost overthrow / Die not, poor death, nor yet canst thou kill me.'"

"Don't say that unless you mean it," Liv a motionless length suddenly.

"He means it," Becca said.

"I do," he said. "Yes."

"It helps in that language, eh?" Liv said, not ironically.

"King James." In the certainly reachable glory of Luther's heaven *dort ueber jenem Sternenmeer.* "Yes."

If he stood in this grave, black hole outlined by a metal frame in the bright red clay, he could probably see more easily through the afternoon light into yonder sea of stars; perhaps as far yonder as that lovely land itself. He so longed to believe it; he did believe it for God is not the God of the dead but of the living. Who said that? The mortician had set Elfie with her crocuses down at one corner of the grave and was guiding the nine coffin-bearing children on either side of it, carefully. His fingertips touched the end of the coffin, it floated over the space and sank onto the frame belts waiting for it, there was not a single grimace of strain on any child's face, not even the smallest when they bent down; as if there was nothing whatever inside. They opened their hands one by one on the long handles and the coffin sat suspended over the hole, a strange calm on their faces and then they obe-

247

diently climbed onto the red mound of clay; they tiered themselves there without apparent instruction while the families clumsily gathered across the coffin from them. There were even chairs for the oldest sisters with their husbands leaning behind them, and the people following came together in a great cloud among the tombstones, the song dying out with the last quavering voice somewhere still under the poplars,

    ... wer weiss, vielleicht schon Morgen.

This is today however, he thought, not tomorrow, and I stand here slightly behind my wife, my daughter on the clay there, and this larger family will not be together like this again; there will never be another reason until one of us is carried out like this, who will it be? which one? And he did not want to think of one detail of any of his sisters' lives, he glanced over them seated in a crooked line so near the framed hole with Olena there between Ruth and Susan and he knew the surface of their living as he knew his own body washing it and not wanting to know one fact of how it actually functioned as it obviously did, if something was wearing out, if cells were running amuck somewhere preying on each other then pray let them do so and leave my thoughts in peace until it is inevitable, don't don't warn me, expect me to worry, to offer years of comfortless dutiful comfort in some fumbled pretense of healing, there are forty-two of you here, in two months forty-four and all of you came and it took four days to get you all together and we had to have this funeral on Sunday afternoon so some of you can leave right after to get your relentless pay for Monday tearing across meridians so fast no thought or emotion and certainly no heavenly aspiration can nick you – but her head is in his lap, she is kissing him so completely his body leaps to her, I can't, can't ... we'll crash oo-o-o, and her tousled head coming up laughing, bright lips a perfect O to hold him, o what a bright way to go, the highway and sky and horizon a flickering screen he is still gasping o, clamped to the life-saving wheel and wanting only her mouth — forty-four and I have more than enough with only three, more than ... some of you I never met until

248

yesterday so let's not pretend that you all have to matter from here to eternity. Who cares whether somebody's kid here gets its shoes scuffed with gumbo? Some mothers, some fathers were frowning at him: apparently he hadn't broken their children's backs with his silly idea but who could tell, yet, between him and that useless mortician who had not even had the courtesy to cover the mound of clay with the usual mat of green plastic grass, who could tell what scarred psyche would surface from this years hence to destroy a marriage or a pregnancy, maybe tiny Elfie would instinctively hate boys because of the deep blue she carried all the way here, what a mess that would be, you could never tell, they really would have to refuse to pay part of the mortuary fee, the man had barely provided a minimum and now even this, the hole just gaping open as if they were shoving any old thing into it, nothing covered one bit as if to rub your nose in it like they were still in the '20s in Russia where the lid had to be peeled back full length and all of them lined behind and staring down gaunt as sticks, thank God the church service had been really nice once they got the coffin lid shut, the children crowding around it one last time it was almost sinful how eager they were to look and even touch and Young Aaron would now certainly have something decent to say too so a person could feel properly sad again, not just so irritated by everything. Really, at a Canadian funeral, nowadays, one should not have to feel *irritated*.

An autumn breeze stirred the heat, and Young Aaron's wispy hair lifted to it. The black book unfolded limp over his hand as fine used leather. He spoke high and nasal, his voice carrying brightly in English for all the children and grand-children and great-grandchildren who knew no word of German:

"The Lord gave, and the Lord hath taken away. Blessed be the name of the Lord. Our beloved mother, grandmother, great-grandmother and great-great-grandmother Liese Ruth Dyck, née Thiessen, who was taken from us by the Lord and Saviour she loved in her eighty-fifth year, gave herself freely, completely to us all. Even though for years she was afflicted with so much pain and suffering. To us who loved her for what she was, herself, she was not only the centre of the family, but the great 'pray-er' in it as well. She prayed for us all, when any of us visited her we prayed together, and she would mention each of us, from the oldest to the youngest and newest great-grandchild, mention each by name. We know she did this every day of her life, and we bring her here now to her final rest which she so often longed for, but we know that she is not here: she is in eternal peace where pain and sorrow come no more. And so I have chosen the great words of Paul to be the last words spoken over her body, First Corinthians 15, beginning at verse 22."

And Young Aaron lifted his black wingy Bible high:

"'For as in Adam all die, even so in Christ shall all be made alive. For he must reign till he hath put all enemies under his feet. And the last enemy that shall be destroyed is death."

Young Aaron glared over the pages at them all in that field of stones, and then suddenly he shouted, "Even so come, Lord Jesus!"

And at his words something wet touched James' face; again and then again. He was staring up into that wispy brilliance of sky, unable to endure Young Aaron's incredibly stupid posturing, dearest God in Heaven why did he have to submit to this at the graveside of his only mother with the Bible full of sweet words for an old, lonely woman who had prayed herself beautiful into eternity. 'Reign,' 'conquer,' as if some macho warrior were stretched out in this brown box the children had carried, a chest-beating ape down the poplar lane to a beneficence of drifting yellow leaves. But rain was falling on him out of a cloudless sky, the blessing of the thunderbird though no thunder had spoken and Young Aaron would have blushed purple at the heathen implication, there it was, well done good and faithful servant, just enough rain to let him know it. And several of the children looked up too – Becca, and David also, he did not know where Gillian was in the crowd. Had rain touched her? Liv in front of him weeping silently?

Olena was wiping her face. Rain or tears? The last enemy to be destroyed is death. How can death be destroyed? Poor death, 'One short sleep past, we wake eternally, / And death

250

shall be no more; death, thou shalt die.' Ah, that were truly to dream someone some happiness; and as he thought this he saw the mortician look over the coffin at Olena with such profound tenderness that the thought materialized in his head as if the look had written it: only love can so destroy.

Which was not what Young Aaron was booming at an abrupt prairie sky, tiered sunlit faces around him stamped in sudden wax.

"When God himself has wiped every tear from every eye and given us to drink freely of the fountain of life, then will his name be written on our foreheads and death shall be no more, it was slain by the sword of the Lord and death and hell will have been cast into the lake of fire. And death shall be no more, death shall be no more death!"

"I find her on the floor," Olena said, "there by the bathroom she falls and she is cold there when I touch, I know it she is gone but I cover her in her bed the night before, seven o'clock like always and I yell at her like always, you get up at night, push the button our nice Jascha fix up for us, I come it don't matter when, I sleep again easy, you just push it when you have to go. But she don't push it, I hear nothing and I know I hear it if she push it, she don't —"

"Of course she didn't, Olena we know," Liv said gently. "She didn't and you couldn't know, it's all right, please."

"You'd have gone," James could finally add. "We know that. We know —"

"I go, if she push it."

"Listen, the doctor said she could have crawled the two steps to the button in the kitchen and buzzed you, the break wasn't that bad, really, if she had wanted to."

"Olena, she did not want you to come," Liv said.

"You understand it?" Olena asked again.

"We understand it," James said slowly. "Everybody understands it."

Olena said, "One or two, they look at me a little...."

"Listen to me!" he hissed, on his knees in front of her and clutching her tight hands between his. "Olena, I put that buzzer there a month ago so it would be easier for you, so you wouldn't have to run back and forth when she didn't need

251

you. I did not put it there so you would be blamed. Mam did not want you to come and everyone, everyone in the family knows that. No one is looking at you."

Olena's broad flat face steadily contemplated him; as a child he had wanted nothing but to kiss it – he had wanted nothing from her but that; he had seen her then not with the eye of his head but with the eye of his navel. And suddenly, he knew something. He asked,

"Did she ever use it?"

"What you say?"

"In that whole month, did she ever push that buzzer, to call you?"

"Why you ask?"

"Olena, please."

She was smiling faintly. "You always know, everything," she said. Her water-rough hand brushed his hair back.

"You were always there anyway, weren't you? Caring for her."

"What do I got to do? We two old women live here, just live, and she always say, 'Olena, if the Lord Jesus let me fall, I don't want you pick me up.'"

She was laughing gloriously, her great body quivering with happiness. "'You don't pick me up, remember, remember!'"

"You were so good to her," Liv murmured behind him, "so lovely." He could say nothing, his face hidden against her knees.

"We sit by the window and she knit when I start the wool right for her and I read her always about de Lazarus, she don't hear but she put down the needle and I put her finger on the verse and she feel de Lazarus like she have eyes there, in her finger, feel the story where de Lazarus die and the Lord Jesus he come and Mary say if he come sooner her brother never die and Jesus cry and go to the grave, de Lazarus not dead he say, just sleeping but Martha say he not sleep at all, he four days in there and stinking now! Jesus say for the Glory of God you take away the stone and they do and he call loud to de Lazarus, 'Come out!' and then he come out, all wrapped like he was dead, white and all wrapped dead, he walk out and even Martha yelling Hallelujah! She know it, that story so good about de Lazarus."

He was weeping between her knees, sobbing aloud as her broad hand fondled his neck where the Cree believed his eternal soul to wander, her delicate voice speaking sorrow out of him like mist rising. He had seen the page in her Bible stroked incomprehensibly grey.

"When she see the story with her hand, 'Olena,' she say, 'the Lord Jesus he let me die like that, then he come and he say, "Liese, you come out now," and I come out just like that. You see,' she say, 'you see.'"

"'Blessed are the dead which die in the Lord,'" Young Aaron had found appropriate words at last to bow over the coffin. 'Where wert thou, brother, those four days? / There lives no record of reply.' "'Yea, saith the Spirit, that they may rest from their labours, and their works do follow them.'"

In the language she had understood well but never truly spoken: always something never quite possible to learn in middle age, always foreign. Another verse from that limp book should have been added: 'Here is the patience of the saints: here are they that keep—not kept, *keep* the commandments of God, and the faith of Jesus,' feeling his spotty recall little better than a curse at that moment, the children terraced on the clay against the humming field of swathed grain, but who has ever had more of all three? Patience, commandments, faith: they will sink here with her like memorials, have already vanished into that brown casing like an essence adrift for a moment in the passing of a stately lady across a long dark room.

Then Young Aaron did something beautiful at last, and James knew that all those clumsy words had really been leading toward this and forgave him, begged him forgiveness for his own mean-hearted, o-so-intellectually-superior sensibilities when Young Aaron was so absolutely sincere no matter how gauche; at the head of the grave he bent his head and lifted both his hands to the strange words of Jesus in the German Mam had breathed and prayed all her life:

"'For what is mortal must clothe itself with immortality. You believe in God, believe also in me. In my father's house are many mansions. I go to prepare a place for you, and after I go to prepare a place I will come again, and take you to myself; so that where I am, you will be also.'"

"Even so, come again, Lord Jesus."

And then Young Aaron closed his book, and turned away. There were no ropes splayed out, no shovels stubbed into the clay. For Eva a young man had dropped down into the grave on the stretched hands of his friends to hammer the box lid into place and scatter the straw evenly that they threw down after him; which only slightly muffled the frozen clods falling, all the men there working furiously, snatching the shovels from each other in turn, fast, faster, while the family faced the earth taking over at last, mound up, seal itself together like everlasting rock. Here the quiet mortician would stay behind and do what needed to be done; that was what he was paid for, and the steel backhoe to fill in what it had clawed out.

Liv turned, put her arm around him and pulled him a little, out of the path of the scattering crowd, the running children. Her body so living warm and fitting.

"I think," she said slowly, "I'd prefer to be burned."

Two thoughts ahead of him again, though he was on the same road. He could almost smile.

"We'll do that little thing for each other," he said.

They stood among numberless stones grey as overused pillows, the dark drift of people ebbing east to the cars glistening beyond trees and fence. Back to church in town where the next hearse was waiting, life that long circular journey following a coffin endlessly. "Here it is," Liv said suddenly, and gestured with her elegant shoe:

Jakob Aaron Dyck
1891 - 1972
Gone but not Forgotten

Flat and sunken like all the other stones in the most recent rows for the mowers to pass over effortlessly.

"My dear sisters," he said, depressed. "Never knowing their horrible ironies, always engraving the banal."

"Didn't you help?" Gillian asked, standing with them.

He shook his head, gone but not forgotten indeed, ashamed of himself but not feeling guilty; as if he had at last been rid of something.

"I never saw this before," he said, and then became aware of her tone. "If that's what you meant."

"Maybe you don't forget enough," she said.

"You think I remember too much?"

"I didn't say that."

"I should just forget more?"

"No. Enough."

"I should forget enough?"

"Well-ll" Gillian seemed unsure of herself; she glanced at Liv. "What do you think?"

"It's a big subject," Liv said heavily. "Too big maybe, here among the stones."

"When we all get to heaven," James sang, "what a day of rejoicing —" But he stopped himself, humiliated.

Mercifully, Liv and Gillian said nothing; they simply turned back to the new grave. "Where's Harold?" Liv asked Gillian, walking.

"The church service was ... fine, but he asked to forgive him the cemetery."

It is of course possible, James thought, for an historian to ignore the existence of cemeteries. The imperial popes tried to do it all the time.

Gillian was moving between stones with the easy tilted motion of a long-thighed woman in heels. "It bothers him," she said. "His father has been in the Calgary hospital for three years dying of cancer. Half the time he thinks they're doing nothing but experiments on him."

"Dearest God," Liv sighed.

The sky mercifully said nothing to James either.

Olena still sat as immovably large as ever in her chair. She held the crocuses while watching the tall mortician show Becca how to turn the mechanism in the frame which lowered the coffin. The belts moved; the coffin seemed to sink of its own volition in such dignified measure that after a moment David knelt beside her and she let him do it too. The

255

coffin settled softly as a sigh into its box. The mortician detached one end of the belts from the frame.

"Okay," he said. "You can wind them up, just turn the switch the other way."

David switched, and belt ends vanished, whirring. "Hey, that works nice," he grinned.

"I want to too," Becca nudged him, and she did.

"Just one more thing," the mortician said. "Put the lid on the box."

"How do you do that?" Becca asked.

"Somebody has to get down there and do it."

"Where's the lid?" David was looking about. He had Young Aaron's intensity but none of his father's implacable Christian benevolence; pray never.

"It's behind the mound, over there," the mortician gestured but did not move.

"Come on," David said to Becca, and immediately she followed him.

James felt himself rid of something. He seemed ... light, what was it? What had happened? He felt himself move, asking, "Can I do that? Fasten the lid down?"

"Sure," the mortician stood with his feet squared to the grave, motionless, his ancient eyes so strange that James stopped at the corner of it.

"What's the matter?" he asked.

"I just ... wondered ... " the mortician paused, slowly bowed his head. He did not seem able to speak; in fact, he seemed to be crying. But he got his emotions under control and said thickly, not looking up, "... wondered if you really want to do that. Or maybe what you really want is get down there and open the coffin."

James stared at him; the very sky roared with silence. Though actually it was what he wanted; though Gillian and Liv were standing there together, that was what he most wanted, he realized that and so finally he could say in a voice he did not recognize as his own, "I've seen her ... enough. She's dead, four days already."

"I know."

And James knew then that that was not the question the

256

mortician was asking him. The children came over the mound with the lid a white rectangle between them and set it on edge beside the grave.

Olena said, "Jascha, do it."

He did not dare look at Liv or Gillian who had come to stand beside him; he simply stepped forward, the mortician took his hand, and he braced his feet against hard clay and walked down the vertical wall with that strong grip an anchor above him, he did not even smudge the cuffs of his black suit and there were his shoes set securely on the thin edges of the box on either side of the coffin. It was wonderfully cool in the earth, and crisp; as if he had become fresh clay on the first spring morning. So he braced himself with one knee and hand against the damp earth and bent down and lifted the coffin lid, open.

She lay as she had lain when the last child touched her in the vestibule of the church. His one, always and only mother a gentle husk. Why had he not spoken the words of Solomon's Song over her: 'Who is this coming up from the wilderness, leaning upon her beloved? I awakened you under the apple tree, there your mother brought you forth; there she was in travail who bore you. Set me as a seal upon your heart, as a seal on your arm: for love is stronger than death, jealousy more cruel than the grave; the coals of love have a most vehement flame, there are no waters on earth to quench them nor can the floods drown them. Rise up, my love, my fair one, and come away. For lo, the winter is past, the rain is over and gone; the flowers appear on the earth and the time for singing is come.'

"Liese, come out!"

She opened her eyes. Reluctantly, but she did at that incontrovertible voice. Then she saw his face above her and she smiled.

"Well, that is nice," she said, and sat up. "Is this bottom half fastened down?"

He found it wasn't when he put his fingers to it; he had to swing his left leg aside to open it. She stood up in front of him among the satin ruffles, raised her arms and the mortician bent and took one hand and the two children the other and she walked up out of the grave. For a moment it seemed they had forgotten him down there; but they hadn't.

His mother and Olena stood together, holding each other's hands. Liv brought Gillian around to them.

"This is our friend from Edmonton, Gillian," she said, and his mother embraced her with a kiss as she had the others.

They all left the mounds and straight lines of stones in the cemetery behind them then and were walking in the wheatfield. The stubble scratched their ankles, but the unharvested swaths gleamed like cloths and ribbons stitched out under the Sunday sun. There was a humming as of pan-flutes in the air, and Becca and David danced around them all, unable to walk.

"You children always surprise me," his mother said to them. One brilliant crocus was on her breast. "After carrying me so far and you still have that much energy."

They threw ears of wheat at her, laughing that she should imagine she could have been heavy for them. Their path was intercepted by a roaring red combine which stopped, its swath motionless in its maw, and they found a white-haired farmer in his cab looking down at them. He cut the motor back and stood up in the glass cab, all its windows open, and continued to eat potato salad out of a plastic box he held against his chest.

"I'm sorry," he shouted to them above the idling whine of the machine, "this is Sunday but the boss says I have to work, I lay around most of August."

"Isn't this your crop?" Gillian asked.

The farmer laughed, looking so familiar with all his false teeth. "I've never owned nothing," he said. "Hey, you people had lunch yet?"

He put the lid on the plastic and clambered down out of the cab. The machine quietened to a kind of hush; a flock of geese was whistling south somewhere high above them. And the crunch of feet coming together.

"Nothing but a bit of salad left, and cold tea," the farmer was offering it to the mortician. His hands were thick, abused by grease and slipped wrenches. "I ate most of it already, going around, there's no use stopping."

"You're very kind," the mortician said, accepting the box and fork and thermos. "There'll be enough for us."

"Becca!" Liv called to the children chasing each other with armsful of straw, leaping and kicking through from swath to swath. "Don't mess that up!"

"There's more than enough for baling," the farmer grinned. "Sure enough for a little fun."

He climbed up and roared off again, the swath pulling his combine along into the distance of slumbering grain. They were inside a globe of nothing but field and sky then; even the water tower and the tops of the elevators were gone where the horizon should have been. The mortician took off his black coat and spread it on a straw swath for his mother to sit, and James did the same for Olena. Everyone settled down in the stubble to the little lunch.

"'... how do you think you'll get all your women to Canada,' his brother Peter was always sneering at him in Moscow. 'You don't have two kopecks to rub together.'"

"He told me that story, too," Olena said. "Again and again."

"Well then, you should have understood him," his mother said. "Peter was the older by twelve years, and of course he inherited the whole farm and Aaron had always worked for him, he gave him work even in the terrible Stalin time when—"

"Hired man for his brother, all his life," Olena nodded heavily, eating.

"Well yes, but in '29 it became impossible and we were all so afraid, we had to get out and we couldn't sell anything because then the spies would know you wanted to run and next morning the NKVD would be there at five o'clock banging on the door, and there was a little saved, a little money but not enough, not really."

"So in Moscow Peter kept it all because there wasn't enough for two families to get out," Olena was rocking back and forth as though she were still keening.

"There was enough to send Peter and all his family to Siberia," his mother said softly. "I always said to my Aaron,

259

'It was Peter brought us to Canada; he made us trust prayer, not money.' But he could never get to that. He stayed hung up on that sneering, after he had always listened to Peter."

"So he got his family to Canada, by God's grace, and then he played 'little god in France' on them in turn. Here he had the control."

"Olena," his mother said steadily. "Now you can forgive."

"O, he never did it to me," Olena stuck the fork into a piece of potato and passed her the plastic box. "What could he do to me there under the water tower?"

"It's always easier to forgive for yourself than for others."

They were both looking at James.

" .... strange?" the mortician said, drinking. "Do you actually think the most brilliant human imaginations can imagine all that God wants to give and will give those who love him?"

"Well," Gillian said doubtfully, and accepted the one used cup from him, "what kind of a God is that, so unimaginably, untouchably other? Don't human beings know something?"

"We certainly can," Liv said.

"Haven't we already lived a little of it?" Gillian added.

"Of course you have," the mortician poured her tea out of the seemingly bottomless thermos. "Start with the most perfect experience of love you've ever had, as a child, or from your mother, or lover, man or woman ... or maybe a love you've never had but dreamed, so perfect it's like plate glass that's more transparent than the air you walk through. That would be a start, a little start."

"I've sometimes thought an animal is the most transparent," Liv said. "A dog gives you .... "

"Would he if you beat him every day?"

"I don't know. But as it is, he gives you everything good he has."

"Or a house," Gillian said, "that protects you in winter."

"You're both getting mushily romantic," the mortician said.

"So what? It's a little start, eh?"

That was Liv, of course, and all three laughed; she was reaching for the cup.

260

"There's still nothing better," Gillian said, "than a woman and a man. For starters."

Liv said, "There's no marriage in heaven, the Bible says."

"That's true," the mortician said. "One for one marriage is for earth, now. Messy as it is, it's still better than indiscriminate casual mating, though human nature seems to pull that way."

"Men's nature a lot more than women's," Liv said, and Gillian and the mortician chuckled. "Well, it's true," she insisted.

"I would have thought you'd say that was the result of a male society – women feel they need the security of one man – rather than their instincts," the mortician grinned.

"Hoist with my own petard," Liv conceded.

"I don't like such a silly heaven," Gillian said wistfully. "Everyone single, alone."

"No," the mortician said slowly, "no. It's not that you aren't married to any one there; you are married to everyone."

They were all seated in that stubble field with a distant rush like pan-flutes whenever they moved, and James realized he was surrounded. By Olena, and his mother, and Becca and David leaving the warm yellow straw to share the fork and potato salad, and Liv, and Gillian. And the mortician serving everyone the sweet delicate tea. He was seated in the centre of them. And when they all had eaten, James' mother was looking at him. She asked him:

"Do you have something to say now?"

"Yes," he said immediately. "Yes."

And he would speak. For a moment he could not quite gather what he had wanted to say, whether he wanted to retrieve something from oblivion or, by saying it, make something that had never quite existed but should have; or both. My soul waits in silence. To teach stones to speak. Be still and know. The past irreversible only in the past, if he could now speak the beginning he could utter the future. And he heard a corner of that silence that was before the world began, called out by the living voice of his mother and he was empty of all his ravaging words, his pre-inspired words were quite gone, he wanted to listen his loved ones into life, now, even the ones who were no longer here. So for a time he looked at each of those who were, the people he loved and who loved him, and he prayed to see them all at once and know them all, not distinct and separate, even himself, but all one. For he understood they all together had to speak or he could never say what was ready to be if only it would be spoken. So he opened his mouth to make that. And much more.